电气专业英语

（第2版）

主　编　徐志成　郑　见

副主编　张一沙　夏　怡　王　琳

北京理工大学出版社
BEIJING INSTITUTE OF TECHNOLOGY PRESS

版权专有　侵权必究

图书在版编目（CIP）数据

电气专业英语 / 徐志成，郑见主编. —2 版. —北京：北京理工大学出版社，2016.8（2023.5重印）

ISBN 978-7-5682-2750-6

Ⅰ.①电⋯　Ⅱ.①徐⋯②郑⋯　Ⅲ.①电气工程–英语–高等学校–教材　Ⅳ.①H31

中国版本图书馆 CIP 数据核字（2016）第 185717 号

出版发行 /	北京理工大学出版社有限责任公司
社　　址 /	北京市海淀区中关村南大街 5 号
邮　　编 /	100081
电　　话 /	（010）68914775（总编室）
	（010）82562903（教材售后服务热线）
	（010）68944723（其他图书服务热线）
网　　址 /	http://www.bitpress.com.cn
经　　销 /	全国各地新华书店
印　　刷 /	北京国马印刷厂
开　　本 /	787 毫米×1092 毫米　1/16
印　　张 /	18.5
字　　数 /	435 千字
版　　次 /	2016 年 8 月第 2 版　2023 年 5 月第 5 次印刷
定　　价 /	48.00 元

责任编辑 / 李志敏
文案编辑 / 李志敏
责任校对 / 周瑞红
责任印制 / 李志强

图书出现印装质量问题，请拨打售后服务热线，本社负责调换

(Preface)

  随着经济全球化的发展，国际技术交流也日益增强，工程技术人员迫切需要阅读和撰写大量的英文技术资料和文献，然而由于科技英语的表达方式，词汇范畴与公共日常英语存在较大差异，所以专业英语课程的开设对于提高专业学生阅读外文技术资料和撰写外文专业文献非常有必要。但是，目前电气专业的英语教材在内容的难易度、合适度上适合高职高专的尚不多。为此，编者从实际应用角度出发，结合电气专业所学课程，从国外原版教材、专著、相关网站及产品说明书等材料中精心挑选课文内容，并结合自己的教学体会给出了相关注释和练习。本书可作为高职高专电气专业及相近专业的专业外语教材，也可供电气专业的工程技术人员阅读参考。

  本教材结合电气类专业的特点，将教材分为五章：第一章（第1~5单元）电工电子基础部分，即与电路元器件、电路网络分析、二极管、运算放大器等知识相关的外文材料；第二章（第6~10单元）电力电子及电机控制部分，即与电力电子及变频技术、直流电机、交流电机及其转速控制等知识相关的外文材料；第三章（第11~16单元）工业自动化部分，即与PLC、单片机等知识相关的外文材料；第四章（第17~21单元）自动控制原理部分，即与传递函数、开环和闭环控制等知识相关的外文材料；第五章（第22~26单元）过程控制技术部分，即与先进控制方法、集散控制系统及传感器等知识相关的外文材料。

  本书由常州机电职业技术学院徐志成、夏怡、王琳以及江苏省常州技师学院英语组郑见联合编写，其中第一章由王琳副教授编写，第二~三章由张一沙、夏怡联合编写，第四~五章由徐志成、郑见联合编写。全书由徐志成、郑见统稿。由于编者经验和水平所限，书中存在不足和疏漏之处，敬请读者批评指正。

编 者

(Contents)

Chapter 1　Electronic Components

Unit 1　Resistors ··· 3
Unit 2　Diodes ·· 15
Unit 3　Transistors ·· 25
Unit 4　Operational Amplifiers ·· 32
Unit 5　Digital Logic Circuits ·· 41

Chapter 2　Power Electronics and Motors

Unit 6　Introduction to Power Electronics ·· 49
Unit 7　How Electric Motors Work ·· 63
Unit 8　DC Motor Control with PWM and H-Bridge ··································· 78
Unit 9　Variable Speed AC Drives and How They Work ······························ 90
Unit 10　Induction Motor Control Circuits ··· 102

Chapter 3　Industrial Automation

Unit 11　PLC Systems ··· 117
Unit 12　PLC Programming ··· 131
Unit 13　Introduction to Fieldbus ·· 142

Unit 14　Why HMIs Are Everywhere……………………………………………153
Unit 15　8051 Microcontroller Architecture……………………………………164
Unit 16　How to Start Working with a Microcontroller………………………185

Chapter 4　Principles of Automatic Control

Unit 17　Introduction to Control…………………………………………………199
Unit 18　Transfer Functions………………………………………………………207
Unit 19　Modes of Control………………………………………………………215
Unit 20　Control Loops……………………………………………………………223
Unit 21　PID Controller……………………………………………………………234

Chapter 5　Process Control Systems

Unit 22　Importance of Process Control…………………………………………243
Unit 23　Process Control Loops…………………………………………………249
Unit 24　Advanced Control Loops………………………………………………257
Unit 25　Computers in Control……………………………………………………266
Unit 26　Introduction to Sensors…………………………………………………277

Chapter 1
Electronic Components

Unit 1

Resistors

Resistors
翻译

Resistors are the most commonly used components in electronics, and their purpose is to create specified values of the current and voltage in a circuit. A number of different resistors are shown in the photos below (The resistors are put on the paper about a millimeter thick, which are spaced out 1 cm apart to give some idea of the dimensions). Fig. 1.1.1 shows some low-power resistors, while Fig. 1.1.2 shows some high-power resistors. Resistors with power dissipation below 5 watt (most commonly used types) are cylindrical in shape, with a wire protruding from each end for connecting to a circuit (Fig. 1.1.1). Resistors with power dissipation above 5 watt are shown below (Fig. 1.1.2).

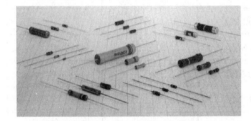 

Fig. 1.1.1 Some low-power resistors   Fig. 1.1.2 High-power resistors and rheostats

The symbol for a resistor is shown in Fig. 1.1.3 (The upper: American symbol, and the lower: European symbol).

The unit for measuring resistance is the OHM (the Greek letter Ω—called Omega). Higher resistance values

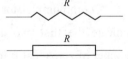

Fig. 1.1.3 Resistor symbols

are represented by "k" (kilo-ohms) and M (megohms). For example, 120,000 Ω is represented as 120 k, while 1,200,000 Ω is represented as 1.2 M. The dot is generally omitted as it can easily be lost in the printing process. In some circuit diagrams, a value such as 8 or 120 represents a resistance in ohms. Another common practice is to use the letter E for resistance in ohms. The letter R can also be used. For examples, 120 E (120 R) stands for 120 Ω, and 1E2 stands for 1R2, etc.

Resistor markings

Resistance value is marked on the resistor body. Most resistors have 4 bands. The first two bands provide the numbers for the resistance, and the third band provides the number of zeros. The fourth band indicates the tolerance. Tolerance values of 5%, 2%, and 1% are most commonly available.

Tab. 1.1.1 shows the colors used to identify resistor values.

Tab. 1.1.1   Resistor values

COLOR	DIGIT	MULTIPLIER	TOLERANCE	TC[①]
Silver		×0.01 Ω	±10%	
Gold		×0.1 Ω	±5%	
Black	0	×1 Ω		
Brown	1	×10 Ω	±1%	±100×10^{-6}/K
Red	2	×100 Ω	±2%	±50×10^{-6}/K
Orange	3	×1 kΩ		±15×10^{-6}/K
Yellow	4	×10 kΩ		±25×10^{-6}/K
Green	5	×100 kΩ	±0.5%	
Blue	6	×1 MΩ	±0.25%	±10×10^{-6}/K
Violet	7	×10 MΩ	±0.1%	±5×10^{-6}/K
Grey	8	×100 MΩ		
White	9	×1 GΩ		±1×10^{-6}/K

A common resistor has 4 bands. It is shown in Fig 1.1.4 (a). The first two bands indicate the first two digits of the resistance; the third band is the multiplier (the number of zeros that is to be added to the number derived from the first two bands); the fourth represents the tolerance.

Marking the resistance with five bands is used for resistors with tolerance values of 2%, 1% and other high-accuracy resistors. The first three bands determine the first three digits, and the fourth is the multiplier, and the fifth represents the tolerance (Fig. 1.1.4 (b)).

---

① TC — Temp. Coefficient, only for SMD devices.

For SMDs (Surface Mounted Devices), the available space on the resistor is very small. 5% of resistors use a 3-digit code, while 1% of resistors use a 4-digit code.

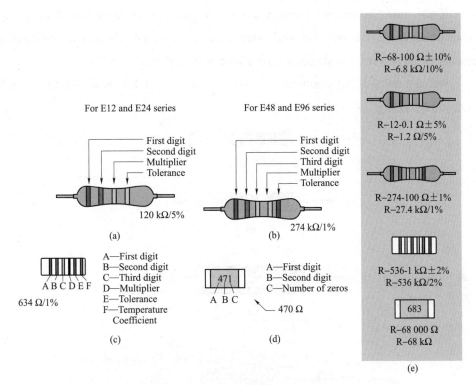

Fig. 1.1.4 Resistors

(a) A four-band resistor; (b) A five-band resistor; (c) A cylindrical SMD resistor;

(d) A flat SMD resistor; (e) Examples

Some SMD resistors are made in the shape of small cylinder while the most common type is flat. Cylindrical SMD resistors are marked with six bands — The first five bands are "read" as with common five-band resistors, while the sixth band determines the Temperature Coefficient (TC), which gives us a value of resistance change upon 1-degree temperature change (Fig. 1.1.4 (c)).

The resistance of a flat SMD resistor is marked with digits printed on their upper side. The first two digits are resistance values, while the third digit represents the number of zeros (Fig. 1.1.4 (d)). For example, the printed number 683 stands for 68,000. That is 68 k.

For some electrical circuits, the resistor tolerance is not important, and it is not specified. In that case, resistors with 5% tolerance can be used. However, devices which require resistors to have a certain amount of accuracy need a specified tolerance.

Resistor dissipation

If the flow of current through a resistor increases, it heats up. And if the temperature exceeds a certain critical value, it can be damaged. The wattage rating of a resistor is the power it can dissipate over a long period of time.

Wattage rating is not identified on small resistors. Fig. 1.1.5 shows the dimensions and wattage rating.

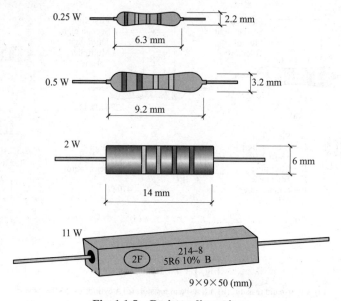

Fig. 1.1.5 Resistor dimensions

Most commonly used resistors in electronic circuits have a wattage rating of 1/2 W or 1/4 W. There are smaller resistors (1/8 W and 1/16 W) and higher ones (1 W, 2 W, 5 W, etc). In place of a single resistor with specified dissipation, another one with the same resistance and higher rating may be used, but its larger dimensions increase the space taken on a printed circuit board as well as the added cost.

Power (in watts) can be calculated according to one of the following formulae, where U is the symbol for Voltage across the resistor (and is in Volts), and I is the symbol for Current in Amps, and R is the resistance in ohms:

$$P = UI$$
$$P = RI^2$$
$$P = \frac{U^2}{R}$$

For example, if the voltage across an 820 Ω resistor is 12 V, the wattage dissipated by the resistors is:

$$P = \frac{U^2}{R} = \frac{12^2}{820} = 0.176 \text{ (W)} = 176 \text{ mW}$$

In this case, a 1/4 W resistor can be used. In many cases, it is not easy to determine the current through or voltage across a resistor. In this case the wattage dissipated by the resistor is determined for the "worst" case. We should assume the highest possible voltage across a resistor, i.e. the full voltage of the power supply (battery, etc).

If we mark this voltage as U_B, the highest dissipation is:

$$P = \frac{U_B^2}{R}$$

For example, if U_B=9 V, the dissipation of a 220Ω resistor is:

$$P = \frac{9^2}{220} = 368 \text{ (mW)}$$

In this case, a 0.5 W or higher wattage resistor should be used.

TECHNICAL WORDS AND PHRASES

resistor	[ri'zistə]	n.	电阻器
component	[kəm'pəunənt]	n.	元件，组（部）件
electronics	[ilek'trɔniks]	n.	电子学
current	['kʌrənt]	n.	电流
voltage	['vəultidʒ]	n.	[电工]电压，伏特数
circuit	['sə:kit]	n.	电路
power	['pauə]	n.	[物]功率
dissipation	[,disi'peiʃən]	n.	损耗
resistance	[ri'zistəns]	n.	电阻，阻抗
ohm	[əum]	n.	[物]欧姆
tolerance	['tɔlərəns]	n.	偏差，公差
cylindrical	[si'lindrik(ə)l]	adj.	圆柱的
multiplier	['mʌltiplaiə]	n.	乘数
formula	['fɔ:mjulə]	n.	公式
wattage	['wɔtidʒ]	n.	瓦特，瓦特数
battery	['bætəri]	n.	电池
wattage rating			额定功率
power supply			电源
four-band resistor			四色环电阻

SMD (Surface Mounted Device)　　　　　表面贴装器件
printed circuit board　　　　　　　　　印刷电路板

NOTES

1. Resistors with power dissipation below 5 watt (most commonly used types) are cylindrical in shape, with a wire protruding from each end for connecting to a circuit.

   译文：功耗低于 5 瓦的电阻（最常使用的类型）为圆柱形，两端伸出的导线用来连接电路。

   句中"with a wire protruding from"为伴随状语。

2. Power (in watts) can be calculated according to one of the following formulae, where U is the symbol for Voltage across the resistor (and is in Volts), and I is the symbol for Current in Amps, and R is the resistance in ohms.

   译文：功率（单位为瓦）可以用下面公式中的一个来计算，其中 U 是电阻两端电压的符号（单位为伏），I 是单位为安培的电流的符号，R 是单位为欧姆的电阻的符号。

   句中"where"引导非限制性定语从句。

EXERCISES

Ⅰ. **Translate the following words into English.**

1. 电压　　　　　　　　　　2. 电流
3. 功率损耗　　　　　　　　4. 滑动变阻器
5. 四色环电阻　　　　　　　6. 温度系数
7. 额定功率　　　　　　　　8. 电源

Ⅱ. **Complete the following sentences.**

1. Most resistors have _____ bands. The first two bands provide the numbers for the _____ and the third band provides the number of _____.
2. Some SMD resistors are made in the shape of small _____ while the most common type is _____.
3. If the flow of current _____ a resistor increases, it heats up. And if the temperature _____ a certain critical value, it can be damaged.
4. Power (in watts) can be calculated according to one of the following formulae, where U is the symbol for Voltage _____ the resistor (and is in Volts), and I is the symbol for _____ in Amps, and R is the resistance in _____.

Supplementary Reading

Reading 1 Capacitors

Capacitors are the common components of electronic circuits, used almost as frequently as resistors. The basic difference between the two is the fact that capacitor resistance (called reactance) depends on the frequency of the signal passing through the item. The symbol for reactance is X_C, and it can be calculated using the following formula:

$$X_C = \frac{1}{2\pi f C}$$

in which f represents the frequency in Hz, and C represents the capacitance in Farad.

For example, 5 nF-capacitor's reactance at $f=125$ kHz equals:

$$X_C = \frac{1}{2 \times 3.14 \times 125\,000 \times 5 \times 10^{-9}} = 255 \ (\Omega)$$

while it is at $f=1.25$ MHz, it equals:

$$X_C = \frac{1}{2 \times 3.14 \times 1\,250\,000 \times 5 \times 10^{-9}} = 25.5 \ (\Omega)$$

A capacitor has an infinitely high reactance for direct current, because $f=0$.

Capacitors are used in circuits for many different purposes. They are common components of filters, oscillators, power supplies, amplifiers, etc.

The basic characteristic of a capacitor is its capacity — the higher the capacity is, the higher the amount of electricity it can hold will be. Capacity is measured in farads (F). As one farad represents fairly high capacity, smaller values such as microfarad (μF), nanofarad (nF) and picofarad (pF) are commonly used. As a reminder, relations between the units are:

$$1 \text{ F} = 10^6 \text{ μF} = 10^9 \text{ nF} = 10^{12} \text{ pF}$$

That is, 1 μF=1,000 nF and 1 nF=1,000 pF. It is essential to remember this notation, as same values may be marked differently in some circuits. For example, 1,500 pF is the same as 1.5 nF, and 100 nF is 0.1 μF. A simpler notation system is used with resistors. If the mark on the capacitor is 120, the value is 120 pF. 1n2 stands for 1.2 nF. n22 stands for 0.22 nF, while .1 μ (or .1 u) stands for 0.1 μF.

Capacitors come in various shapes and sizes, depending on their capacity, working voltage, type of insulation, temperature coefficient and other factors. All capacitors can be divided into two groups: one with changeable capacity values and the other with fixed capacity values. These will be covered in the following chapters.

Block-capacitors

Capacitors with fixed values (the so-called block-capacitors) consist of two thin metal plates (these are called "electrodes" or sometimes called the "foil"), separated by a thin insulating material such as plastic. The most commonly used material for the "plates" is aluminum, while the common materials used for insulator include paper, ceramic, mica, etc. after which the capacitors get named. A number of different block-capacitors are shown in Fig. 1.1.6. A symbol for a capacitor is in the upper right corner of the figure.

Fig. 1.1.6   Block capacitors

Most of the capacitors, block-capacitors included, are non-polarized components, meaning that their leads are equivalent in respect of the way the capacitor can be placed in a circuit. Electrolytic capacitors represent the exception as their polarity is important.

Marking the block-capacitors

Commonly, capacitors are marked by a set of numbers representing the capacity. Beside this value is another number representing the maximal working voltage, and sometimes tolerance, temperature coefficient and some other values are printed as well. But on the smallest capacitors (such as surface-mount) there are not markings at all, and you must not remove them from their protective strips until they are needed. The size of a capacitor is never an indication of its value as the dielectric and the number of layers or "plates" can vary from manufacturer to manufacturer. The value of a capacitor on a circuit diagram, marked as 4n7/40 V, means the capacitor is 4,700 pF, and its maximal working voltage is 40 V. Any other 4n7 capacitor with higher maximal working voltage can be used, but they are larger and more expensive.

Sometimes, capacitors are identified with colors, similar to the 4-band system used for resistors (Fig. 1.1.7 and Tab. 1.1.2). The first two colors (A and B) represent the first two digits, and the third color (C) is the multiplier, and the fourth color (D) is the tolerance, and the fifth color (E) is the working voltage.

With disk-ceramic capacitors (Fig. 1.1.7 (b)) and tubular capacitors (Fig. 1.1.7 (c)) working voltage is not specified, because these are used in circuits with low DC voltage. If a tubular capacitor has five color bands on it, the first color represents the temperature coefficient, while the other four specify the capacity in the previously described way.

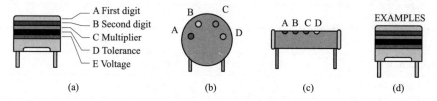

Fig. 1.1.7 Marking the capacity using colors

Tab. 1.1.2 Capacitor values

COLOR	DIGIT	MULTIPLIER	TOLERANCE	VOLTAGE
Black	0	×1 pF	±20%	
Brown	1	×10 pF	±1%	
Red	2	×100 pF	±2%	250 V
Orange	3	×1 nF	±2.5%	
Yellow	4	×10 nF		400 V
Green	5	×100 nF	±5%	
Blue	6	×1 µF		
Violet	7	×10 µF		
Grey	8	×100 µF		
White	9	×1,000 µF	±10%	

Fig. 1.1.8 and Tab. 1.1.3 show how the capacity of miniature tantalum electrolytic capacitors is marked by colors. The first two colors represent the first two digits and have the same values as with resistors. The third color represents the multiplier, to get the capacity expressed in µF. The fourth color represents the maximal working voltage.

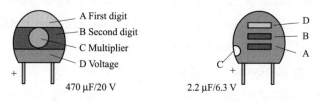

Fig. 1.1.8 Marking tantalum electrolytic capacitors

Tab. 1.1.3 Capacity of miniature tantalum electrolytic capacitors

COLOR	DIGIT	MULTIPLIER	VOLTAGE
Black	0	×1 µF	10 V
Brown	1	×10 µF	
Red	2	×100 µF	
Orange	3		
Yellow	4		6.3 V
Green	5		16 V
Blue	6		20 V
Violet	7		
Grey	8	×.01 µF	25 V
White	9	×.1 µF	3 V
Pink			35 V

One important note on the working voltage: The voltage across a capacitor must not exceed the maximal working voltage as the capacitor may get destroyed. In the case when the voltage is unknown, the "worst" case should be considered. There is the possibility that, due to malfunction of some other components, the voltage on the capacitor equals the power supply voltage. If, for example, the supply is 12 V, the maximal working voltage for the capacitor should be higher than 12 V.

Electrolytic capacitors

Electrolytic capacitors represent the special type of capacitors with fixed capacity value. Thanks to special construction, they can have exceptionally high capacity, ranging from one to several thousand µF. They are most frequently used in the circuits for filtering, however they also have other purposes.

Electrolytic capacitors are polarized components, meaning they have positive and negative leads, which is very important when they are connected to a circuit. The positive lead or pin has to be connected to the point with a higher positive voltage than the negative lead. If it is connected in reverse, the insulating layer inside the capacitor will be "dissolved," and the capacitor will be permanently damaged.

Explosion may also occur if a capacitor is connected to the voltage that exceeds its working voltage. In order to prevent such instances, one of the capacitor's connectors is very clearly marked with a + or −, while the working voltage is printed on the case.

Several models of electrolytic capacitors, as well as their symbols, are shown in the picture below (Fig. 1.1.9).

Fig. 1.1.9   Electrolytic capacitors

Tantalum capacitors represent a special type of electrolytic capacitors. Their parasitic inductance is much lower than standard aluminum electrolytic capacitors so that tantalum capacitors with significantly (even ten times) lower capacity can completely substitute aluminum electrolytic capacitors.

Variable capacitors

Variable capacitors are capacitors with variable capacity. Their minimal capacity ranges from 1 pF and their maximum capacity goes as high as few hundred pF (500 pF max). Variable capacitors are manufactured in various shapes and sizes, but common features for them are a set of fixed plates (called the stator) and a set of movable plates. These plates are fitted into each other and can be taken into and out of mesh by rotating a shaft. The insulator (dielectric) between the plates is air or a thin layer of plastic, hence the name variable capacitor. When adjusting these capacitors, it is important that the plates do not touch.

Below are the photos of air-dielectric capacitors as well as mylar-insulated variable capacitors (Fig. 1.1.10 (a)).

Fig. 1.1.10 (a) shows a "ganged capacitor" in which two capacitors are rotated at the same time. This type of capacitor is used in radio receivers. The larger is used for the tuning circuit, and the smaller one in the local oscillator. The symbol for these capacitors is also shown in the figure.

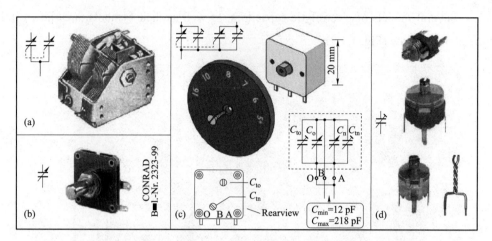

Fig. 1.1.10 (a), (b), and (c) Variable capacitors; d. Trimmer capacitors

Beside capacitors with air dielectric, there are also variable capacitors with solid insulators. With these, thin insulating material such as mylar occupies the space between the stator and the rotor. These capacitors are much more resistant to mechanical damage. They are shown in Fig. 1.1.10 (b).

The most common devices containing variable capacitors are radio receivers, where these are used for frequency adjustment. Semi-variable or trim capacitors are miniature capacitors, with capacity ranging from several picofarads to several tens of picofarads. These are used for fine tuning radio receivers, radio transmitters, oscillators, etc. Three trimmers, along with their symbol, are shown in Fig. 1.1.10 (d).

Unit 2

Diodes

Diodes
翻译

In electronics, a diode is a two-terminal device. Diodes have two active electrodes between which the signal of interest may flow, and most are used for their unidirectional electric current property. The varicap diode is used as an electrically adjustable capacitor.

The directionality of current flow most diodes exhibit is sometimes generically called the rectifying property. The most common function of a diode is to allow an electric current to pass in one direction (called the forward biased condition) and to block the current in the opposite direction (the reverse biased condition). Thus, the diode can be thought of as an electronic version of a check valve.

Real diodes do not display such a perfect on-off directionality but have a more complex non-linear electrical characteristic, which depends on the particular type of diode technology. Diodes also have many other functions in which they are not designed to operate in this on-off manner.

Early diodes included "cat's whisker" crystals and vacuum tube devices. Today the most common diodes are made from semiconductor materials such as silicon or germanium.

Semiconductor diodes

Most modern diodes are based on semiconductor p-n junctions. In a p-n diode, conventional current can flow from the p-type side (the anode) to the n-type side (the cathode), but cannot flow in the opposite direction. Another type of semiconductor diode, the Schottky diode, is formed from the contact between a metal and a semiconductor rather than by a p-n junction.

Current-voltage characteristic

A semiconductor diode's current-voltage characteristic, or *I-V* curve, is related to the transport of carriers through the so-called depletion layer or depletion region that exists at the p-n junction between differing semiconductors. When a p-n junction is first created, conduction band (mobile) electrons from the N-doped region diffuse into the P-doped region where there is a large population of holes (places for electrons in which no electron is present) with which the electrons "recombine." When a mobile electron recombines with a hole, both the hole and electron vanish, leaving behind an immobile positively charged donor on the N-side and negatively charged acceptor on the P-side. The region around the p-n junction becomes depleted of charge carriers and thus behaves as an insulator.

However, the depletion width cannot grow without limit. For each electron-hole pair that recombines, a positively-charged dopant ion is left behind in the N-doped region, and a negatively charged dopant ion is left behind in the P-doped region. As recombination proceeds and more ions are created, an increasing electric field develops through the depletion zone which acts to slow and then finally stop recombination. At this point, there is a "built-in" potential across the depletion zone.

If an external voltage is placed across the diode with the same polarity as the built-in potential, the depletion zone continues to act as an insulator, preventing any significant electric current flow. This is the reverse bias phenomenon. However, if the polarity of the external voltage opposes the built-in potential, recombination can once again proceed, resulting in substantial electric current through the p-n junction. For silicon diodes, the built-in potential is approximately 0.6 V. Thus, if an external current is passed through the diode, about 0.6 V will be developed across the diode such that the P-doped region is positive with respect to the N-doped region and the diode is said to be "turned on" as it has a forward bias.

A diode's *I-V* characteristic can be approximated by four regions of operation (Fig. 1.2.1).

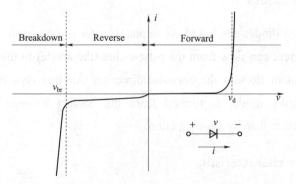

Fig. 1.2.1　The *I-V* characteristic of a p-n junction diode

At very large reverse bias, beyond the peak inverse voltage or PIV, a process called reverse breakdown occurs, which causes a large increase in current that usually damages the device permanently. The avalanche diode is deliberately designed for use in the avalanche region. In the zener diode, the concept of PIV is not applicable. A zener diode contains a heavily doped p-n junction allowing electrons to the tunnel from the valence band of the p-type material to the conduction band of the n-type material, such that the reverse voltage is "clamped" to a known value (called the zener voltage), and avalanche does not occur. Both devices, however, do have a limit to the maximum current and power in the clamped reverse voltage region.

The second region, at reverse biases more positive than the PIV, has only a very small reverse saturation current. In the reverse bias region for a normal P-N rectifier diode, the current through the device is very low (in the μA range).

The third region is forward but small bias, where only a small forward current is conducted.

As the potential difference is increased above an arbitrarily defined "cut-in voltage" or "on-voltage" or "diode forward voltage drop (Vd)", the diode current becomes appreciable (the level of current considered "appreciable" and the value of cut-in voltage depends on the application), and the diode presents a very low resistance.

The current-voltage curve is exponential. In a normal silicon diode at rated currents, the arbitrary "cut-in" voltage is defined as 0.6 to 0.7 volts. The value is different for other diode types — Schottky diodes can be as low as 0.2 V and red light-emitting diodes (LEDs) can be 1.4 V or more and blue LEDs can be up to 4.0 V.

At higher currents the forward voltage drop of the diode increases. A drop of 1 V to 1.5 V is typical at full rated current for power diodes.

Types of semiconductor diodes

There are several types of junction diodes(Fig. 1.2.2), which either emphasize a different physical aspect of a diode often by geometric scaling, doping level, choosing the right electrodes, are just an application of a diode in a special circuit, or are really different devices like the Gunn and laser diode and the MOSFET:

Normal (p-n) diodes, which operate as described above, are usually made of doped silicon or, more rarely, germanium. Before the development of modern silicon power rectifier diodes, cuprous and later selenium were used; its low efficiency gave it a much higher forward voltage drop (typically 1.4–1.7 V per "cell," with multiple cells stacked to increase the peak inverse voltage rating in high voltage rectifiers), and

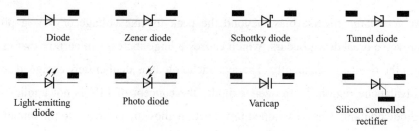

Fig. 1.2.2 Some diode symbols

required a large heat sink (often an extension of the diode's metal substrate), much larger than a silicon diode of the same current ratings would require. The vast majority of all diodes are the p-n diodes found in CMOS integrated circuits, which include two diodes per pin and many other internal diodes.

Applications

Radio demodulation

The first use for the diode was the demodulation of amplitude modulated (AM) radio broadcasts. The history of this discovery is treated in depth in the radio article. In summary, an AM signal consists of alternating positive and negative peaks of voltage, whose amplitude or "envelope" is proportional to the original audio signal. The diode (originally a crystal diode) rectifies the AM radio frequency signal, leaving an audio signal which is the original audio signal. The audio is extracted using a simple filter and fed into an audio amplifier or transducer, which generates sound waves.

Power conversion

Rectifiers are constructed from diodes, where they are used to convert alternating current (AC) into direct current (DC). Automotive alternators are a common example, where the diode, which rectifies the AC into DC, provides better performance than the commutator of the earlier dynamo. Similarly, diodes are also used in Cockcroft-Walton voltage multipliers to convert AC into higher DC voltages.

Over-voltage protection

Diodes are frequently used to conduct damaging high voltages away from sensitive electronic devices. They are usually reverse-biased (non-conducting) under normal circumstances. When the voltage rises above the normal range, the diodes become forward-biased (conducting). For example, diodes are used in (the stepper motor and H-bridge) motor controllers and relay circuits to de-energize coils rapidly without damaging voltage spikes that would otherwise occur (Any diode used in such an application is called a flyback diode). Many integrated circuits also incorporate diodes on the connection pins to prevent external voltages from damaging their sensitive transistors. Specialized diodes are used to protect from over-voltages at higher power (see Diode types above).

TECHNICAL WORDS AND PHRASES

diode	[ˈdaiəud]	n.	二极管
electrode	[iˈlektrəud]	n.	电极
unidirectional	[ˌjuːnidiˈrekʃənəl]	adj.	单向的，单向性的
varicap	[ˌværiˈkæp]	n.	变容二极管
directionality	[diˌrekʃənˈæliti]	n.	方向性
rectify	[ˈrektifai]	vt.	[电子学] 把……整流
silicon	[ˈsilikən]	n.	[化] 硅，硅元素
germanium	[dʒəːˈmeiniəm]	n.	锗
conventional	[kənˈvenʃənl]	adj.	惯例的，常规的
depletion	[diˈpliːʃən]	n.	耗散
doped	[dəupt]	adj.	掺杂质的
hole	[həul]	n.	[物理学] 空穴
electron	[iˈlektrɔn]	n.	电子
immobile	[iˈməubail]	adj.	静止的
donor	[ˈdəunə]	n.	供体
acceptor	[əkˈseptə(r)]	n.	受体
deplete	[diˈpliːt]	vt.	耗尽
dopant	[ˈdəupənt]	n.	掺杂物，掺杂剂
substantial	[səbˈstænʃəl]	adj.	实质的，真实的
breakdown	[ˈbreikdaun]	n.	[电学] 击穿
avalanche	[ˈævəˌlɑːnʃ]	n.	雪崩
tunnel	[ˈtʌnl]	n.	隧道，地道
clamp	[klæmp]	vt.	钳制
saturation	[ˌsætʃəˈreiʃən]	n.	饱和（状态）
appreciable	[əˈpriːʃiəbl]	adj.	可感知的
exponential	[ˌekspəuˈnenʃəl]	adj.	指数的，幂数的
selenium	[siˈliːniəm]	n.	[化] 硒

extension	[iks'tenʃən]	n.	扩大，伸展
substrate	['sʌbstreit]	n.	衬底，基片，基体
pin	[pin]	n.	引脚，管脚
anode	['ænəud]	n.	[电]阳极，正极
cathode	['kæθəud]	n.	阴极
demodulation	[ˌdiːˌmɔdjuː'leiʃən]	n.	[讯]解调，检波
envelope	['enviləup]	n.	包迹(线)，包络(线或面)
rectifier	['rektifaiə]	n.	整流器
audio	['ɔːdiəu]	adj.	音频的
frequency	['friːkwənsi]	n.	频率
extract	[iks'trækt]	vt.	推断出，引出
filter	['filtə]	n.	滤波器
commutator	['kɔmjuteitə]	n.	换向器，转接器
dynamo	['dainəməu]	n.	发电机
relay	['riːlei]	n.	继电器
spike	[spaik]	n.	[无]尖峰信号，测试信号
varicap diode			变容二极管
forward biased			正偏的
reverse biased			反偏的
check valve			单向阀
cat's whisker			触须
p-n junction			p-n 结
Schottky diode			肖特基二极管
current-voltage characteristic			伏—安特性
N-doped region			N 型掺杂区
avalanche diode			雪崩二极管
zener diode			稳压二极管
valence band			价电子带
tunnel diode			隧道二极管
cut-in voltage			开启电压，阈值电压
light-emitting diode(LED)			发光二极管
geometric scaling			几何尺寸
Gunn		adj.	[电子]耿氏效应的，基于耿氏效应的
cuprous oxide			氧化亚铜

heat sink	散热片，散热装置
integrated circuit	集成电路
amplitude modulated (AM) radio broadcast	调幅无线广播
automotive alternator	机动车交流发电机
Cockcroft-Walton voltage multiplier	科克罗夫—瓦耳电压倍增器
stepper motor	步进电机
H-bridge	H 桥电路
de-energize	去激励
flyback diode	回扫二极管

NOTES

1. Semiconductor diode's current-voltage characteristic, or *I-V* curve, is related to the transport of carriers through the so-called depletion layer or depletion region that exists at the p-n junction between differing semiconductors.

   译文：半导体二极管的电流－电压特性，即 *I-V* 曲线，与载流子流过的耗散层或耗散区有关，耗散层或耗散区位于不同类型半导体间形成的 p-n 结上。

   句中"that"引导定语从句，修饰"depletion layer"和"depletion region"。

2. Automotive alternators are a common example, where the diode, which rectifies the AC into DC, provides better performance than the commutator of the earlier dynamo.

   译文：机动车交流发电机是一个常用的例子，其中二极管，把交流变为直流，比早期的发电机换向器提供更好的性能。

   句中"where"引导非限制性定语从句，从句的谓语为"provides"。

3. For example, diodes are used in (the stepper motor and H-bridge) motor controllers and relay circuits to de-energize coils rapidly without damaging voltage spikes that would otherwise occur.

   译文：例如，二极管用在（步进电动机和 H 桥电路）电动机控制器和继电器电路中，对线圈快速地去激励时，不会产生可能出现的具有危害性的电压尖峰。

   句中"to"引导目的状语。

EXERCISES

Ⅰ. **Mark the following statements with T (true) or F (false) according to the text.**

1. Diodes are used for their bidirectional electric current property. (   )
2. Today the most common diodes are made from semiconductor materials such as silicon or germanium. (   )

3. In a p-n diode, conventional current can flow from the n-type side (the cathode) to the p-type side (the anode). (　)
4. Rectifiers are constructed from diodes, where they are used to convert alternating current (AC) into direct current (DC). (　)
5. Many integrated circuits also incorporate diodes on the connection pins to prevent external voltages from damaging their sensitive transistors. (　)

II. Complete the following sentences.

1. Most modern diodes are based on semiconductor _____. In a p-n diode, conventional current can flow from the _____ side (the anode) to the _____ side (the cathode), but cannot flow in the _____ direction.
2. If an external voltage is placed across the diode with the same polarity as the _____ potential, the depletion zone continues to act as an _____, preventing any significant electric current flow.
3. In a normal silicon diode at rated currents, the arbitrary "cut-in" voltage is defined as _____ to 0.7 V.
4. The audio is extracted using a simple _____ and fed into an _____ or transducer, which generates sound waves.
5. _____ diodes are used to protect from _____ at higher power.

Supplementary Reading

Reading 2　Voltage Regulators

Voltage Regulators, also known as voltage stabilizers, are semiconductor devices that output a constant and stable DC voltage at a specified level, despite fluctuations in its input voltage or variations in its load. Voltage regulator ICs have already become available in so many forms and characteristics that they've virtually eliminated the need to build voltage regulating circuits from discrete components.

Factors that spurred the growth of the voltage regulator IC business include: ① ease with which zener diodes and balanced amplifiers can be built into ICs; ② improved IC heat dissipation capabilities; ③ advances in overload protection techniques; and of course, ④ a high demand for voltage regulators in almost all fields of the electronics industry, especially in power supply applications.

Important considerations when selecting a voltage regulator include: ① the desired output voltage level and its regulation capability; ② the output current capacity; ③ the applicable input voltages; ④ conversion efficiency (P_{out}/P_{in}); ⑤ the transient response time; ⑥ ease of use; and if applicable, ⑦ the ability to step-down or step-up output voltages. In switch-mode regulators, the switching frequency is also a consideration.

There are several types of voltage regulators, which may be classified in terms of how they operate or what type of regulation they offer. The most common regulator IC is the standard linear regulator. A typical linear voltage regulator operates by forcing a fixed voltage at the output through a voltage-controlled current source. It has a feedback mechanism that continuously adjusts the current source output based on the level of the output voltage. A drop in voltage would excite the current source into delivering more current to the load to maintain the output voltage. Thus, the capacity of this current source is generally the limiting factor for the maximum load current that the linear regulator can deliver while maintaining the required output level. The amount of time needed for the output to adjust to a change in the input or load is the transient response time of the regulator.

The feedback loop used by linear regulators need some forms of compensation for stability. In most linear regulator ICs, the required feedback loop compensation is already built into the circuit, thereby requiring no external components for this purpose. However, some regulator ICs, like the low-dropout ones, do require that a capacitor be connected between the output and ground to ensure stability. The main disadvantage of linear regulators is their low efficiency, since they are constantly conducting.

The switching voltage regulator is another type of regulator ICs. It differs from the linear regulator in the sense that it employs pulse width modulation (PWM) to regulate its output. The output is controlled by current that is switched at a fixed frequency ranging from a few Hz to a few kHz but with varying duty cycles. The duty cycle of the pulses increases if the output of the regulator needs to supply more load current to maintain the output voltage and decreases if the output needs to be reduced. Switching regulators are more efficient than linear regulators because they only supply power when necessary. Complexity, output ripples, and limited current capacity are the disadvantages of switching regulators.

There is also a group of regulator ICs known as low drop-out (LDO) regulators. The drop-out voltage is the minimum voltage across the regulator that's required to maintain the output voltage at the correct level. The lower the drop-out voltage is, the less the power dissipated internally within the regulator will be, and the higher the regulation efficiency will be. In LDO regulators, the drop-out voltage is typically just about 0.6 V. Even at maximum current, the drop-out voltage increases to just about 0.7–0.8 V.

Examples of applications of regulator ICs include the following: ① regulated power supplies; ② data conversion (ADC/DAC) circuits; ③ sensor and triggering systems; ④ DC-to-DC voltage converters; ⑤ measurement and instrumentation systems; ⑥ motor control; and ⑦ battery charging.

Unit 3

Transistors

Transistors
翻译

In electronics, a transistor is a semiconductor device commonly used to amplify or switch electronic signals. A transistor is made of a solid piece of a semiconductor material, with at least three terminals for connection to an external circuit. A voltage or current applied to one pair of the transistor's terminals changes the current flowing through another pair of terminals. Because the controlled (output) power can be much larger than the controlling (input) power, the transistor provides amplification of a signal. The transistor is the fundamental building block of modern electronic devices, and is used in radio, telephone, computer and other electronic systems. Some transistors are packaged individually but most are found in integrated circuits.

Types

Transistors are categorized by:
- Semiconductor materials: germanium, silicon, gallium arsenide, silicon carbide, etc.
- Structures: BJT, JFET, IGFET (MOSFET), IGBT, "other types."
- Polarity: NPN, PNP (BJTs); N-channel, P-channel (JFETs).
- Maximum power rating: low, medium, high.
- Maximum operating frequency: low, medium, high, radio frequency (RF), microwave (The maximum effective frequency of a transistor is denoted by the term FT, an abbreviation for "frequency of transition." The frequency of transition is the frequency at which the transistor yields unity gain).
- Applications: switch, general purpose, audio, high voltage, super-beta, matched pair.
- Physical packaging: through hole metal, through hole plastic, surface mount, ball grid array, power modules.

- Amplification factor h_{fe} (transistor beta).

Thus, a particular transistor may be described as: silicon, surface mount, BJT, NPN, low power, high frequency switch.

BJT and JFET symbols are shown in Fig. 1.3.1.

Usage

In the early days of transistor circuit design, the bipolar junction transistor, or BJT, was the most commonly used transistor. Even after MOSFETs became available, the BJT remained the transistor of choice for digital and analog circuits because of its ease of manufacture. However, desirable properties of MOSFETs, such as their utility in low-power devices, have made them the ubiquitous choice for use in digital circuits and a very common choice for use in analog circuits.

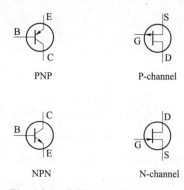

Fig. 1.3.1   BJT and JFET symbols

Transistor as a switch

Transistors are commonly used as electronic switches, for both high power applications including switched-mode power supplies and low power applications such as logic gates.

It can be seen from the graph (Fig. 1.3.2) that once the base voltage reaches a certain level, shown at B, no more current will exist and the output will be held at a fixed voltage. The transistor is then said to be saturated. Hence, the values of the input voltage can be chosen such that the output is either completely off, or completely on. The transistor is acting as a switch, and this type of operation is common in digital circuits where only "on" and "off" values are relevant.

Transistor as an amplifier

The common emitter amplifier below (Fig. 1.3.3) is designed so that a small change in voltage (in V_{in}) changes the small current through the base of the transistor, and the transistor's current amplification combined with the properties of the circuit means that small swings in V_{in} produce large changes in V_{out}.

It is important that the operating parameters of the transistor be chosen and the circuit be designed such that as far as possible the transistor operates within a linear portion of the graph, otherwise the output signal will suffer distortion.

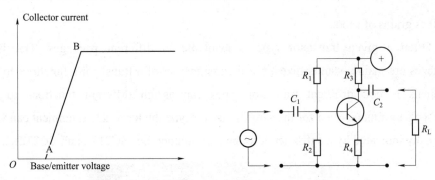

Fig. 1.3.2　The operation of a transistor　　Fig. 1.3.3　A common emitter amplifier

Various configurations of a single transistor amplifier are possible, with some providing current gain, some voltage gain, and some both.

From mobile phones to televisions, vast numbers of products include amplifiers for sound reproduction, radio transmission, and signal processing. The first discrete transistor audio amplifiers barely supplied a few hundred milliwatts, but power and audio fidelity gradually increased as better transistors became available and amplifier architecture evolved.

Modern transistor audio amplifiers of up to a few hundred watts are common and relatively inexpensive. Transistors have replaced valves (electron tubes) in instrument amplifiers.

Some musical instrument amplifier manufacturers mix transistors and vacuum tubes in the same circuit, as some believe tubes have a distinctive sound.

Packaging

Transistors come in many different packages (chip carriers) (See Fig. 1.3.4). The two main categories are through-hole (or leaded), and surface-mount, also known as surface mount device (SMD). The ball grid array (BGA) is the latest surface mount package (currently only for large transistor arrays). It has solder "balls" on the underside in place of leads. Because they are smaller and have shorter interconnections, SMDs have better high frequency characteristics but lower power rating.

Transistor packages are made of glass, metal, ceramic or plastic. The package often dictates the power rating and frequency characteristics. Power transistors have large packages that can be clamped to heat sinks for enhanced cooling. Additionally, most power transistors have the collector or drain physically connected to the metal can/metal plate. At the other extreme, some surface-mount microwave transistors are as small as grains of sand.

Often a given transistor type is available in different packages. Transistor packages are mainly standardized, but the assignment of a transistor's functions to the terminals is not: different transistor types can assign different functions to the package's terminals. Even for the same transistor type the terminal assignment can vary (normally indicated by a suffix letter to the part number, i.e. BC212L and BC212K).

Fig. 1.3.4　Transistors

TECHNICAL WORDS AND PHRASES

transistor	[træn'zistə]	n.	[电子]晶体管
amplification	[ˌæmplifi'keiʃən]	n.	放大
package	['pækidʒ]	vt.	封装
gallium	['gæliəm]	n.	镓
arsenide	['ɑːsənaid]	n.	[化]砷化物
carbide	['kɑːbaid]	n.	[化]碳化物
ubiquitous	[juː'bikwitəs]	adj.	到处存在的，（同时）普遍存在的
relevant	['relivənt]	adj.	有关的，相应的
emitter	[i'mitə]	n.	发射极
swing	[swiŋ]	n.	波动，改变
distortion	[dis'tɔːʃən]	n.	失真
barely	['bɛəli]	adv.	仅仅
fidelity	[fi'deliti]	n.	保真度
architecture	['ɑːkitektʃə]	n.	结构
ceramic	[si'ræmik]	n.	陶瓷制品
collector	[kə'lektə]	n.	集电极
drain	[drein]	n.	漏极

grain	[grein]	n.	细粒
assignment	[ə'sainmənt]	n.	分配
integrated circuit			集成电路
gallium arsenide			砷化镓
ball grid array			球栅阵列
heat sink			散热片

NOTES

1. The common emitter amplifier below (Fig. 1.3.3) is designed so that a small change in voltage (in V_{in}) changes the small current through the base of the transistor, and the transistor's current amplification combined with the properties of the circuit means that small swings in V_{in} produce large changes in V_{out}.

   译文：下图（图1.3.3）给出的共射放大电路中，输入电压微小的变化会使基极电流发生微小的变化，晶体管的电流放大性能和电路的性质合起来意味着 V_{in} 的很小变化会使 V_{out} 发生很大的变化。

   句中"so that"引导结果状语从句。

2. It is important that the operating parameters of the transistor be chosen and the circuit be designed such that as far as possible the transistor operates within a linear portion of the graph, otherwise the output signal will suffer distortion.

   译文：晶体管的工作参数的选择和电路的设计很重要，晶体管应尽可能工作于图形的线性部分，否则输出信号将会失真。

   句中"it"为形式主语。

EXERCISES

Ⅰ. **Translate the following words into English.**

1. 表面贴装
2. 高频开关
3. 共射放大器
4. 失真
5. 球栅阵列
6. 集电极
7. 功率晶体管
8. 真空管

Ⅱ. **Complete the following sentences.**

1. In electronics, a transistor is a _____ device commonly used to _____ or _____ electronic signals.
2. Some transistors are packaged _____ but most are found in _____.
3. Various configurations of a single transistor amplifier are possible, with some

providing current _____, some voltage gain, and some _____.
4. Transistors come in many different packages. The two main categories are _____ (or leaded), and _____, also known as surface mount device (SMD).
5. Power transistors have large _____ that can be clamped to _____ for enhanced cooling.

Supplementary Reading

Reading 3 Field-effect Transistors

The field-effect transistor (FET) relies on an electric field to control the shape and hence the conductivity of a channel of one type of charge carrier in a semiconductor material. FETs are sometimes called unipolar transistors to contrast their single-carrier-type operation with the dual-carrier-type operation of bipolar (junction) transistors (BJT). The concept of the FET predates the BJT, though it was not physically implemented until after BJTs due to the limitations of semiconductor materials and the relative ease of manufacturing BJTs compared with FETs at the time.

Terminals

All FETs have a gate, drain, and source terminal that correspond roughly to the base, collector, and emitter of BJTs (Fig. 1.3.5). Aside from the JFET, all FETs also have a fourth terminal called the body, base, bulk, or substrate. This fourth terminal serves to bias the transistor into operation; it is rare to make non-trivial use of the body terminal in circuit designs, but its presence is important when we set up the physical layout of an integrated circuit. The size of the gate, length L in the diagram, is the distance between the source and drain. The width is the extension of the transistor, in the diagram perpendicular to the cross section. Typically the width is much larger than the length of the gate. A gate length of 1 μm limits the upper frequency to about 5 GHz, 0.2 μm to about 30 GHz.

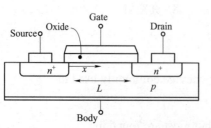

Fig. 1.3.5 The cross section of an n-type MOSFET

The names of the terminals refer to their functions. The gate terminal may be thought of as controlling the opening and closing of a physical gate. This gate permits electrons to flow through or blocks their passage by creating or eliminating a channel between the source and drain. Electrons flow from the source terminal towards the drain terminal if influenced by an applied voltage. The body simply refers to the bulk of the semiconductor in which the gate, source and drain lie. Usually the body terminal is connected to the highest or lowest voltage within the circuit, depending on its type. The body terminal and the source terminal are sometimes connected together since the source is also sometimes connected to the highest or lowest voltage within the circuit, however there are several uses of FETs which do not have such a configuration, such as transmission gates and cascode circuits.

Composition

The FET can be constructed from a number of semiconductors, silicon being by far the most common. Most FETs are made with conventional bulk semiconductor processing techniques, using the single crystal semiconductor wafer as the active region, or channel.

Among the more unusual body materials are amorphous silicon, polycrystalline silicon or other amorphous semiconductors in thin-film transistors or organic field effect transistors that are based on organic semiconductors and often apply organic gate insulators and electrodes.

Uses

IGBTs see application in switching internal combustion engine ignition coils, where fast switching and voltage blocking capabilities are important.

The most commonly used FET is the MOSFET. The CMOS (complementary-symmetry metal oxide semiconductor) process technology is the basis for modern digital integrated circuits. This process technology uses an arrangement where the (usually "enhancement-mode") p-channel MOSFET and n-channel MOSFET are connected in series such that when one is on, the other is off.

The fragile insulating layer of the MOSFET between the gate and channel makes it vulnerable to electrostatic damage during handling. This is not usually a problem after the device has been installed in a properly designed circuit.

In FETs electrons can flow in either direction through the channel when operated in the linear mode, and the naming convention of drain terminal and source terminal is somewhat arbitrary, as the devices are typically (but not always) built symmetrically from the source to the drain. This makes FETs suitable for switching analog signals between paths (multiplexing).

Unit 4
Operational Amplifiers

Operational Amplifiers 翻译

An operational amplifier, often called an op-amp, is a DC-coupled high-gain electronic voltage amplifier with differential inputs and, usually, a single output. Typically the output of an op-amp is controlled either by negative feedback, which largely determines the magnitude of its output voltage gain, or by positive feedback, which facilitates regenerative gain and oscillation. High input impedance at the input terminals and low output impedance are important typical characteristics.

Op-amps are among the most widely used electronic devices today, being used in a vast array of consumer, industrial, and scientific devices. Many standard IC op-amps cost only a few cents in moderate production volume; however some integrated or hybrid operational amplifiers with special performance specifications may cost over $100 US in small quantities.

Modern designs are electronically more rugged than earlier implementations and some can sustain direct short-circuits on their outputs without damage.

Circuit notation

The circuit symbol for an op-amp is shown in Fig. 1.4.1, where:

V_+: non-inverting input
V_-: inverting input
V_{out}: output
V_{S+}: positive power supply
V_{S-}: negative power supply

Fig. 1.4.1 The op-amp symbol

The power supply pins (V_{S+} and V_{S-}) can be labeled in different ways. Despite different labeling, the function remains the same. Often these pins are left out of the diagram for clarity, and the power configuration is described or assumed from the circuit. The positions of the inverting and non-inverting inputs may be reversed in the diagrams where appropriate; the power supply pins are not commonly reversed. For example, IC741 is an operational amplifier. It is used for doing arithmetic operations on analog computers, instrumentation and other control systems. Operational amplifier is in the class of linear ICs. Linear ICs have a peculiarity that they can take continuous voltage signals like their analog counterparts. These are highly used today because of their high reliability and low cost. They are mainly used as voltage amplifiers. The basic operational amplifier works similar to the following sequence.

input stage--->intermediate stage--->level shifter--->output stage

The input stage consists of high input impedance that amplifies the difference between the given input signals. The intermediate stage consists of cascaded amplifiers to amplify the signals from the input. Due to high amplification the DC level of the signals goes up. So in order to bring them down to the rated value, the level shifter or level translator is used. The output stage consists of class AB/ class B power amplifier in order to amplify the power of the output signal.

Operation of ideal op-amps

The amplifier's differential inputs consist of an inverting input and a non-inverting input, and ideally the op-amp amplifies only the difference in voltage between the two. This is called the "differential input voltage." In its most common use, the op-amp's output voltage is controlled by feeding a fraction of the output signal back to the inverting input. This is known as negative feedback. If that fraction is zero, i.e., there is no negative feedback, the amplifier is said to be running "open loop" and its output is the differential input voltage multiplied by the total gain of the amplifier, as shown by the following equation:

$$V_{out} = (V_+ - V_-) * G_{openloop}$$

where V_+ is the voltage at the non-inverting terminal, V_- is the voltage at the inverting terminal, and G is the total open-loop gain of the amplifier.

Because the magnitude of the open-loop gain is typically very large and not well controlled by the manufacturing process, op-amps are not usually used without negative feedback. Unless the differential input voltage is extremely small, open-loop operation results in op-amp saturation. An example of how the output voltage is calculated when negative feedback exists is shown below in the basic non-inverting amplifier circuit.

Another typical configuration of op-amps is the positive feedback, which takes a fraction of the output signal back to the non-inverting input. Its important application is the comparator with hysteresis.

For any input voltages the ideal op-amp has:
- Infinite open-loop gain;
- Infinite bandwidth;
- Infinite input impedances (resulting in zero input currents);
- Zero offset voltage;
- Infinite slew rate;
- Zero output impedance and zero noise.

Applications

Use in electronics system design

The use of op-amps as circuit blocks is much easier and clearer than specifying all their individual circuit elements (transistors, resistors, etc.), whether the amplifiers used are integrated or discrete. In the first approximation op-amps can be used as if they were ideal differential gain blocks; at a later stage limits can be placed on the acceptable range of parameters for each op-amp.

Circuit design follows the same lines for all electronic circuits. A specification is drawn up governing what the circuit is required to do, with allowable limits. For example, the gain may be required to be 100 times, with a tolerance of 5% but drift of less than 1% in a specified temperature range; the input impedance not less than 1 megohm; etc.

A basic circuit is designed, often with the help of circuit modeling (on a computer). Specific commercially available op-amps and other components are then chosen, which meet the design criteria within the specified tolerances at acceptable cost. If not all the criteria can be met, the specification may need to be modified.

Basic non-inverting amplifier circuits

The general op-amp has two inputs and one output. The output voltage is a multiple of the difference between the two inputs:

$$V_{out} = G(V_+ - V_-)$$

in which G is the open-loop gain of the op-amp. The inputs are assumed to have very high impedance; negligible current will flow into or out of the inputs. Op-amp outputs have very low source impedance.

If the output is connected to the inverting input (Fig. 1.4.2), after being scaled by a voltage divider $K = R_1/(R_1 + R_2)$, then:

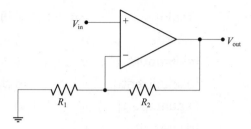

Fig. 1.4.2   A non-inverting amplifier circuit

$$V_+ = V_{in}$$
$$V_- = KV_{out}$$
$$V_{out} = G(V_{in} - KV_{out})$$

Solving for V_{out}/V_{in}, we see that the result is a linear amplifier with gain:

$$V_{out}/V_{in} = G/(1+GK)$$

If G is very large, V_{out}/V_{in} comes close to $1/K$, which equals $1+(R_2/R_1)$.

This negative feedback connection is the most typical use of an op-amp, but many different configurations are possible, making it one of the most versatile of all the electronic building blocks.

When connected in a negative feedback configuration, the op-amp will try to make V_{out} whatever voltage is necessary to make the input voltages as nearly equal as possible. This, and the high input impedance, is sometimes called the two "golden rules" of op-amp design (for circuits that use negative feedback):

- No current will flow into the inputs.
- The input voltages will be nearly equal.

Most single, dual and quad op-amps available have a standardized pin-out which permits one type to be substituted for another without wiring changes. A specific op-amp may be chosen for its open loop gain, bandwidth, noise performance, input impedance, power consumption, or a compromise between any of these factors.

TECHNICAL WORDS AND PHRASES

differential	[ˌdifəˈrenʃəl]	adj.	差动的
feedback	[ˈfiːdbæk]	n.	反馈
magnitude	[ˈmægnitjuːd]	n.	大小
regenerative	[riˈdʒenərətiv]	adj.	再生的
oscillation	[ˌɔsiˈleiʃən]	n.	振荡
array	[əˈrei]	n.	大批
volume	[ˈvɔljuːm]	n.	量, 大量, 音量

rugged	['rʌgid]	adj.	坚固的
clarity	['klæriti]	n.	清楚，透明
arithmetic	[ə'riθmətik]	n.	算术，算法
peculiarity	[pi,kju:li'æriti]	n.	特性
counterpart	['kauntəpɑ:t]	n.	副本，极相似的人（物）
reliability	[ri,laiə'biliti]	n.	可靠性
cascade	[kæs'keid]	n.	级联
comparator	['kɔmpəreitə]	n.	比较器
hysteresis	[,histə'ri:sis]	n.	迟滞
offset	['ɔ:fset]	n.	失调
tolerance	['tɔlərəns]	n.	误差
drift	[drift]	n.	漂移
versatile	['və:sətail]	adj.	通用的，万能的
quad	[kwɔd]	n.	同类4个的一套或一组
consumption	[kən'sʌmpʃən]	n.	消耗
compromise	['kɔmprəmaiz]	n.	折中
short-circuit		n.	短路
DC-coupled			直流耦合
non-inverting input			同相输入
inverting input			反相输入
voltage amplifier			电压放大器
level shifter			电平转换器
level translator			电平转换
slew rate			延迟率
open loop gain			开环增益
operational amplifier			运算放大器

NOTES

1. Typically the output of an op-amp is controlled either by negative feedback, which largely determines the magnitude of its output voltage gain, or by positive feedback, which facilitates regenerative gain and oscillation.

   译文：运放的输出端受负反馈或正反馈控制，负反馈在很大程度上决定输出电压增益的大小，正反馈可以促进再生增益并产生振荡。

   句中"which"引导非限制性定语从句。

2. This negative feedback connection is the most typical use of an op-amp, but many different configurations are possible, making it one of the most versatile of all the

electronic building blocks.

译文：负反馈连接是运放的最典型应用，但是可能有很多种不同的结构，使得其成为最通用的电子模块之一。

句中"making it one of the most versatile of all the electronic building blocks"作句子的补语。

EXERCISES

Ⅰ. **Mark the following statements with T (true) or F (false) according to the text.**

1. Low input impedance at the input terminals and high output impedance are important typical characteristics of operational amplifiers. (   )
2. An operational amplifier is in the class of nonlinear ICs. (   )
3. The amplifier's differential inputs consist of an inverting input and a non-inverting input, and ideally the op-amp amplifies only the difference in voltage between the two. (   )
4. In the first approximation op-amps can be used as if they were ideal differential gain blocks. (   )
5. The general op-amp has one input and two outputs. (   )

Ⅱ. **Complete the following sentences.**

1. An operational amplifier, often called an op-amp, is a _____ high-gain electronic voltage amplifier with _____ inputs and, usually, a single output.
2. The input stage consists of high _____ that amplifies the _____ between the given input signals.
3. In its most common use, the op-amp's _____ voltage is controlled by feeding a fraction of the output signal back to the _____ input.
4. Unless the differential input voltage is extremely _____, _____ operation results in op-amp saturation.
5. A specific op-amp may be chosen for its _____, bandwidth, noise performance, _____, power consumption, or a compromise between any of these factors.

Supplementary Reading

Reading 4   System in a Package

The term "System in a Package" or SIP refers to a semiconductor device that incorporates multiple chips that make up a complete electronic system into a single package. Electronic devices like mobile phones conventionally consist of several individually packaged ICs handling different functions, e.g., logic circuits for information processing, memory for storing information, and I/O circuits for information exchange with the outside world. In a system-in-a-package, all of these individual chips are assembled into a single package, allowing tremendous space savings and significant down-sizing of electronic gadgets.

SIP must not be confused with SOC, or system-on-a-chip, which is a complete electronic system, built on a single chip. SOCs suffer from long development time and high development costs; mainly because it is difficult to make an entire system of differently functioning circuit blocks work on a single chip. SIP technology, on the other hand, simply takes several readily available chips put together in a single package.

The predecessor of the SIP is the multichip module (MCM) of the early 1990's, wherein several specialized chips are also assembled in a single ceramic package as a system solution using traditional assembly processes. Some people consider the SIP and the MCM as still the same thing, but most people prefer to give SIP its own distinct identity because of its mass-production nature and use of cutting edge assembly technologies. For instance, the chips in an MCM are mounted on the same plane (the cavity substrate), whereas SIP employs die stacking as its natural configuration (Fig. 1.4.3).

Fig. 1.4.3　An example of an MCM, the predecessor of the SIP

The ability to take existing chips to come up with a totally new system in a single package has one clear advantage: It drastically reduces development time and risk to bring new products to the market more quickly. With SIP technology, vendors are able to cram multiple flash devices, SRAMs, DRAMs, microcontrollers, ASICs, DSPs, and passive components into very thin packages that can fit into sleeker, more stylish, and yet more complex electronic gadgets.

Aside from shorter time-to-market, SIP manufacturing reduces its over-all assembly and test costs, since only one package will be assembled and tested to come up with the system. Better electrical performance is also achieved because of the shorter interconnections within the SIP. The SIP also simplifies the process of assembling the final application module by requiring simpler PCB lay-outs, since the complex interconnections required by the system have already been taken care of inside the SIP.

The challenge in SIP manufacturing lies in the assembly process itself. Touted as the next-level multi-chip module (MCM) assembly technology, it requires the ability to assemble and interconnect several dies not only horizontally (wherein dies are placed side by side), but vertically as well (wherein several dies are placed on top of each other).

Mounting dies on top of each other and interconnecting them are known as die stacking, a new technology that is harnessed extensively in state-of-the-art SIP manufacturing. This extensive use of stacked die configuration is the reason why SIP is also known as the 3-D package.

One challenge posed by die stacking is the need to keep the stack thermally and mechanically stable on the substrate, while allowing good interconnection among the dies, and keeping the package as thin as possible in doing so. Needless to say, package thickness largely depends on the number of dies that are vertically stacked inside. For instance, current technology would generally require a 1.4-mm chip scale package (CSP) to accommodate a six-die stack whereas a four-die stack can fit within a 1.2-mm CSP.

Flip chip bonding is also used in SIP interconnection, either on its own or as a complement to wire bonding. Flip chip configuration may be applied either to the upper dies or the lower ones, depending on the intent of the design. Flip chipping a bottom die directly onto the substrate enables that die to operate at a high speed. On the other hand, flip chipping a top die eliminates the use of long wires for connection to the substrate (Fig. 1.4.4).

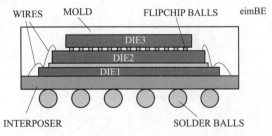

Fig. 1.4.4   An example of a 3-die SIP configuration employing both wire bonding and flip chip bonding

Heat dissipation is another challenge in the development of SIPs. Taking chips off-the-shelf and using them in SIPs aren't always easy from the thermal point of view, since these chips were designed to dissipate heat through their own packages. Crowding them all together inside a SIP can accumulate enough heat to be of major concern in the field. Thermal management is therefore an important ingredient of any SIP development process.

SIP manufacturing not only offers assembly challenges, but test challenges as well. SIPs combine microelectromechanical systems, optoelectronic devices, various sensors, linear and digital circuits, etc., which were built by different wafer fab process technologies and therefore have varying excitation requirements. Add to this the fact that each of these system blocks require special test methods of its own. A test solution to meet the various test resources and methods required by a complex SIP can turn out to be expensive.

For these test issues, some quarters propose a cost-effective solution in the form of an open-architecture automated test equipment (OA-ATE) that allows semiconductor manufacturers to specify their own test resource and instrumentation requirements. "Specialization" of test capability nonetheless requires some standardized vital elements: ① an industry-standard bus structure; ② compatibility with industry-standard data formats; ③ browser technology to access and control resources; ④ a modular hardware and software structure to enable reconfigurability; and ⑤ partitioned test supported by ATE and EDA tools.

Successful implementation of SIP manufacturing brings in many advantages that are important to the semiconductor industry of the future: shorter time-to-market, lower cost, flexibility, smaller size, etc. To get there, however, requires a monumental engineering effort to address all technical obstacles along the way.

Unit 5
Digital Logic Circuits

Digital Logic
Circuits
翻译

Number systems

The number system with which we are most familiar is the base 10, or decimal system. Recent technological developments have created the need for other number systems. The electronic computer, for example, required the development of system that was easily adapted to electronic processes. These number systems were the binary (base 2), octal (base 8), and hexadecimal (base 16). The binary system is the primary language of the computer. The octal and hexadecimal systems are usually used for communication with the computer and for storage of information within the computer. Since computers can only process binary numbers or numbers coded in other systems such as octal and hexadecimal, the decimal system must be converted to one of these other systems before it can be processed by the computer. When the computer finishes its operations on the information, the output is printed or displayed in the number system other than the decimal one, and this too must be converted, this time back to the decimal system.

Digital electronics is a "logical" science. Logic, generally speaking, is the science of formal principles of reasoning. Digital logic is the science of reasoning with numbers, a special circuit called a gate which can perform nearly all-digital functions. If the logic operation is too complex for one gate, it can almost always be implemented through the use of a combination of gates. These extended logic circuits are combinational logic.

Logical gates

AND gates and NAND gates

Two of the most basic logic functions are the AND and the NAND. The difference between these functions is that they are complements. This means they are opposite in function.

The AND gate provides a function in digital logic which gives a high output when all of its inputs are high. Fig. 1.5.1 shows the symbol used to represent an AND gate. In this case, there are two inputs, A and B, and one output, C. Gates with as many as eight inputs are available.

An AND gate will provide an output high (1) only when both inputs (or all inputs if there are more than two) are high (1). This relationship is usually written in the following way:

$$AB = C$$

Above expressing is normally said in the following way: "If A equals 1 and B equals 1, then C will equal 1" or "A and B equals C."

The NAND gate is a more common gate than the AND gate (as shown in Fig. 1.5.2). It is the complement of the AND gate, meaning that it is just the opposite in logic state.

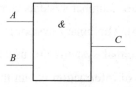
Fig. 1.5.1 The AND gate

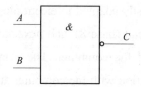
Fig. 1.5.2 The NAND gate

NAND gates frequently are cheaper and easier to use than AND gates because electronically they are simpler. The **N** in front of the AND means "not" AND.

The logic is also written differently for an N gate when it is placed in a formula. An overscore of bar is used to indicate a NOT or inverted (complement) condition. For example: $AB = \overline{C}$.

It means "A and B equals NOT C." In the case of the NAND gate the output will be high (1) except when the inputs are all high. When all inputs are high, the output of the NAND gate will be low (0).

OR gates

The OR gate (as shown in Fig. 1.5.3) provides a function that will give a high output (1) when any one of the inputs is at a high (1) logic level. This function is usually written in the following way: $A + B = C$.

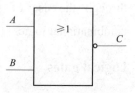
Fig. 1.5.3 The OR gate

The plus (+) sign is the symbol used to indicate an OR logic function. This expression is spoken in the following way: "If A OR B equals 1, then *C* equals 1."

Combination logic functions

Individual logic gates are building blocks. They can stand alone if only a single logic function is needed, or they can be combined with other gates for more complex operations. There are times when it is advantageous to substitute one kind of gate for another. What does a circuit designer do, for instance, if an AND gate is needed and only NAND gates are available? It is an indicator of the versatility and flexibility of digital integrated circuits that the designer can configure the gates on hand to meet the circuit needs.

Flip-flops and clocks

Microprocessors employ both latches and flip-flops. The basic RS latch is not a flip-flop because it is an asynchronous device (it is unlocked). That is a latch function at arbitrary times, whenever data pulses may be inputted. On the other hand, we will see that a flip-flop is a synchronous device, it is clocked, and it can change state only on the arrival of a clock pulse. Clock pulses are basically square waves that may have a very low repetition, or may have a very high repetition rate.

Note that the simple arrangement depicted in Fig. 1.5.4 operates as a flip-flop, as the RS latch function is locked in step with the clock input. This is an active-low configuration: the R and S outputs can be complemented only while the clock is logic-low.

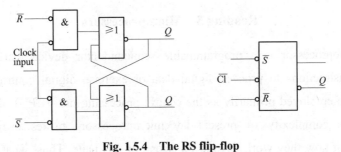

Fig. 1.5.4 The RS flip-flop

TECHNICAL WORDS AND PHRASES

flip-flop	['flipflɔp]	n.	触发器
latch	[lætʃ]	n.	门闩，碰锁
asynchronous	[ei'siŋkrənəs]	adj.	[电] 异步的

arbitrary	[ˈɑːbitrəri]	adj.	任意的
synchronous	[ˈsiŋkrənəs]	adj.	[物]同步的
arrangement	[əˈreindʒmənt]	n.	电路，装置

EXERCISES

Ⅰ. **Match the items listed in the following two columns.**

1. digital logic circuit   2. 数字系统
3. number system   4. 六进制
5. octal system   6. 逻辑门
7. hexadecimal system   8. 数字逻辑电路
9. logical gate   10. 组合逻辑功能
11. combination logic function   12. 八进制

Ⅱ. **Complete the following sentences.**

1. The number system with which we are most familiar is the _____ system.
2. The _____ system is the primary language of the computer.
3. The AND gate provides a function in digital logic which gives a high output when all of its inputs are_____.
4. If A OR B equals 1, then C equals_____.
5. On the other hand，we will see that a flip-flop is a_____device.

Supplementary Reading

Reading 5 Microprocessors

  A microprocessor is a programmable semiconductor device that is used for executing instructions to process digital data or exercise digital control over other devices. It is employed primarily as the central processing unit (CPU) of a computer system. The complexity of present-day microprocessors makes even a modest description of how they work beyond the scope of this page. Thus, what is presented below is the architecture of a typical microprocessor from a couple of decades ago. The following discussion, simple as it is, nonetheless gives a reasonable understanding of how microprocessors in general work.

  As mentioned, a microprocessor is used to execute a series of steps or instructions, which collectively constitute a "program." Every microprocessor has a unique set of instructions that can be executed. This set of instructions is known as its, well, instruction set. Every instruction on the instruction set does something unique, and has different requirements in terms of which part(s) of the microprocessor to utilize or what data to work on.

A basic microprocessor circuit has the following parts:

(1) An arithmetic and logic unit (ALU), which is where the arithmetic and logic operations of the microprocessor take place;

(2) A data bus system where data that need to be processed are transported;

(3) An address bus system that provides the address of the memory location being accessed;

(4) A control unit for orchestrating the program execution of the microprocessor;

(5) An instruction register/decoder where instructions are loaded one at a time and "interpreted";

(6) A program counter that indicates the memory address where the next instruction will come from;

(7) Various registers, flags, and pointers.

A microprocessor executes a program stored in memory by fetching the instructions of the program (and whatever data they require) one at a time and performing these instructions. Memory in this context basically refers to external memory devices that complement the microprocessor and the input/output devices of the computer system. The manner in which the next instruction will be executed depends on the results of the last operation. Thus, the output of the microprocessor depends on the instructions and the input data provided to it.

Microprocessors with different ALU designs have different arithmetic and logic capabilities. For instance, some ALUs can handle all the basic arithmetic functions directly, while the simplest ones only perform addition and shift operations, which are also the steps used to emulate all other arithmetic functions such as multiplication and division. The logic capability of the ALU also varies from one microprocessor to another, but almost all ALUs can perform the AND, OR and EXOR.

The instructions being followed by a microprocessor come in the form of instruction codes. Instruction execution cannot occur haphazardly, and must be controlled precisely as it happens. The control unit of the microprocessor is the one responsible for controlling the sequencing of events needed for the execution of an instruction, as well as the timing of this sequence of events. The control unit is complemented by a clock or timing generator that helps it trigger the occurrence of each event at the correct point in time.

The program counter of a microprocessor indicates where the next instruction bytes are located in memory. It is indexed by the control unit by 1 every time an instruction code is transferred from memory to the microprocessor.

A microprocessor uses the instruction register to store the instruction code last fetched from memory. The first byte of an instruction code is fed by the instruction register to the instruction decoder, which "decodes" it to determine which operation must be carried out, how many bytes of data will be processed, and where to get these data. After instruction decoding, the execution of the instruction proceeds.

Registers are elements composed of a set of flip-flops where data are stored temporarily for subsequent processing or transfer, as the microprocessor goes about its task of executing its instructions one at a time. The accumulator is a special register used by the microprocessor for holding operands, or data to be manipulated by the ALU. Aside from the accumulator, several general-purpose registers are also available to the microprocessor for holding data that need to be operated on.

Microprocessors also have Status Flags, which are really just special registers for storing the state of a condition that results from a previous operation. Examples of status flags include: ① the Carry Status Flag, which indicates if there's a need to do a "carry" after addition or a "borrow" after subtraction; ② the Zero Status Flag, which indicates if a given operation in the ALU results in a "zero"; ③ the Sign Status Flag, which indicates whether the result of an ALU operation is negative or positive; ④ the Overflow Status Flag, which indicates if an operation produces a result that can't fit into the specified word length; and ⑤ the Parity Status Flag, a flag (used in error detection) that is set if the result of an operation contains an even number of 1.

The microprocessor has been around for more than two decades already. It now comes in many forms, sizes and levels of sophistication, powering all kinds of applications that rely on "computer control." Although it is the central processing unit of a computer system, it also needs to interact with other semiconductor devices in order to perform its functions. These "other" devices include the memory and input/output devices that constitute the rest of the computer system.

Chapter 2
Power Electronics and Motors

Unit 6
Introduction to Power Electronics

Introduction to Power Electronics 翻译

Definition

Power electronics refers to control and conversion of electrical power by power semiconductor devices wherein these devices operate as switches as shown in Fig. 2.6.1. Example: An electric vehicle drive must convert the DC input to the AC output that has variable voltage and variable frequency.

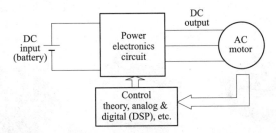

Fig. 2.6.1 Power electronics as power processing and control circuits

The advent of silicon-controlled rectifiers, abbreviated as SCRs, led to the development of a new area of application called the power electronics. Prior to the introduction of SCRs, mercury-arc rectifiers were used for controlling electrical power, but such rectifier circuits were part of industrial electronics and the scope for applications of mercury-arc rectifiers was limited. Once SCRs were available, the application area spread to many fields such as drives, power supplies, aviation electronics, high frequency inverters and power electronics.

Main task of power electronics

Power electronics has applications that span the whole field of electrical power systems, with the power range of these applications extending from a few VA/Watts to several MVA / MW.

The main task of power electronics is to control and convert electrical power from one form to another. The four main forms of conversion are:
- Rectification referring to conversion of AC voltage to DC voltage;
- DC-to-AC conversion;
- DC-to DC conversion;
- AC-to-AC conversion.

"Electronic power converter" is the term that is used to refer to a power electronic circuit that converts voltage and current from one form to another. These converters can be classified as:
- Rectifiers converting an AC voltage to a DC voltage;
- Inverters converting a DC voltage to an AC voltage;
- Choppers or switch-mode power supplies that convert a DC voltage to another DC voltage;
- Cycloconverters and cycloinverters converting an AC voltage to another AC voltage.

In addition, SCRs and other power semiconductor devices shown in Fig. 2.6.2 are used as static switches.

Fig. 2.6.2 Power semiconductor devices

Rectification

Rectifiers can be classified as uncontrolled and controlled rectifiers, and the controlled rectifiers can be further divided into semi-controlled and fully-controlled rectifiers. Uncontrolled rectifier circuits are built with diodes, and fully-controlled rectifier circuits are built with SCRs. Both diodes and SCRs are used in semi-controlled rectifier circuits.

The popular rectifier configurations are listed below:
- Single-phase semi-controlled bridge rectifiers;
- Single-phase fully-controlled bridge rectifiers;
- Three-phases three-pulse, star-connected rectifiers;
- Double three-phase, three-pulse, star-connected rectifiers with inter-phase transformers (IPT);
- Three-phase semi-controlled bridge rectifiers;
- Three-phase fully-controlled bridge rectifiers;
- Double three-phase fully-controlled bridge rectifiers with IPTs.

Apart from the configurations listed above, there are series-connected and 12-pulse rectifiers for delivering high power output.

Power rating of a single-phase rectifier tends to be lower than 10 kW. Three-phase bridge rectifiers are used for delivering higher power output, up to 500 kW at 500 V DC or even more. For low voltage, high current applications, a pair of three-phase, three-pulse rectifiers interconnected by an inter-phase transformer(IPT) is used. For a high current output, rectifiers with IPTs are preferred to connecting devices directly in parallel. There are many applications for rectifiers. Some of them are:
- Variable speed DC drives;
- Battery chargers;
- DC power supplies and power supplies for a specific application like electroplating.

DC-to-AC conversion

The converter that changes a DC voltage to an alternating voltage is called an inverter. Earlier inverters were built with SCRs. Since the circuitry required to turn the SCR off tends to be complex, other power semiconductor devices such as bipolar junction transistors, power MOSFETs, insulated gate bipolar transistors (IGBT) and MOS-controlled thyristors (MCTs) are used nowadays. Currently only the inverters with a high power rating, such as 500 kW or higher, are likely to be built with either SCRs or gate turn-off thyristors (GTOs). There are many inverter circuits, and the techniques for controlling an inverter vary in complexity.

Some of the applications of an inverter are listed below:
- Emergency lighting systems;
- AC variable speed drives;

- Uninterrupted power supplies;
- Frequency converters.

DC-to-DC conversion

When the SCR came into use, a DC-to-DC converter circuit was called a chopper. Nowadays, an SCR is rarely used in a DC-to-DC converter. Either a power BJT or a power MOSFET is normally used in such a converter, and this converter is called a switch-mode power supply. A switch-mode power supply can be of one of the types listed below:

- Step-down switch-mode power supplies;
- Step-up choppers;
- Fly-back converters;
- Resonant converters.

The typical applications for a switch-mode power supply or a chopper are:

- DC drives;
- Battery chargers;
- DC power supplies.

AC-to-AC conversion

A cycloconverter or a cycloinverter converts an AC voltage, such as the mains supply, to another AC voltage. The amplitude and the frequency of input voltage to a cycloconverter tend to be fixed values, whereas both the amplitude and the frequency of output voltage of a cycloconverter tend to be variable. On the other hand, the circuit that converts an AC voltage to another AC voltage at the same frequency is known as an AC-chopper. A typical application of a cycloconverter is to use it for controlling the speed of AC traction motor, and most of these cycloconverters have a high power output, of the order a few megawatts and SCRs are used in these circuits. In contrast, low cost, low power cycloconverters for low power AC motors are also in use, and many of these circuits tend to use triacs in place of SCRs. Unlike an SCR which conducts in only one direction, a triac is capable of conducting in either direction and like an SCR. It is also a three terminal device. It may be noted that the use of a cycloconverter is not as common as that of an inverter, and a cycloinverter is rarely used.

Additional insights into power electronics

There are several striking features of power electronics, the foremost among which being the extensive use of inductors and capacitors. In many applications of power electronics, an inductor may carry a high current at a high frequency. The implications of operating an inductor in this manner are quite a few, such as necessitating the use of litz wires in place of single-stranded or multi-stranded copper wires at frequencies above 50 kHz, using a proper core to limit the losses in the core, and shielding the inductor properly so that the fringing that occurs at the air-gaps in the magnetic path does not lead to electromagnetic interference. Usually the capacitors used in a power electronic application are also stressed. It is typical for a capacitor to be operated at a high frequency with current surges passing through it periodically. This means that the current rating of the capacitor at the operating frequency should be checked before its use. In addition, it may be preferable if the capacitor has self-healing property. Hence an inductor or a capacitor has to be selected or designed with care, taking into account the operating conditions, before its use in a power electronic circuit.

In many power electronic circuits, diodes play a crucial role. A normal power diode is usually designed to be operated at 400 Hz or less. Many of the inverter and switch-mode power supply circuits operate at a much higher frequency, and these circuits need diodes that turn ON and OFF fast. In addition, it is also desired that the turning-off process of a diode should not create undesirable electrical transients in the circuit. Since there are several types of diodes available, selection of a proper diode is very important for reliable operation of a circuit.

Analysis of power electronic circuits tends to be quite complicated, because these circuits rarely operate in steady-state. Traditionally steady-state response refers to the state of a circuit characterized by either a DC response or a sinusoidal response. Most of the power electronic circuits have a periodic response, but this response is not usually sinusoidal. Typically, the repetitive or the periodic response contains both a steady-state part due to the forcing function and a transient part due to the poles of the network. Since the responses are nonsinusoidal, harmonic analysis is often necessary. In order to obtain the time response, it may be necessary to resort to the use of a computer program.

Power electronics is a subject of interdisciplinary nature. To design and build control circuitry of a power electronic application, one needs knowledge of several areas, which are listed below:
- Design of analogue and digital electronic circuits, to build the control circuitry.
- Microcontrollers and digital signal processors for use in sophisticated applications.

- Many power electronic circuits have an electrical machine as their load. In an AC variable speed drive, it may be a reluctance motor, an induction motor or a synchronous motor. In a DC variable speed drive, it is usually a DC shunt motor.
- In a circuit such as an inverter, a transformer may be connected at its output, and the transformer may have to operate with a nonsinusoidal waveform at its input.
- A pulse transformer with a ferrite core is used commonly to transfer the gate signal to the power semiconductor device. A ferrite-cored transformer with a relatively higher power output is also used in an application such as a high frequency inverter.
- Many power electronic systems are operated with negative feedback. A linear controller such as a PI controller is used in relatively simple applications, whereas a controller based on digital or state-variable feedback techniques is used in more sophisticated applications.
- Computer simulation is often necessary to optimize the design of a power electronic system. In order to simulate, knowledge of software package such as MATLAB and the know-how to model nonlinear systems may be necessary.

The study of power electronics is an exciting and challenging experience. The scope for applying power electronics is growing at a fast pace. New devices keep coming into the market, sustaining development work in power electronics.

TECHNICAL WORDS AND PHRASES

conversion	[kən'və:ʃən]	n.	转变，变换
rectification	[ˌrektifi'keiʃən]	n.	整流
rectifier	['rektifaiə]	n.	整流器
chopper	['tʃɔpə]	n.	斩波器
cycloconverter	[ˌsaikləukən'və:tə]	n.	周波变换器
cycloinverter	[ˌsaikləuin'və:tə]	n.	（交流供电时的）双向离子变频器
inverter	[in'və:tə]	n.	逆变器
amplitude	['æmplitju:d]	n.	幅值
megawatt	['megəwɔt]	n.	兆瓦
triac	['traiæk]	n.	双向晶闸管
striking	['straikiŋ]	adj.	显著的，惊人的
shield	[ʃi:ld]	n. & v.	防护物，护罩
fringing	['frindʒiŋ]	n.	漏磁，边缘通量（的

形成）

transient	['trænziənt]	adj.	短暂的，瞬时的
interdisciplinary	[ˌintə(:)'disiplinəri]	adj.	各学科间的
sophisticated	[sə'fistikeitid]	adj.	非常复杂的，精密或尖锐的
simulation	[ˌsimju'leiʃən]	n.	仿真

power electronics	电力电子学
power semiconductor device	电力半导体器件
silicon-controlled rectifier	可控硅整流器
mercury-arc rectifier	汞弧整流器
aviation electronics	航空电子学
high frequency inverter	高频逆变器
switch-mode power supply	开关电源
static switch	静态开关
uncontrolled and controlled rectifier	不可控和可控整流器
semi-controlled and fully-controlled rectifier	半控和全控整流器
single-phase semi-controlled bridge rectifier	单相半控桥式整流器
single-phase fully-controlled bridge rectifier	单相全控桥式整流器
bipolar junction transistor	双极结型晶体管
power MOSFET	功率 MOSFET
insulated gate bipolar transistor(IGBT)	绝缘栅双极型晶体管
MOS-controlled thyristor (MCT)	金属氧化物可控晶体管
uninterrupted power supply	不间断电源
frequency converter	变频器
emergency lighting system	应急照明系统
step-down switch-mode power supply	降压式开关电源
step-up chopper	升压式斩波器
fly-back converter	反激式变换器
resonant converter	谐振变换器
fixed value	固定值
of the order	大约
three terminal device	三端器件
litz wire	漆包绞线，李兹线
multi-stranded	多股的
single-stranded	单股的

copper wire	铜线
electromagnetic interference	电磁干扰
air-gap	空气隙
magnetic path	磁路
current surge	电流浪涌，电流冲击
steady-state	稳态
sinusoidal response	正弦响应
periodic response	周期响应
harmonic analysis	谐波分析
time response	时间响应
shunt motor	并励电动机
ferrite core	铁氧体磁心，铁心
state-variable feedback	状态变量反馈

NOTES

1. Power electronics refers to control and conversion of electrical power by power semiconductor devices wherein these devices operate as switches.

   译文：电力电子学是研究如何通过电力半导体器件来实现电能的控制和转换的学科。该学科中电力半导体器件作为开关器件来使用。

   其中 "wherein" = "in which" 引导定语从句修饰 "power electronics"。

2. "Electronic power converter" is the term that is used to refer to a power electronic circuit that converts voltage and current from one form to another.

   译文："电能变换器"是一个术语，用来表示将电压和电流从一种形式变换成另一种形式的电力电子电路。

   该句中第一个 "that" 引导一个定语从句，修饰 "term"；第二个 "that" 引导定语从句，修饰 "power electronic circuit"。

3. The amplitude and the frequency of input voltage to a cycloconverter tend to be fixed values, whereas both the amplitude and the frequency of output voltage of a cycloconverter tend to be variable.

   译文：周波变换器的输入电压的幅值和频率一般是固定值，而周波变换器的输出电压的幅值和频率一般都是可调的。

   该句为 "whereas" 引导的对比从句，翻译为 "然而" 或 "而"。

4. The implications of operating an inductor in this manner are quite a few, such as necessitating the use of litz wires in place of single-stranded or multi-stranded copper wires at frequencies above 50 kHz, using a proper core to limit the losses in

the core, and shielding the inductor properly so that the fringing that occurs at the air-gaps in the magnetic path does not lead to electromagnetic interference.

译文：电感的某些使用方式是非常少见的，如频率在 50 kHz 以上必须用李兹线来代替单芯或多股铜线，用合适的铁心来限制铁心上的损耗，并且要适当地屏蔽电感，从而让磁路空隙处产生的漏磁不至于导致电磁干扰。

该句中"such as"用做关系代词，用以引导定语从句，修饰"this manner"。该定语部分由 3 个并列部分组成："necessitating…50 kHz"，"using … core"，"shielding… electromagnetic interference"。

5. Hence an inductor or a capacitor has to be selected or designed with care, taking into account the operating conditions, before its use in a power electronic circuit.

译文：因此在将电感或电容用于电力电子电路前，必须小心选择和设计，要考虑其运行条件。

该句为连词 before 引导的时间状语从句，其本义是"在……之前"，而这里强调主句动作发生在从句动作之前，句子侧重在主句，从句译文前置。"take into account"为"考虑"的意思。

EXERCISES

Ⅰ. **Fill in the blanks with English words and translate them into Chinese.**

1. "Electronic power converter" can be classified as: _____ converting an AC voltage to a DC voltage converting a DC voltage to an AC voltage; _____ or a _____ that converts a DC voltage to another DC voltage; _____ and _____ converting an AC voltage to another AC voltage.

2. Rectifiers can be classified as _____ and _____ rectifiers, and the controlled rectifiers can be further divided into _____ and _____ rectifiers.

3. There are several _____ features of power electronics, the foremost among them being the extensive use of _____ and _____.

4. Most of the power electronic circuits have a _____, but this response is not usually _____.

5. A pulse transformer with a ferrite core is used commonly to transfer the _____ to the _____.

Ⅱ. **Translate the following sentences into Chinese.**

1. The amplitude and the frequency of input voltage to a cycloconverter tend to be fixed values, whereas both the amplitude and the frequency of output voltage of a cycloconverter tend to be variable.

2. Unlike an SCR which conducts in only one direction, a triac is capable of conducting in either direction and like an SCR; it is also a three terminal device.
3. There are several striking features of power electronics, the foremost among which being the extensive use of inductors and capacitors.
4. A linear controller such as a PI controller is used in relatively simple applications, whereas a controller based on digital or state-variable feedback techniques is used in more sophisticated applications.
5. In order to simulate, knowledge of software package such as MATLAB and the know-how to model nonlinear systems may be necessary.

Ⅲ. **Answer the following questions according to the text.**
1. What's the main task of power electronics?
2. According to the text, when do we use single-phase rectifiers and when do we use three-phase bridge rectifiers?
3. According to the text what's the periodic response feature of the power electronic circuit?

Supplementary Reading

Reading 6　Evolution of Power Semiconductor Devices

Power semiconductor devices are used to control the energy transfer of electronic systems. Over the last two decades the technology of power semiconductors has made impressive progress. The power function (switching or protection) is achieved through the combined use of low-voltage data and signal processing circuits with power devices. The evolution naturally involves the integration of the whole or part of the low-voltage elements with the power devices in order to improve performance and to reduce the chip (or system) size. The application of IC technologies on power semiconductor devices has offered efficient protection components, simple drive characteristics, and good control dynamics together with a direct interface to the monolithic integration with the signal processing circuitry on the same chip. As a result, power electronic systems have greatly benefited from advances in power semiconductor technology. In consumer and industrial environments, designers make big efforts of improving the efficiency, to reduce the size and weight of components by combining the functions of several ICs and discrete power semiconductors. Thereby the system costs can be lowered, and the system design is simplified by reducing the number of components.

There are two distinct concepts for the development of power semiconductor devices. One concept involves discrete vertical power devices for medium- and high-power applications, and the other uses the lateral power devices for high-voltage (low-current) and smart power applications, and for monolithic integration with low-voltage circuitry. Discrete vertical power devices have evolved from bipolar devices (diodes, thyristors, GTOs, and BJTs) to power MOSFETs, IGBTs and MCTs. Applications of discrete power devices are in the computer, telecommunication, and automotive industry for devices operated at below 300 V and motor control, robotics, and power distribution for devices operated at above 300 V. The most important step in the development of a new generation of power devices was the introduction of power MOSFETs. The development of these new devices provided a direct link between integrated circuits and power devices. This evolution has led to power device development in terms of structure, design, size reduction, and manufacturing. The design rules reduction in discrete power MOSFETs has allowed a drastic reduction in the on-resistance drastically and in power dissipation. Another important breakthrough in the field of discrete devices has been the development of IGBTs combining the advantages of MOS transistors, such as low power drives by using MOS gate and fast switching, with the advantages of bipolar devices, such as low forward voltage drop by conductivity modulation in the drift region. Improvements in these new power devices, MOSFETs and IGBTs, are related to advances in standard MOS technology. These devices are produced in the same production facilities which were used for integrated circuits. The introduction of MOS technology in power electronics made it easy to integrate power devices into standard technology, and integrated circuits have become compatible. For medium- and high-voltage applications IGBTs have been the dominated devices due to scaling of their voltage ratings and refinements to their gate structure achieved by using very large scale integration (VLSI) technology and trench gate regions. Fig. 2.6.3 shows the development of power MOSFETs and IGBTs. In the past ten years, MOSFET technology has benefited from the drastic improvements achieved in the trench technology and in the characteristics of vertical super-junctions, while IGBT technology has shown improvements in performance due to lifetime control technology and structure enhancements.

Several types of MOS-gated thyristors have also been introduced, resulting in some promising improvements in the trade-off between on-state power loss, switching power loss, and the safe operating area. Improvements in power rectifiers have been

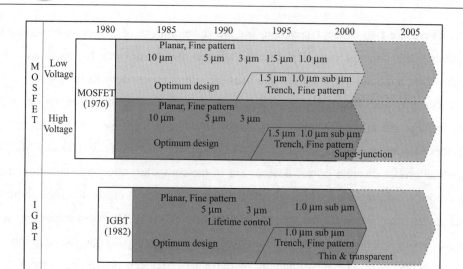

Fig. 2.6.3 Developments in power MOSFET and IGBT technology

achieved at low-voltage ratings using Schottky rectifier structures containing trenches and at high-voltage ratings using structures that combine junction and Schottky barrier contacts.

One of the most promising approaches in the field of power semiconductor devices is the use of new materials such as silicon carbide (SiC) and gallium nitride (GaN). SiC Schottky rectifiers, power MESFETs, and power MOSFETs offer a significant improvement in the trade-off between R_{sp} and the BV and in high-temperature environments. The defect density and cost of the starting materials determine the progress of commercialization of this technology.

Fig. 2.6.4 shows the application areas of discrete power semiconductors. As shown in the figure, MOSFETs and IGBTs are used for high-frequency applications, and SCRs and GTOs are mainly used for high-power applications. For medium-power applications such as the uninterruptible power supply (UPS), automotive, and robots IGBT or power MOSFET modules, which are constructed with series and parallel connection of power devices inside a plastic package, are used.

According to the area of application and the required performance, different modes of integration have been developed. A distinction must be made between monolithic and hybrid integrations. The different developments have clearly shown that the medium- and high-power range can be implemented using hybrid integration which makes use of power parts and low-voltage parts in a package. For the low-power range (current (I)<10 A, voltage (V)<600 V) it can be implemented using monolithic integration of power semiconductor components and integrated circuits.

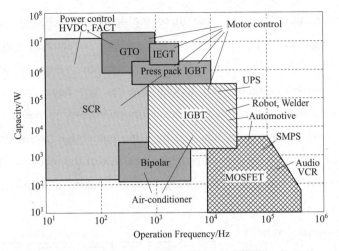

Fig. 2.6.4 Applications of discrete power semiconductors

The evolution of lateral power device structures has created a market for monolithic power integrated circuits that can incorporate sensors and protection functions.

Traditionally power semiconductor technology has always followed advances in VLSI technology. In addition to the improvements in photo-lithography and trench etching processes for power semiconductor structures, the capability for the integration of bipolar and CMOS structures with high-voltage devices has been greatly improved during the past fifteen years.

The basis for smart power technology is the integration of interface circuits, sensors, and protection circuitry with power devices. The interface function is made with CMOS circuits specially designed to operate in noisy and high temperature environments.

The high-voltage portion of the IC can either provide the entire power control function as in the case of monolithic motor drives and lamp ballast chips, or serve as the drive electronics for medium and high-power devices in modules. The implementation of the monolithic power IC technology was first done using junction isolation as shown in Fig. 2.6.5 (a). An important breakthrough in the performance of high-voltage lateral MOSFETs which was required for the applications was achieved by using the reduced surface field (RESURF) principle, where the charge coupling between the drift region and the p-substrate is used to reduce the electric field along the surface. With this approach, devices capable of supporting more than 1,200 V have been made. Some of the drawbacks of junction isolation are the inability to integrate bipolar structures due to mutual interaction and the high leakage currents at elevated temperatures. To overcome these problems, the RESURF concept was successfully extended to dielectrically isolated structures, such as the SOI-LDMOSFET (See Fig. 2.6.5 (b)). A systematic study of a variety of dielectrically isolated unipolar and bipolar devices has been conducted for the purpose of integration. Recently, significant improvements in the performance of lateral power devices have been achieved by using innovative lateral structures with charge coupled regions. This section provides a review of the recent developments in power semiconductor integration technology that are making a significant impact on electronic systems.

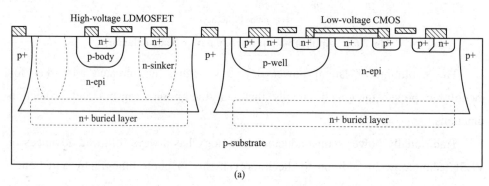

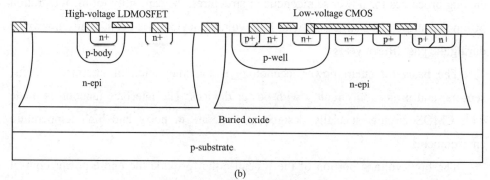

Fig. 2.6.5 Device cross sections of junction isolation and dielectric isolation

(a) Junction isolation; (b) Dielectric isolation

Unit 7

How Electric Motors Work

How Electric Motors Work 翻译

Inside an electric motor

Let's start by looking at the overall plan of a simple two-pole DC electric motor. A simple motor has six parts, as shown in the diagram below:

- An armature or rotor;
- A commutator;
- Brushes;
- An axle;
- Field magnets;
- A DC power supply of some sort.

An electric motor is all about magnets and magnetism: A motor uses magnets to create motion. If you have ever played with magnets, you know about the fundamental law of all magnets: opposites attract and likes repel. So if you have two bar magnets with their ends marked "north" and "south," then the north end of one magnet will attract the south end of the other. On the other hand, the north end of one magnet will repel the north end of the other (and similarly, the south end will repel the south end of the other). Inside an electric motor, these attracting and repelling forces create rotational motion.

In Fig. 2.7.1, you can see two magnets in the motor: The armature (or rotor) is an electromagnet, while the field magnet is a permanent magnet (the field magnet could be an electromagnet as well, but in most small motors it isn't in order to save power).

Toy motors

The motor being dissected in Fig. 2.7.2 is a simple electric motor that you would typically find in a toy.

You can see that this is a small motor, about as big around as a dime. From the outside you can see the steel can that forms the body of the motor, an axle, a nylon end cap and two battery leads. If you hook the battery leads of the motor up to a flashlight battery, the axle will spin. If you reverse the leads, it will spin in the opposite

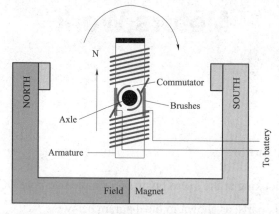

Fig. 2.7.1   Motor image gallery (Parts of an electric motor)

Fig. 2.7.2   A toy motor

direction. Fig. 2.7.3 is two other views of the same motor. (Note the two slots in the side of the steel can in the second shot — their purpose will become more evident in a moment.)

Fig. 2.7.3   Other views of a toy motor

The nylon end cap shown in Fig. 2.7.4 is held in place by two tabs that are part of the steel can. By bending the tabs back, you can free the end cap and remove it. Inside the end cap are the motor's brushes. These brushes transfer power from the battery to the commutator as the motor spins.

 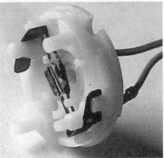

Fig. 2.7.4   Nylon end caps

More motor parts

The axle holds the armature and the commutator. The armature is a set of electromagnets, in this case three. The armature in this motor is a set of thin metal plates stacked together, with thin copper wires coiled around each of the three poles of the armature. The two ends of each wire (one wire for each pole) are soldered onto a terminal, and then each of the three terminals is wired to one plate of the commutator. Fig. 2.7.5 makes it easy to see the armature, terminals and commutator.

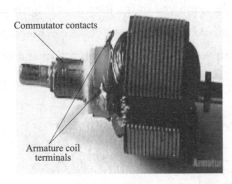 

Fig. 2.7.5   The armature, terminals and commutator of a motor

The final piece of any DC electric motor is the field magnet. The field magnet in this motor is formed by the can itself plus two curved permanent magnets.

One end of each magnet rests against a slot cut into the can, and then the retaining clip presses against the other ends of both magnets as shown in Fig. 2.7.6.

Fig. 2.7.6　The field magnet of a motor

Electromagnets and motors

To understand how an electric motor works, the key is to understand how the electromagnet works. (See Reading 7 "How Electromagnets Work" for complete details.)

An electromagnet is the basis of an electric motor. You can understand how things work in the motor by imagining the following scenario. Say that you created a simple electromagnet by wrapping 100 loops of wires around a nail and connecting it to a battery. The nail would become a magnet and have a north and south pole while the battery is connected.

Now say that you take your nail electromagnet, run an axle through the middle of it and suspend it in the middle of a horseshoe magnet as shown in Fig. 2.7.7. If you were to attach a battery to the electromagnet so that the north end of the nail appeared as shown, the basic law of magnetism tells you what would happen: The north end of the electromagnet would be repelled from the north end of the horseshoe magnet and attracted to the south end of the horseshoe magnet. The south end of the electromagnet would be repelled in a similar way. The nail would move about half a turn and then stop in the position shown.

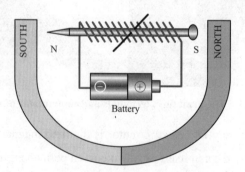

Fig. 2.7.7　The electromagnet in a horseshoe magnet

You can see that this half-turn of motion is simply due to the way magnets naturally attract and repel one another. The key to an electric motor is to then go one step further so that, at the moment that this half-turn of motion completes, the field of the electromagnet flips. The flip causes the electromagnet to complete another half-turn of motion. You flip the magnetic field just by changing the direction of the electrons flowing in the wire (you do that by flipping the battery over). If the field of the electromagnet were flipped at precisely the right moment at the end of each half-turn of motion, the electric motor would spin freely.

Armatures, commutators and brushes

Consider the image on the previous page. The armature takes the place of the nail in an electric motor. The armature is an electromagnet made by coiling thin wires around two or more poles of a metal core.

The armature has an axle, and the commutator is attached to the axle. In Fig. 2.7.8, you can see three different views of the same armature: the front, the side and the end-on. In the end-on view, the winding is eliminated to make the commutator more obvious. You can see that the commutator is simply a pair of plates attached to the axle. These plates provide the two connections for the coil of the electromagnet.

The "flipping the electric field" part of an electric motor is accomplished by two parts: the commutator and the brushes.

Fig. 2.7.9 shows how the commutator and brushes work together to let current flow to the electromagnet, and also to flip the direction that the electrons are flowing at just the right moment. The contacts of the commutator are attached to the axle of the electromagnet, so they spin with the magnet. The brushes are just two pieces of springy metal or carbon that make contact with the contacts of the commutator.

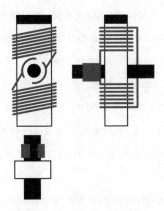
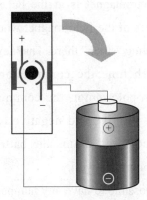

Fig. 2.7.8   An armature   Fig. 2.7.9   Brushes and a commutator

Putting it all together

When you put all of these parts together, what you have is a complete electric motor.

In Fig. 2.7.10, the armature winding has been left out so that it is easier to see the commutator in action. The key thing to notice is that as the armature passes through the horizontal position, the poles of the electromagnet flip. Because of the flip, the north pole of the electromagnet is always above the axle so it can repel the field magnet's north pole and attract the field magnet's south pole.

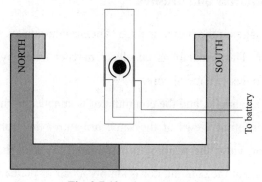

Fig. 2.7.10 An armature

If you ever have the chance to take apart a small electric motor, you will find that it contains the same pieces described above: two small permanent magnets, a commutator, two brushes, and an electromagnet made by winding wires around a piece of metal. Almost always, however, the rotor will have three poles rather than the two poles as shown in this article. There are two good reasons for a motor to have three poles:

- It causes the motor to have better dynamics. In a two-pole motor, if the electromagnet is at the balance point, perfectly horizontal between the two poles of the field magnet when the motor starts, you can imagine the armature getting "stuck" there. That never happens in a three-pole motor.
- Each time the commutator hits the point where it flips the field in a two-pole motor, the commutator shorts out the battery (directly connects the positive and negative terminals) for a moment. This shorting wastes energy and drains the battery needlessly. A three-pole motor solves this problem as well.

It is possible to have any number of poles, depending on the size of the motor and the specific application it is being used in.

Unit 7 How Electric Motors Work

Motors everywhere

Look around your house and you will find that it is filled with electric motors. Here's an interesting experiment for you to try: Walk through your house and count all the motors you find. Starting in the kitchen, we find motors in:

- The fan over the stove and in the microwave oven;
- The blender;
- The can opener;
- The refrigerator — two or three in fact: one for the compressor, one for the fan inside the refrigerator, as well as one in the icemaker;
- The mixer;
- The tape player in the answering machine;
- Probably even the clock on the oven.

In the utility room, there is an electric motor in:

- The washer;
- The dryer;
- The electric screwdriver;
- The vacuum cleaner and the dustbuster mini-vac;
- The electric saw;
- The electric drill;
- The furnace blower.

Even in the bathroom, there's a motor in:

- The fan;
- The electric toothbrush;
- The hair dryer;
- The electric razor.

Your car is loaded with electric motors:

- Power windows (a motor in each window);
- Power seats (up to seven motors per seat);
- Fans for the heater and the radiator;
- Windshield wipers;
- The starter motor;
- Electric radio antennas.

Plus, there are motors in all sorts of other places:

- Several in the VCR;

- Several in a CD player or tape deck;
- Many in a computer (each disk drive has two or three, plus there's a fan or two);
- Most toys that move have at least one motor;
- Electric clocks;
- The garage door opener;
- Aquarium pumps.

In walking around my house, I counted over 50 electric motors hidden in all sorts of devices. Everything that moves uses an electric motor to accomplish its movement.

TECHNICAL WORDS AND PHRASES

motor	['məutə]	n.	发动机，电动机
magnet	['mægnit]	n.	磁
electromagnet	[ilektrəu'mægnit]	n.	电磁体，电磁铁
pole	[pəul]	n.	磁极，电极
armature	['ɑːmətjuə]	n.	电枢（电机的部件）
rotor	['rəutə]	n.	[机] 转子
commutator	['kɔmjuteitə]	n.	换向器，转接器
brush	[brʌʃ]	n.	电刷
axle	['æksl]	n.	转轴
magnetism	['mægnitizəm]	n.	磁，磁力，吸引力，磁学
repel	[ri'pel]	v.	[物理学] 排斥
dime	[daim]	n.	<美>一角硬币
flashlight	['flæʃlait]	n.	手电筒，闪光灯
spin	[spin]	v.	旋转
solder	['sɔldə]	v.	焊接
scenario	[si'nɑːriəu]	n.	情景，场面
loop	[luːp]	n.	环，线（绳）圈
flip	[flip]	v.	翻转
electron	[i'lektrɔn]	n.	电子
carbon	['kɑːbən]	n.	炭棒
horizontal	[ˌhɔri'zɔntl]	adj.	地平线的，水平的
dynamic	[dai'næmik]	adj.	动态的
blender	['blendə]	n.	搅拌器，搅和器
compressor	[kəm'presə]	n.	压缩机

mixer	['miksə]	n.	搅拌器，
mechanical movement			机械运动
overall plan			总体方案
field magnet			[物] 场磁铁
rotational motion			旋转运动
nylon end cap			尼龙端盖
copper wire			铜线
permanent magnet			[物] 永久磁铁
retaining clip			固定夹
horseshoe magnet			马蹄形磁铁
metal core			铁心
front, side and end-on view			正视图、侧视图和端视图
microwave oven			微波炉
electric screwdriver			电动螺丝起子
vacuum cleaner			真空吸尘器
dustbuster mini-vacuum			小型的真空吸尘器
electric drill			电钻
electric saw			电锯
furnace blower			鼓风机
hair dryer			吹风机
electric razor			电动剃须刀
windshield wiper			挡风雨雪刷
aquarium pump			鱼缸的水泵

NOTES

1. So if you have two bar magnets with their ends marked "north" and "south," then the north end of one magnet will attract the south end of the other.

   译文：因此，如果你有两个条形磁铁，它们的两端分别标有"南极"和"北极"，那么一个磁铁的北极将吸另一个磁铁的南极。

   该句为"If"引导的条件状语从句，主句用一般将来时，从句用一般现在时。

2. The armature in this motor is a set of thin metal plates stacked together, with thin copper wires coiled around each of the three poles of the armature.

   译文：在本例中电枢是由一些薄的硅钢片叠压而成，并且在每个电枢的极上都有铜线绕组，每个电枢绕组两端的引线被焊到连接片上。

该句中"stacked together"为过去分词做定语，修饰"metal plates"；而"with …armature"为 with + n./pron. + done 的复合结构，表行为方式或伴随情况。

3. Now say that you take your nail electromagnet, run an axle through the middle of it and suspend it in the middle of a horseshoe magnet as shown in the figure below.

译文：现在假定你拿起你的铁钉做的电磁铁，在它的中间穿一根转轴，并且将它悬挂于马蹄形磁铁的中间，如下图所示。

"say that"为"如果""假定"的意思。"that"引导3个并列的宾语从句，由于主语都为"you"，故后两个从句省略主语。

4. If you were to attach a battery to the electromagnet so that the north end of the nail appeared as shown, the basic law of magnetism tells you what would happen: The north end of the electromagnet would be repelled from the north end of the horseshoe magnet and attracted to the south end of the horseshoe magnet. The south end of the electromagnet would be repelled in a similar way. The nail would move about half a turn and then stop in the position shown.

译文：如果你将电池接到电磁铁上，那么铁钉的北极就如图所示，磁力学的基本定律可以告诉你将要发生的一切：电磁铁的北极将受到马蹄形磁铁北极的排斥，被马蹄形磁铁的南极吸引过去。同样，电磁铁的南极将被马蹄形磁铁南极排斥。铁钉将转过半圈，然后停留在图示位置。

该句中"if"引导的是条件状语从句。从句部分为"If you …appeared as shown"。从句部分含一个"so that"引导的目的状语从句，主句为"the basic law …in the position shown"。该主句又包含了一个"what"引导的宾语从句。

5. Fig. 2.7.9 shows how the commutator and brushes work together to let current flow to the electromagnet, and also to flip the direction that the electrons are flowing at just the right moment.

译文：图 2.7.9 显示了换向器和电刷如何一起让电流流进电磁铁，并且在恰当的时候改变电流的方向。

该句中"how"引导的是宾语从句，主语为"Fig. 2.7.9"，谓语为"shows"，宾语为"how the commutator a… right moment"。

6. In a two-pole motor, if the electromagnet is at the balance point, perfectly horizontal between the two poles of the field magnet when the motor starts, you can imagine the armature getting "stuck" there.

译文：在两极电机中，当电机启动时，如果电磁铁位于平衡点上，即磁场两极的绝对水平点上，你可以想象到电枢将"卡"在那儿，而在三极电机中就不会出

Unit 7　How Electric Motors Work 73

现这种情况。

该句中 if 引导的是条件状语从句。从句部分为"when"引导的时间状语从句，其中"perfectly horizontal … magnet"为对"balance point"进一步补充说明。

EXERCISES

Ⅰ. **Fill in the blanks with English words and translate them into Chinese (Fig. 2.7.11).**

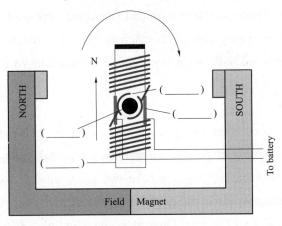

Fig. 2.7.11

Ⅱ. **Translate the following sentences into Chinese.**

1. An electric motor consists of two essential elements. The first, a static component which consists of magnetic materials and electrical conductors to generate magnetic fields of a desired shape, is known as the stator. The second, which also is made from magnetic and electrical conductors to generate shaped magnetic fields which interact with the fields generated by the stator, is known as the rotor.

2. A simple DC motor has a coil of wire that can rotate in a magnetic field. The current in the coil is supplied via two brushes that make moving contact with a split ring. The coil lies in a steady magnetic field. The forces exerted on the current-carrying wires create a torque on the coil.

Ⅲ. **Answer the following questions according to the text.**

1. How does the electromagnet work?
2. Please explain the purpose of brushes.
3. Why do most motors have three poles rather than two poles?

Supplementary Reading

Reading 7　How Electromagnets Work

The basic idea behind an electromagnet is extremely simple: By running electric current through a wire, you can create a magnetic field.

By using this simple principle, you can create all sorts of things, including motors, solenoids, read/write heads for hard disks and tape drives, speakers, and so on. In this article, you will learn exactly how electromagnets work. You will also have the chance to try several experiments with an electromagnet that you create yourself.

A regular magnet

Before talking about electromagnets, let's talk about normal "permanent" magnets like the ones you have on your refrigerator and that you probably played with as a kid.

You likely know that all magnets have two ends, usually marked "north" and "south," and that magnets attract things made of steel or iron. And you probably know the fundamental law of all magnets: Opposites attract and likes repel. So, if you have two bar magnets with their ends marked "north" and "south," the north end of one magnet will attract the south end of the other. On the other hand, the north end of one magnet will repel the north end of the other (and similarly, the south end will repel the south end of the other).

An electromagnet is the same way, except it is "temporary" — The magnetic field only exists when electric current is flowing.

An electromagnet

An electromagnet starts with a battery (or some other source of power) and a wire. What a battery produces is electrons.

If you look at a battery, say at a normal D-cell from a flashlight, you can see that there are two ends, one marked plus (+) and the other marked minus (−). Electrons collect at the negative end of the battery, and, if you let them, they will gladly flow to the positive end. The way you "let them" flow is with a wire. If you attach a wire directly between the positive and negative terminals of a D-cell, three things will happen:

• Electrons will flow from the negative side of the battery to the positive side as fast as they can.

• The battery will drain fairly quickly (in a matter of several minutes). For that reason, it is generally not a good idea to connect the two terminals of a battery to one another directly. Normally, you connect some kind of load in the middle of the wire so the electrons can do useful work. The load might be a motor, a light bulb, a radio or whatever.

• A small magnetic field is generated in the wire. It is this small magnetic field that is the basis of an electromagnet.

The magnetic field

The part about the magnetic field might be a surprise to you, yet this definitely happens in all wires carrying electricity. You can prove it to yourself with the following experiment. You will need:

• One AA, C or D-cell battery;
• A piece of wire (If you have no wire around the house, go buy a spool of insulated thin copper wire down at the local electronics or hardware store. Four-strand telephone wire is perfect — cut the outer plastic sheath and you will find four perfect wires within.);
• A compass.

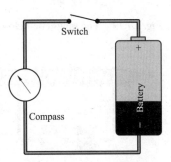

Fig. 2.7.12 A compass

Put the compass on the table and, with the wire near the compass, and connect the wire between the positive and negative ends of the battery for a few seconds. What you will notice is that the compass needle swings. Initially, the compass will be pointing toward the Earth's north pole (whatever direction that is for you), as shown in Fig. 2.7.12 on the right. When you connect the wire to the battery, the compass needle swings because the needle is itself a small magnet with a north and south end. Being small, it is sensitive to small magnetic fields. Therefore, the compass is affected by the magnetic field created in the wire by the flow of electrons.

The coil

Fig. 2.7.13 below shows the shape of the magnetic field around the wire. In this figure, imagine that you have cut the wire and are looking at it end-on. A circular magnetic field develops around the wire, as shown by the circular lines in the illustration below. The field weakens as you move away from the wire (so the lines are farther apart as they get farther from the wire). You can see that the field is perpendicular to the wire and that the field's direction depends on which direction the current is flowing in the wire. The compass needle aligns itself with this field (perpendicular to the wire). Using the contraption, you created in the previous section. If you flip the battery around and repeat the experiment, you will see that the compass needle aligns itself in the opposite direction.

Because the magnetic field around a wire is circular and perpendicular to the wire, an easy way to amplify the wire's magnetic field is to coil the wire, as shown in Fig. 2.7.14.

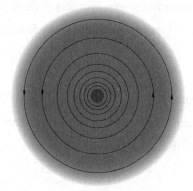

Fig. 2.7.13   The magnetic field of a wire   Fig. 2.7.14   One loop's magnetic field

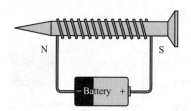

Fig. 2.7.15   A simple electromagnet

For example, if you wrap your wire around a nail 10 times, connect the wire to the battery and bring one end of the nail near the compass, you will find that it has a much larger effect on the compass. In fact, the nail behaves just like a bar magnet, as shown in Fig. 2.7.15.

However, the magnet exists only when the current is flowing from the battery. What you have created is an electromagnet! You will find that this magnet is able to pick up small steel things like paper clips, staples and thumb tacks.

Experiments to try

- What is the magnetic power of a single coil wrapped around a nail? Of 10 turns of wire? Of 100 turns? Experiment with different numbers of turns and see what happens. One way to measure and compare a magnet's "strength" is to see how many staples it can pick up.
- What difference does voltage make in the strength of an electromagnet? If you

hook two batteries in series to get 3 volts, what does that do to the strength of the magnet? (Please do not try any more than 6 volts, and please do not use anything other than flashlight batteries. Please do not try house current coming from the wall in your house, as it can kill you. Please do not try a car battery, as its current can kill you as well.)

- What is the difference between an iron and an aluminum core for the magnet? For example, roll up some aluminum foil tightly and use it as the core for your magnet in place of the nail. What happens? What if you use a plastic core, like a pen?

- What about solenoids? A solenoid is another form of electromagnet. It is an electromagnetic tube generally used to move a piece of metal linearly. Find a drinking straw or an old pen (remove the ink tube). Also find a small nail (or a straightened paperclip) that will slide inside the tube easily. Wrap 100 turns of wire around the tube. Place the nail or paperclip at one end of the coil and then connect the coil to the battery. Notice how the nail moves. Solenoids are used in all sorts of places, especially locks. If your car has power locks, they may operate using a solenoid. Another common thing to do with a solenoid is to replace the nail with a thin, cylindrical permanent magnet. Then you can move the magnet in and out by changing the direction of the magnetic field in the solenoid. (Please be careful if you try placing a magnet in your solenoid, as the magnet can shoot out.)

- How do I know there's really a magnetic field? You can look at a wire's magnetic field using iron filings. Buy some iron filings, or find your own iron filings by running a magnet through playground or beach sand. Put a light dusting of filings on a sheet of paper and place the paper over a magnet. Tap the paper lightly and the filings will align with the magnetic field, letting you see its shape!

Unit 8
DC Motor Control with PWM and H-Bridge

DC Motor Control with PWM and H-Bridge 翻译

PWM or Pulse Width Modulation refers to the concept of rapidly pulsing the digital signal of a wire to simulate a varying voltage on the wire. This method is commonly used for driving motors at varying speeds.

A few terms are associated with PWM:
- Period — how long each complete pulse cycle takes.
- Frequency — how often the pulses are generated. This value is typically specified in Hz (cycles per second).
- Duty cycle — refers to the amount of time in the period that the pulse is active or high. Duty cycle is typically specified as a percentage of the full period.

In Fig. 2.8.1, the duty cycle is shown at 50%. The pink line shows the average output and you can see that at 50% duty cycle, the average output is roughly 6 V or 50% of full power. Fig. 2.8.2 is a diagram of what a 25% duty cycle PWM signal looks like.

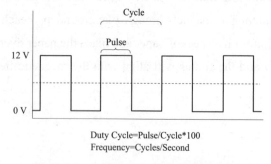

Fig. 2.8.1　A 50% duty cycle PWM signal

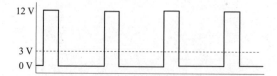

Fig. 2.8.2　A 25% duty cycle PWM signal

Unit 8 DC Motor Control with PWM and H-Bridge

> Note 1: The human ear can hear frequencies up to roughly 20 kHz. When using PWM at frequencies below this, the device being driven can often be heard to buzz. Higher frequencies avoid this.
>
> Note 2: When controlling motors, much greater PWM efficiency is achieved at frequencies above 20-30 kHz. This is because the current (induction) in the windings of the motor doesn't get a chance to collapse and leave the motor when the OFF-period is short. The collapse of this induction field takes some time; driving the motor at high PWM frequencies keeps this induction current in the motor at all times, resulting in much higher efficiencies.

An H-bridge is a bipolar driver circuit that is often used to control a load such as a brush type DC motor. This article covers the most basic concepts of a simplified H-bridge circuit. Later articles dig deeper into the details of practical H-bridge operation and design.

The H-bridge consists of four switches — two half-bridges with the load connected between them. The switches are usually solid-state devices such as bipolar transistors or power MOSFET's. For now let's depict them as mechanical switches.

When S_1 and S_4 are on as shown in Fig. 2.8.3, current tends to flow along the positive rail of the power supply through the motor from left to right and then to ground. If instead we turn on S_3 and S_2 as shown in Fig. 2.8.3, the current is driven the opposite direction through the motor. Obviously, these modes can be used to run a DC motor in a forward and reverse direction.

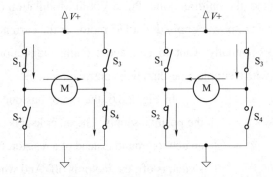

Fig. 2.8.3 H-bridge running a DC motor in a forward or reverse direction

There is also a third mode where the motor leads are effectively shorted together as shown in Fig. 2.8.4. This can be done by turning on both high side or both low side switches. This allows current to recirculate through the motor freely. When done briefly as the "off" portion of a PWM cycle, it allows current to decay slowly. When held in this state while a DC motor is spinning, the back-EMF of the motor will ease a recirculating current to flow, which will rapidly brake the motor to a stop. This is known as "dynamic braking."

Note: Your control logic must never turn on both the high side and the low side switches in the same half-bridge at the same time. This condition is called "shoot-through" as shown in Fig. 2.8.5 and it creates a dead-short circuit straight from power to ground. Most bridge drive IC's are designed to lock-out any command to do this. However, you must also be sure that one switch is fully off before the other switch even starts to turn on. We'll cover the details of this in a later article.

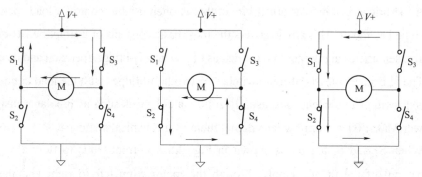

Fig. 2.8.4 Dynamic braking　　　　　　Fig. 2.8.5 Shoot-through

Unidirectional pulse width modulation

First we will show the unidirectional Pulse Width Modulation (PWM) and how it can be used to control the power applied to a DC motor or the current in a stepper motor winding. While we eventually want to talk about doing bidirectional PWM with an h-bridge, we'll start with a simple, one-direction control circuit.

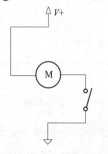

Fig. 2.8.6 Unidirectional Pulse Width Modulation (PWM)

In Fig. 2.8.6, the motor has one lead hard-wired to the positive supply. The other lead is connected through a switch to ground instead of a resistor. Obviously when the switch is off, the motor is off. And when the switch is on, the motor will run at full speed. What happens if we rapidly flick the switch on and off, say, thousands of times a second? You can imagine that if the "on" time and the "off" time of the switch are about equal, the average voltage applied to the motor will effectively be half of the supply voltage, and the motor will run at about half speed. During the "off" time, no current is being drawn from the power supply, so no energy is being wasted. You can also imagine that the ratio of the "on" time to the "off" time will determine the effective voltage that the motor sees. This relationship is sometimes called the "duty cycle" and is often expressed as a percentage of "on" time versus the total cycle time.

Up to this point, we've purposely left out something important, and now is the time to tackle it. A motor is an inductive load, and current through an inductor cannot change instantaneously.

In a mechanical analogy, think of inductance as mass or inertia. Current flow is speed and voltage is force. It takes force and time to build up speed or slow the mass to a stop. To stop quickly, it takes more force. A heavy mass that runs into a solid stop will result in a lot of force.

In Fig. 2.8.6, when the switch is opened, the current flowing through the motor has nowhere to go. In reality, the voltage across the switch would quickly rise until it was high enough to arc across the switch contacts or, in a solid state switch, cause voltage break down. We need to provide a safe path for the current to continue flowing.

Fortunately, this can be achieved by simply adding a diode as shown in Fig. 2.8.7. When the switch is on, the current through the motor increases. When the switch opens, the motor current simply redirects through the diode and recirculates through the motor, gradually decaying.

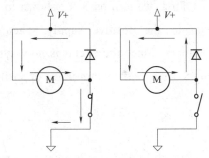

Fig. 2.8.7 Adding a diode

The diode works fine, but it does have an inherent 0.6 volt drop across it that can start to waste significant power at high current levels. What if we add another switch in parallel with the diode? When the bottom switch is off, we can turn the high side switch on, bypassing the diode with a nice efficient switch as shown in Fig. 2.8.8. This technique is known as synchronous rectification.

Unfortunately, we can't eliminate the diode entirely, because there always must be a brief time period after turning one switch fully off before the other switch begins to turn on, and the diode must be there to conduct during that time. Every switching event takes place in three steps. First, the lower switch opens. Current then flows through the diode for a short period. When the upper switch closes, current flows through it and

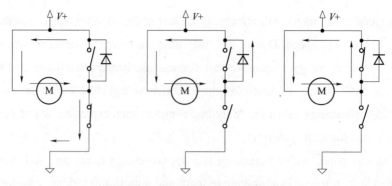

Fig. 2.8.8   Synchronous rectification

current through the diode stops. Next, moving back from right to left, the upper switch opens and current again flows through the diode until the lower switch closes.

Bidirectional PWM motor control

Once you understand unidirectional PWM of an inductive motor load, we can expand the concept to a bidirectional h-bridge PWM circuit.

Let's start by using our h-bridge circuit to mimic the unidirectional PWM circuit (in the previous article). For clarity, we'll leave out the diodes for the moment.

First, we turn on S_1 as shown in Fig. 2.8.9 and keep it on to connect one motor lead to the positive supply. Then we alternately modulate S_3 and S_4. Look familiar? Since the circuit is now symmetrical, we can hold S_3 on and modulate S_1 and S_2 to drive the motor in the opposite direction as shown in Fig. 2.8.10.

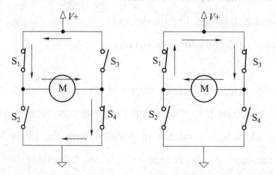

Fig. 2.8.9   A bidirectional H-bridge PWM circuit driving a motor in forward direction

This technique is called sign-magnitude modulation. The sign of the signal determines which side of the bridge is modulated and the magnitude determines the duty cycle of the modulation. Sign-magnitude modulation is often used for electric vehicles and other applications where the motor spends most of its time turning in one direction.

Unit 8   DC Motor Control with PWM and H-Bridge

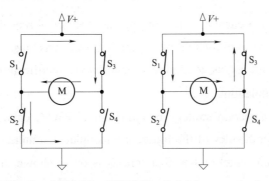

Fig. 2.8.10 A bidirectional H-bridge PWM circuit driving a motor in reverse direction

Note that we can also just choose to hold a low-side switch on instead of a high-side switch as shown in Fig. 2.8.11. As mentioned briefly in the H-bridge basics article, when both high side (or both low side) switches are on, this is known as "recirculating" or "slow decay" mode.

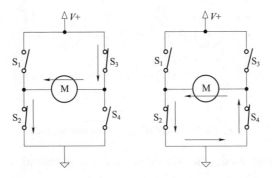

Fig. 2.8.11 "Recirculating" or "slow decay" mode

Now let's put the diodes back in and imagine that we start with S_1 and S_4 closed as before, causing current to flow through the motor. What if we suddenly open all the switches? Current must continue flowing through the motor, at least for a moment, so it takes the only path available, through the freewheeling diodes as shown in Fig. 2.8.12.

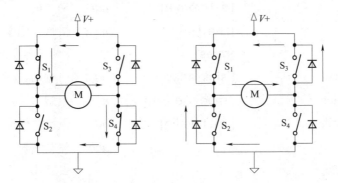

Fig. 2.8.12 A bidirectional h-bridge PWM circuit with the freewheeling diodes

Current is actually flowing the "wrong" way, pumping power back into the power supply rails. Since the current is flowing against the full force of the power supply voltage, it decays more rapidly. For this reason it is known as "fast decay." We might as well turn on S_3 and S_2 as a kind of synchronous rectification like we did for sign-magnitude modulation.

This leads to a second strategy of bidirectional PWM, called locked-antiphase. With this method, both sides of the bridge are modulated simultaneously. When S_1 is on, S_4 is on. And alternately when S_2 is on, S_3 is on as shown in Fig. 2.8.13. If the system spends the same amount of time in both states, the net effective voltage applied to the motor is zero. If the time spent in one state is increased and/or the other is decreased, the motor will be driven in the corresponding direction.

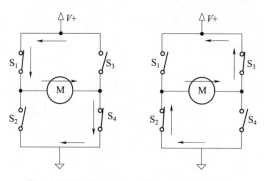

Fig. 2.8.13 Locked-antiphase modulation

Locked-antiphase modulation is often used for industrial servo motor controls where the motor is frequently accelerating, decelerating and reversing.

TECHNICAL WORDS AND PHRASES

period	['piəriəd]	n.	周期
frequency	['fri:kwənsi]	n.	频率
dynamic	[dai'næmik]	adj.	动力的
inertia	[i'nə:ʃjə]	n.	惯性，惯量
mass	[mæs]	n.	[物理学] 质量
synchronous	['siŋkrənəs]	adj.	同时的，[物] 同步的
modulation	[ˌmɔdju'leiʃən]	n.	调制
freewheeling	['fri:'hwi:liŋ]	adj.	惯性滑行的，随心所欲的
PWM		abbr.	脉宽调制
duty cycle			占空比
solid-state device			固态电子元件
bipolar transistor			双极型晶体管

Unit 8　DC Motor Control with PWM and H-Bridge

mechanical switch	机械开关
dynamic braking	能耗制动
shoot-through	直通
effective voltage	有效电压
inductive load	感性负载
break down	击穿
volt drop	压降
synchronous rectification	同步整流
sign-magnitude modulation	S\M 调制
slow decay	慢速衰减
freewheeling diode	续流二极管
locked-antiphase	锁相

NOTES

1. This is because the current (induction) in the windings of the motor doesn't get a chance to collapse and leave the motor when the OFF-period is short.

   译文：这是由于当关断时间较短时，电机绕组中的电流（感应）就来不及下降或消失。

   该句中"because"引导的是表语从句。该表语从句中又包含一个"when"引导的时间状语从句。

2. Driving the motor at high PWM frequencies keeps this induction current in the motor at all times, resulting in much higher efficiencies.

   译文：用高频率的 PWM 驱动电机，可让电机中的感应电流一直存在，从而获得更高的效率。

   "Driving the motor at high PWM frequencies"为分词短语做主语。"resulting in …efficiencies"为分词短语做状语，有结果意味。

3. When held in this state while a DC motor is spinning, the back-EMF of the motor will ease a recirculating current to flow, which will rapidly brake the motor to a stop.

   译文：当处在这种状态下而直流电机仍在转动的话，电机的反电势将会阻碍这个循环电流的流动，从而将电机快速制动，直到停止。

   "When… while … spinning"为条件状语从句；"which will rapidly… stop"为"which"引导的结果状语从句。

4. You can imagine that if the "on" time and the "off" time of the switch are about equal, the average voltage applied to the motor will effectively be half of the supply

voltage, and the motor will run at about half speed.

译文：可以想象到如果开关接通（闭合）的时间和断开的时间相等，那么加到电机两端的平均电压将为电源电压的一半，因而电机将以半速运行（全压时运行速度的一半）。

该句中"that"引导的是宾语从句，宾语从句部分为"that if … at about half speed"。该从句又包含一个"if"引导的条件状语从句，其主句为"and"连接的两个并列句。句中"applied to the motor"为过去分词，做"the average voltage"的定语。

5. Unfortunately, we can't eliminate the diode entirely, because there always must be a brief time period after turning one switch fully off before the other switch begins to turn on, and the diode must be there to conduct during that time.

译文：不幸的是，我们无法完全去除二极管，因为在将一个二极管完全断开后及另一个二极管开始闭合前存在一个很短的时间，因而在那段时间内必须有一个二极管来给电流提供流通的回路。

该句中"because"引导的是原因状语从句，主句为"we … entirely"，从句为"because …during that time"。原因状语从句为"and"连接的并列句，前后分句中存在因果的意义关系，前一个分句为"after ... before …"引导的时间状语从句。

EXERCISES

Ⅰ. **Translate the following words into English.**

1. 脉宽调制   2. 占空比
3. 双极型晶体管   4. 能耗制动
5. 直通   6. 同步整流
7. 慢速衰减   8. 续流二极管

Ⅱ. **Select an answer from the four choices.**

1. In the following diagram (Fig. 2.8.14) the frequency is _____, and the Duty Cycle is _____.
   A. 10 MHz, 10%   B. 50 MHz, 20%
   C. 20 MHz, 20%   D. 20 MHz, 60%

2. When using PWM at frequencies of _____, the device being driven can often be heard to buzz.
   A. 15 kHz   B. 25 kHz   C. 35 kHz   D. 40 kHz

3. In the following picture (Fig. 2.8.15), the DC motor is in the period of _____.

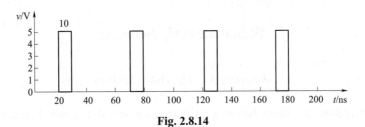

Fig. 2.8.14

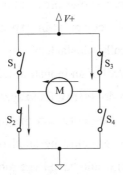

Fig. 2.8.15

A. forward rotation
B. reverse rotation
C. dynamic braking
D. all of the above

4. When the motor is in "fast decay" mode, the _____ decays more rapidly.

   A. frequency   B. plus   C. current   D. period

5. In a bidirectional h-bridge PWM circuit as shown in the following diagram (Fig. 2.8.16), _____, which is known as synchronous rectification.

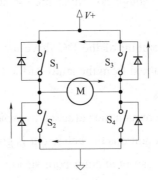

Fig. 2.8.16

A. turning on S_3 and S_2
B. turn on S_3 and S_2
C. turning off S_3 and S_2
D. turn off S_3 and S_2

Supplementary Reading

Reading 8　Thyristor Drives

The thyristor DC drive remains an important speed-controlled industrial drive, especially where the higher maintenance cost associated with the DC motor brushes is tolerable. The controlled thyristor rectifier provides a low-impedance adjustable "DC" voltage for the motor armature, thereby providing speed control.

Until the 1960s, the only really satisfactory way of obtaining the variable-voltage DC supply needed for speed control of an industrial DC motor was to generate it with a DC generator. The generator was driven at a fixed speed by an induction motor, and the field of the generator was varied in order to vary the generated voltage.

The motor/generator (MG) set could be sited remote from the DC motor, and multi-drive sites (e.g. steelworks) would have large rooms full of MG sets, one for each variable-speed motor on the plant. Three machines (all of the same power rating) were required for each of these "Ward Leonard" drives, which were good business for the motor manufacturer. For a brief period in the 1950s they were superseded by grid-controlled mercury arc rectifiers, but these were soon replaced by thyristor converters which have lower cost, higher efficiency (typically over 95%), smaller size, less maintenance, and faster response to changes in set speed.

The disadvantages of rectified supplies are that the waveforms are not pure DC, that the overload capacity of the converter is very limited, and that a single converter is not capable of regeneration. Though no longer pre-eminent, study of the DC drive is valuable for several reasons:

- The structure and operation of the DC drive are reflected in almost all other drives, and lessons learned from the study of the DC drive therefore have close parallels to other types.
- The DC drive tends to remain the yardstick by which other drives are judged.
- Under constant-flux conditions the behaviour is governed by a relatively simple set of linear equations, so predicting both steady-state and transient behaviour is not difficult. When we turn to the successors of the DC drive, notably the induction motor drive, we will find that things are much more complex, and that in order to overcome the poor transient behaviour, the strategies adopted are based on emulating the DC drive.

Thyristor DC drives-general

For motors up to a few kilowatts the armature converter can be supplied from either single-phase or three-phase mains, but for larger motors the three-phase is always used. A separate thyristor or diode rectifier is used to supply the field of the motor: The power is much less than the armature power, so the supply is often single-phase, as shown in Fig. 2.8.17.

The arrangement shown in Fig. 2.8.17 is typical of the majority of DC drives and provides for closed-loop speed control.

The main power circuit consists of a six-thyristor bridge circuit, which rectifies the incoming AC supply to produce a DC supply to the motor armature. The assembly of thyristors, mounted on a heatsink, is usually referred to as the "stack." By altering the firing angle of the thyristors the mean value of the rectified voltage can be varied, thereby allowing the motor speed to be controlled.

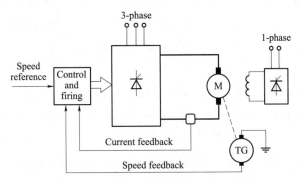

Fig. 2.8.17 Schematic diagram of a speed-controlled DC motor drive

The controlled rectifier produces a crude form of DC with a pronounced ripple in the output voltage. This ripple component gives rise to pulsating currents and fluxes in the motor, and in order to avoid excessive eddy-current losses and commutation problems, the poles and frame should be of laminated construction.

It is accepted practice for motors supplied for use with thyristor drives to have laminated construction, but older motors often have solid poles and/or frames, and these will not always work satisfactorily with a rectifier supply. It is also the norm for drive motors to be supplied with an attached "blower" motor as standard. This provides continuous, thorough ventilation and allows the motor to operate continuously at full torque even down to the lowest speed without overheating.

Unit 9

Variable Speed AC Drives and How They Work

Variable Speed AC Drives and How They Work 翻译

An AC drive is a device that is used to control the speed of an electrical motor, either an induction motor or a synchronous motor. AC drives are also known by various other names such as adjustable speed drives (ASD) or adjustable frequency drives (AFD) or variable frequency drives (VFD) or variable speed drives (VSD) or frequency converters (FC).

The first electrical AC motor was designed in 1899. Electrical motors convert electric energy into mechanical energy by electromagnetic induction. These motors are characterized by:

- Fixed speed, determined by the frequency of the power supply;
- Fixed torque.

Obviously, a fixed speed is not suitable for all the processes in all circumstances; thus, the need for adjusting the speed according to need.

Industrial machinery is often driven by electrical motors that have provisions for speed adjustment. Such motors are simply larger, more powerful versions of those driving familiar appliances such as food blenders or electric drills. These motors normally operate at a fixed speed.

If speed control is required, that controller is called an (variable speed) AC drive. AC drives are used in a wide variety of industrial applications. To give an easy example, AC drives are often used with fans to provide adjustable airflow in large heating and air conditioning systems. The flow of water and chemicals in industrial processes is often controlled by adjusting the speed of pumps.

However, variable speed AC drives are commonly used in more complex and difficult environments such as water and wastewater processing, paper mills, tunnel boring, oil drilling platforms or mining.

Technologies

The synchronous rotational speed of the rotor (i.e. the theoretical unloaded speed with no slip) is controlled by the number of pole pairs (number of windings in the stator) and by the frequency of the supply voltage. Before the development of cheap power electronics, it was difficult to vary the frequency to the motor and therefore the uses for the induction motor were limited.

The general term for a power electronic device that controls the speed of motors as well as other parameters is inverter. A typical unit will take the mains AC supply, rectify and smooth it into a "link" DC voltage, and, then convert it into the desired AC waveform as shown in Fig. 2.9.1. In general, a DC-to-AC converter is called an inverter, which is probably where the motor-control inverter gets its name.

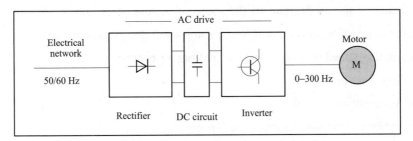

Fig. 2.9.1 The main components of an AC drive: the rectifier, DC circuit and inverter

Because the induction motor has no brushes and is easy to control, many older DC motors are being replaced with induction motors and accompanying inverters in industrial applications.

The speed is controlled by changing the frequency of the electrical supply to the motor. The 3-phase voltage in the national electrical grid connected to a motor creates a rotating magnetic field in it. The rotor of the electrical motor will follow this rotating magnetic field. An AC drive converts the frequency of the network to anything between 0 Hz to 300 Hz or even higher, and thus controls the speed of motors proportionally to the frequency.

Rectifier units

The AC drive is supplied by the electrical network via a rectifier. The rectifier unit can be uni-or bi-directional. When unidirectional, the AC drive can accelerate and run the motor by taking energy from the network. If bidirectional, the AC drive can also take the mechanical rotation energy from the motor and process and feed it back to the electrical network.

DC circuits

The DC circuit will store the electrical energy from the rectifier for the inverter to use. In most cases, the energy is stored in high-power capacitors.

Inverter units

The inverter unit takes the electrical energy from the DC circuit and supplies it to the motor. The inverter uses modulation techniques to create the needed 3-phase AC voltage output for the motor. The frequency can be adjusted to match the need of the process. The higher the frequency of the output voltage is, the higher the speed of the motor will be, and thus, the output of the process.

Benefits

The types of motors that AC drives control are normally operating at a constant speed. Enabling the user to control the speed of motors potentially gives him various benefits in terms of process control, system stress and energy savings.

Adjusting speed as a means of controlling a process

- Smoother operation;
- Acceleration control;
- Different operating speed for each process;
- Compensate for changing process variables;
- Adjust the rate of production;
- Allow accurate positioning;
- Control torque or tension.

System stress

- Reducing the start-up current, which allows the use of smaller fuses and supply connections and reduces peak loads on the electrical network;
- Reducing the mechanical shock in start and stop situations.

Saving energy by using AC drives

Fans and pumps are the most common energy saving applications. In these applications, energy savings are typically 20%–50%.

When a fan is driven by a fixed speed motor, the airflow may sometimes be higher than it needs to be. Airflow can be regulated by using a damper to restrict the flow, but it is more efficient to regulate the airflow by regulating the speed of the motor.

Case study: AC drives in HVAC applications

40% of all the energy in Europe and North America is consumed in buildings. The biggest share of this energy is consumed in heating, ventilation and air conditioning (HVAC) applications as shown in Fig. 2.9.2.

With the rising energy cost and concerns about the CO_2 levels and global warming, it is crucial to use all the means available to reduce the energy consumption in HVAC applications. The savings potential is big.

The key thing is to start looking more at lifetime costs of HVAC systems, where energy cost plays a big role, rather than the initial investment in HVAC systems. To give an example, 90% of the lifetime costs of the pump or fan is energy.

The majority of HVAC applications where AC drives are used are:

- Fans;
- Pumps;
- Compressors.

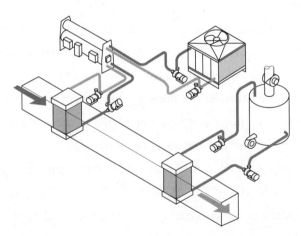

Fig. 2.9.2 The main components of an HVAC system: air circulation, water cooling circuits and water heating circuits

Fans and pumps

Using an AC drive to control the fan or pump output rather than using dampers, vanes, valves or on/off control brings substantial energy savings as shown in Fig. 2.9.3, if the required output is less than the nominal most of the time.

The AC drive controls the speed of the pump and fan by changing the electrical energy supplied rather than damping the air- or water-flow. It is like reducing the speed of a car by pressing less on the accelerator instead of using the brake to slow down the speed. The payback time of an AC drive is typically one year or less.

Other benefits of using AC drives to control the speed of fans or pumps are:
- Smooth ramp up and ramp down causes less stress to the mechanics of fans and pumps and to air ducts and water piping;

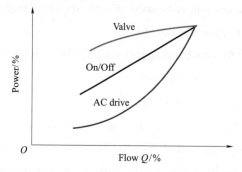

Fig. 2.9.3　Electrical power consumed by pump at partial loads being significantly less with an AC drive than with valve or on/off control

- Slowing down the speed rather than damping the output will result in lower noise levels.

Compressors

Compressors in HVAC systems are often used in chillers for cooling water, which again are used for cooling air. Utilizing AC drives in compressor applications will bring energy savings compared with on/off control.

Energy savings are achieved by optimising the system setup of compressors. The optimum set point for chilled water temperature and condenser water temperature is based on outdoor and indoor temperature and humidity.

The energy savings are most effectively achieved by tuning the system rather than optimizing individual functions. The AC drive gives the flexibility of tuning the setup of the system to operate in the most energy efficient operational point.

Other benefits
- Reduced number of starts and stops reduces the wear of the compressor.
- The piping and mechanics are stressed less in ramp-up or -down situations.
- Reduced noise level in low load situations.
- Possibility to use high speed compressors.

TECHNICAL WORDS AND PHRASES

appliance	[əˈplaiəns]	n.	家用电器
rotational	[rəuˈteiʃənəl]	adj.	旋转的，循环的
rectify	[ˈrektifai]	vt.	整流

Unit 9　Variable Speed AC Drives and How They Work

smooth	[smu:ð]	n.	滤波
accelerate	[æk'seləreit]	v.	加速，促进
damper	['dæmpə]	n.	风门，节气阀
ventilation	[ˌventi'leiʃən]	n.	通风，流通空气
compressor	[kəm'presə]	n.	压缩机
duct	[dʌkt]	n.	管，输送管
optimize	['ɔptimaiz]	vt.	使最优化
condenser	[kən'densə]	n.	冷凝器
humidity	[hju:'miditi]	n.	湿度

AC drive			交流驱动
induction motor			感应电机，异步电机
synchronous motor			同步电机
adjustable speed drive (ASD)			调速驱动
adjustable frequency drive (AFD)			调频驱动
electromagnetic induction			电磁感应
synchronous rotational speed			同步速度，同步转速
water and wastewater processing			水和污水处理
paper mill			卷纸
tunnel boring machine			隧道挖掘机
oil drilling platform			石油钻井平台
pole pair			极对
a "link" DC voltage			直流侧电压
national electrical grid			国家电网
high-power			大功率
peak load			最大负荷
mechanical shock			机械冲击
heating, ventilation and air conditioning (HVAC) applications			供暖、通风和空调应用
initial investment			初始投资
condenser water temperature			冷凝水温度
chilled water temperature			冷却水温度

NOTES

1. In general, a DC-to-AC converter is called an inverter, which is probably where the motor-control inverter gets its name.

译文：一般而言，将交直流变换器叫做逆变器，这可能就是电机控制逆变器取名的原因。

该句含有一个"which"引导的非限定性定语从句，该从句中又含有一个"where"引导的表语从句。

2. The key thing is to start looking more at lifetime costs of HVAC systems, where energy cost plays a big role, rather than the initial investment in HVAC systems.

译文：问题的关键是要开始更为关注供暖、通风和空调系统其终身的费用，其中占据很大份额的是能耗费，而不是初始投资成本。

"The key thing is"意思为"问题的关键是"。"to… HVAC systems"为不定式做表语，该表语结构为"start looking more… rather than…"意为"开始关注……而不是……"。

3. Using an AC drive to control the fan or pump output rather than using dampers, vanes, valves or on/off control brings substantial energy savings, if the required output is less than the nominal most of the time.

译文：如果大部分时间中风扇或泵所需的输出值比额定值小，那么用交流驱动代替风门（节气阀）、叶片、阀或开关来控制风扇或泵的输出可以节省大量的能源。

该句中"if"引导的是条件状语从句。主句结构为：主语"Using… on/off control"+谓语"brings"+宾语"substantial energy savings"。主句主语为现在分词短语做主语。

EXERCISES

Ⅰ. Fill in the blanks with English words and explain their functions (Fig. 2.9.4).

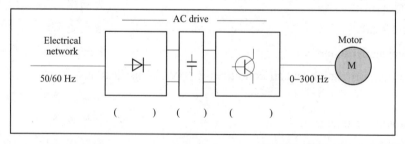

Fig. 2.9.4

Ⅱ. Mark the following statements with T(true) or F(false) according to the text.

1. Adjustable speed drives (ASDs) can be used to control the speed of induction motors.
（　　）

2. The speed of induction motors can be changed by changing the number of pole pairs.

( )
3. The DC circuit will store the electrical energy from the inverter for the rectifier to use. (   )
4. It is more efficient to use AC drives to regulate the airflow of the fan by regulating the speed of the motor. (   )
5. Compressors in HVAC systems are only used in chillers for cooling water. (   )

III. Answer the following questions according to the text.
1. Why do we need to adjust the speed of the electrical AC motor?
2. How does an AC drive adjust the speed of a motor?
3. What're the benefits of AC drives?
4. Please depict the operation process of an AC drive.

Supplementary Reading

Reading 9   Induction motors

An induction motor (IM) is a type of alternating current motor where power is supplied to the rotating device by means of electromagnetic induction.

An electric motor converts electrical power to mechanical power in its rotor (rotating part). There are several ways to supply power to the rotor. In a DC motor this power is supplied to the armature directly from a DC source, while in an induction motor this power is induced in the rotating device. An induction motor is sometimes called a rotating transformer because the stator (stationary part) is essentially the primary side of the transformer, and the rotor (rotating part) is the secondary side. Induction motors are widely used, especially polyphase induction motors, which are frequently used in industrial drives (Fig. 2.9.5).

Fig. 2.9.5   Three-phase induction motors

Induction motors are now the preferred choice for industrial motors due to their rugged construction, absence of brushes (which are required in most DC motors) and—thanks to modern power electronics — the ability to control the speed of the motor.

History

The induction motor with a wrapped rotor was invented by Nikola Tesla in 1882 in France but the initial patent was issued in 1888 after Tesla had moved to the United States. In his scientific work, Tesla laid the foundations for understanding the way the motor operates. The induction motor with a cage was invented by Mikhail Dolivo-Dobrovolsky about a year later in Europe. Technological development in the field has improved where a 100 hp (74.6 kW) motor from 1976 takes the same volume as a 7.5 hp (5.5 kW) motor did in 1897. Currently, the most common induction motor is the cage rotor motor. *Comments to be changed and corrected later once verified: Tesla had basically patented all useful versions of the alternating motor. Currently General Electric uses the same design today, minus the semiconductors, which Tesla had designed in his patents. Whomever edits and researches this, please get a physics major to look at all his patents regarding the AC motor. You will find this information. Patent No. 382,280 shows the motors used in a polyphase system (including processes from generator to motor that makes the rotor move). Patent No. 417,794 is the patent, with all the other numerous patents Tesla had on a polyphase motor, that basically adds up to the modern GE induction motor. You will also find Tesla's design that is a brushless pulse DC motor in patent No.424,036. Westinghouse profited off these designs until Edison's company and General Electric (owned by JPMorgan) merged and forced Westinghouse into a corner. Please do right by the gentleman who should be hailed as a national hero in both the United States and Canada; as well as the rest of modern human civilizations, and read through the patents I have pointed at as well as his other patents on the induction motor. You will find that at the time these were published, Tesla was the global authority on polyphase motors.

Principles of operation and comparison with synchronous motors

The basic difference between an induction motor and a synchronous AC motor is that in the latter a current is supplied onto the rotor. This then creates a magnetic field which, through magnetic interaction, links to the rotating magnetic field in the stator which in turn causes the rotor to turn. It is called synchronous because in a steady state the speed of the rotor is the same as the speed of the rotating magnetic field in the stator.

By way of contrast, the induction motor does not have any direct supply onto the rotor; instead, a secondary current is induced in the rotor. To achieve this, stator windings are arranged around the rotor so that when energised with a polyphase supply, they create a rotating magnetic field pattern which sweeps past the rotor as shown in Fig. 2.9.6. This changing magnetic field pattern induces currents in the rotor conductors. These currents interact with the rotating magnetic field created by the stator and in effect causes a rotational motion on the rotor.

However, for these currents to be induced, the speed of the physical rotor and the speed of the rotating magnetic field in the stator must be different, or else the magnetic field will not be moving relative to the rotor conductors, and no currents will be induced as shown in Fig. 2.9.6. If by some chance this happens, the rotor typically slows slightly until a current is re-induced, and then the rotor continues as before. The ratio of this difference between the speed of the rotor and the speed of the rotating magnetic field in the stator to the speed of the rotating stator field is called slip. In other words, it is the ratio of the relative speed of the magnetic field as seen by the rotor (the slip speed) to the speed of the rotating stator field. Due to this an induction motor is sometimes referred to as an asynchronous machine.

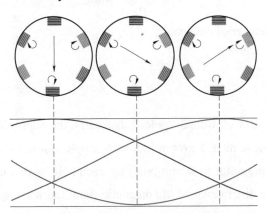

Fig. 2.9.6 A 3-phase power supply providing a rotating magnetic field in an induction motor

Formulae

The relationship between the supply frequency f, the number of poles p, and the synchronous speed (speed of rotating field) n_s is given by:

$$f = \frac{pn_s}{120}$$

From this relationship, we can get the synchronous speed:

$$n_s = \frac{120f}{p} \quad [\text{rpm}]$$

where

n = revolutions per minute (rpm);

f = AC power frequency (Hz);

p = number of poles (an even number).

The rotor speed is:
$$n_r = n_s(1-s)$$
where s is the slip.

Slip is calculated using:
$$s = \frac{n_s - n_r}{n_s}$$

A synchronous motor always runs at the synchronous speed with 0% slip.

Note on the use of p: Some texts refer to the number of pole pairs instead of the number of poles. For example, a six-pole motor would have 3 pole pairs. The equation of synchronous speed then becomes:
$$n_s = \frac{60f}{p} \quad [\text{rpm}]$$
where p is the number of pole pairs.

Construction

The stator consists of wound "poles" that carry the supply current to induce a magnetic field that penetrates the rotor. In a very simple motor, there would be a single projecting piece of the stator (a salient pole) for each pole, with windings around it. In fact, to optimize the distribution of the magnetic field, the windings are distributed in many slots located around the stator, but the magnetic field still has the same number of north-south alternations. The number of "poles" can vary between motor types but the poles are always in pairs (i.e. 2, 4, 6, etc.).

Induction motors are most commonly built to run on single-phase or three-phase power, but two-phase motors also exist. In theory, two-phase and more-than-three-phase induction motors shown in Fig. 2.9.5 are possible; many single-phase motors having two windings and requiring a capacitor can actually be viewed as two-phase motors, since the capacitor generates a second power phase 90 degrees from the single-phase supply and feeds it to a separate motor winding. Single-phase power is more widely available in residential buildings, but cannot produce a rotating field in the motor (the field merely oscillates back and forth), so single-phase induction motors must incorporate some kind of starting mechanism to produce a rotating field. They would, using the simplified analogy of salient poles, have one salient pole per pole number; a four-pole motor would have four salient poles. Three-phase motors have three salient poles per pole number, so a four-pole motor would have twelve salient poles. This allows the motor to produce a rotating field, allowing the motor to start with no extra equipment and run more efficiently than a similar single-phase motor.

There are three types of rotors:

- Squirrel-cage rotors

The most common rotor is a squirrel-cage rotor. It is made up of bars of either solid copper (most common) or aluminum that span the length of the rotor, and are connected through a ring at each end. The rotor bars in squirrel-cage induction motors are not straight, but have some skew to reduce noise and harmonics.

- Slip ring rotors

A slip ring rotor replaces the bars of the squirrel-cage rotor with windings that are connected to slip rings. When these slip rings are shorted, the rotor behaves similarly to a squirrel-cage rotor; they can also be connected to resistors to produce a high-resistance rotor circuit, which can be beneficial in starting.

- Solid core rotors

A rotor can be made from a solid mild steel. The induced current causes the rotation.

[awaiting approval] A rotor can also be made with coils wrapped around the rotor with each coil set being shorted.

Unit 10

Induction Motor Control Circuits

Induction Motor
Control Circuits
翻译

Starting circuits

Star-delta starters
Star-delta connections

The star-delta connection is mainly used for low and medium powered machines. During starting the stator winding is star-switched and subsequently delta-switched during acceleration.

In order to be switchable from star to delta the stator windings must be laid out for interlinked (conductor) voltage.

Fig. 2.10.1 shows that a star connection to a winding strand only receives $1/\sqrt{3}$ of the network voltage. The current decreases by the same factor. Moreover as both the conductor and strand current in the star connection remain identical (in the delta connection $I_{Str} = \dfrac{I_L}{\sqrt{3}}$), a further current reduction by the factor 1/3 ensues vis-a-vis the star delta connection.

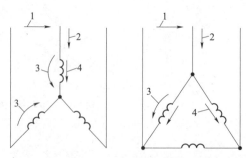

Fig. 2.10.1 The values of voltage and current during delta starting

1—Conductor voltage; 2—Conductor current; 3—Strand voltage (voltage through a winding);
4—Strand current (current in a winding)

The considerable starting current is effectively restricted by switching the stator winding from the operational delta connection to the star connection. The conductor current of the star connection is one third of the value of the delta connection.

Moreover, the diminished voltage in the star connection not only causes diminished stator current, the following also applies.

$$\frac{M_\lambda}{M_\Delta} = \frac{\dfrac{c \cdot \Phi \cdot I_2}{\sqrt{3} \cdot \sqrt{3}} \cos\varphi_2}{c \cdot \Phi \cdot I_L \cos\varphi_2} = \frac{1}{\sqrt{3} \cdot \sqrt{3}}$$

$$\frac{M_\lambda}{M_\Delta} = \frac{1}{\sqrt{3} \cdot \sqrt{3}}$$

The initial torque in the star connection is but one third of its value in the delta connection. The advantage of the star-delta connection for limiting the considerable starting current in an effective manner is, however, only possible through a further reduction in the already minimal initial torque. In many cases it will be necessary when we employ this starting procedure to start up the motor without load.

Circuitry (See Fig.2.10.2)

Circuitry description

Fig. 2.10.2 shows the starting up of the squirrel cage motor via K_1 and K_3 in star connection. Switch the stator winding to delta connection by means of K_2. Actuate S_2

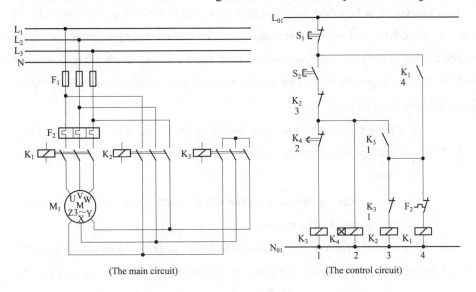

(The main circuit) (The control circuit)

Fig. 2.10.2 Automatic star-delta connection

L—External conductor; N—Neutral conductor; F_1—Fuses; F_2—Thermal cut-out; K_1—Main contactor;

K_2—Delta contactor; K_3—Star contactor; M_1—Three-phase motor;

S_1, S_2—Switches; K_1...K_3—Relay; K_4—Time relay

by switching K_3 and the time relay K_4 (starting delay). K_1 is switched by means of K_3 closer. K_1 holds itself alone above its closer. Following the adjustment period the opening contact of K_4 switches K_3 off whilst K_2 is switched on by means of the opening contact of K_3.

Resistance stators

Modes of operation

A further possibility of diminishing stator voltage, thereby reducing motor current whilst starting, is to connect resistors in series to the stator windings. Ohmic resistors are advantageous for lesser powered motors whilst series reactors are more economical for higher powered motors.

Curtailing voltage at the stator windings serves to reduce the starting current and the starting torque as also applies in other starting procedures (Fig. 2.10.3).

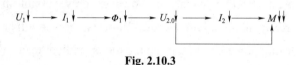

Fig. 2.10.3

An effective reduction in the starting current is attained by connecting resistors in series within the stator circuit in conjunction with a pronounced decline in the starting torque.

This procedure is however only suitable for no-load running motors. In order to ensure a smoother and slower starting (i.e. to exclude torque impulses from impact-switched gears) it is sufficient whilst starting to connect an ohmic resistance or a coil in a lead (Kusa circuit). The significance of this resistance is illustrated as follows for both limit values:

$R_v \to \infty$ $\begin{cases} \text{The limit current motor is fed from one side only from the stator.} \\ \text{Consequently there is no rotating field and the motor does not develop} \\ \text{a torque.} \end{cases}$

$R_v = 0$ $\begin{cases} \text{The asynchronous motor is connected directly. The motor develops the} \\ \text{maximum possible torque.} \end{cases}$

With the help of the resistor R_v in a lead it becomes possible to adjust the possible starting torques between zero and the possible maximum value. Then an impact-free starting becomes possible. As a result of the circuit asymmetry the conduction currents are distributed unequally in the three leads. An effective reduction of the starting current is not possible. The current only declines in the strand with the series connected resistor.

Unit 10 Induction Motor Control Circuits   105

Circuitry (See Fig. 2.10.4)
Circuitry description

In Fig. 2.10.4 starting ensues via protection K_2 and the series resistor R_1. Diminish the voltage at the stator winding, curtail the starting current to ensure smooth starting up. Switching over to network voltage by means of protection K_1 without currentless interruption.

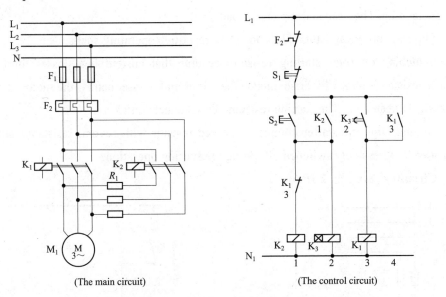

Fig. 2.10.4 **Starting connection by means of series resistors**

K_2—Starting contactor; R_1—Starting resistance; K_3—Time relay

Actuating S_2 switches on protection K_2 and the time relay K_2 (initial torque delay). K_2 retains itself independently over its closer in the current path "2." Following the adjustment spell the K_3 closer in the current path "3" switches K_1 on whilst K_1 switches K_2 through its opener in the current path "1."

Slip ring motors
Modes of operation

In Fig. 2.10.5 the ends of the rotor winding are attached to the slip rings which give rise to the designation of this rotor.

The torque and the rotor current can be aligned in the desired values during the starting operation

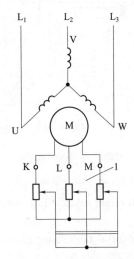

Fig. 2.10.5 **The slip-ring rotor with rotor starting resistance**

1—Rotor starting resistance;
K, L, M—Connecting terminals

with the assistance of the additional resistors which may be switched on via the slip rings of the rotor winding. The internal electrical properties of this motor can be undertaken by switching on the resistors from outside. Starting can thus ensue with substantially less current than in the case of squirrel cage motors whilst the initial torque attains substantial values because of the greater ohmic share in the rotor current.

Slip ring motors develop a pronounced initial torque notwithstanding minimal current take-up. They can start up under load.

Slip ring motors are suitable for long and repetitive operating spells.

Switching on rotor starting resistors ensures that current heat losses through greater resistance generally arise outside the motor and, consequently, the motor is not excessively heated up. The starting resistors dissipate heat quickly.

By and large the starter comprises a fixed resistor with several resistance steps which are progressively switched off during the starting operation.

Circuitry (See Fig. 2.10.6)

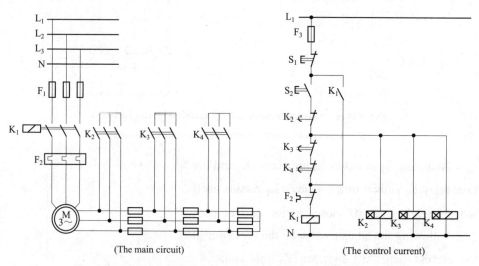

(The main circuit) (The control current)

Fig. 2.10.6 Automatic starting connection for the slip-ring motor

Circuitry description

Fig. 2.10.6 features an automatic starting circuit for ring motors. The starting resistors are switched off by protectors with turn-on delayed closers in three stages.

Rotational reversing circuits

Circuitry (See Fig. 2.10.7)
Circuitry description

Fig. 2.10.7 shows the rotational direction selection without cut-off compulsion.

The K_1 is switched clockwise by actuating S_3. K_2 is locked in the current path "3" by the openers of K_1 and S_3. K_2 drive is switched counterclockwise by the dead and simultaneous actuation of S_2 and K_1.

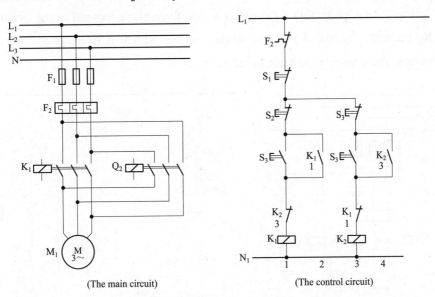

Fig. 2.10.7 Rotational direction turnover voltage

Braking circuits

Counter-current braking
Modes of operation

Braking by means of counter-current is the simplest way to attain standstill of an asynchronous drive, for instance in pumping stations. Two stator leads are interchanged to this end during motor operation. This changes the rotational direction of the rotating field. The rotor thus runs counter to the rotational direction of the rotating field. This connection can be used both for squirrel cage and slip ring motors. No additional devices are required.

The braking effect during counter-current braking is based on the altered rotational field direction. The motor tries to accelerate in the other rotational direction.

The motor must be disconnected in good time from the mains so that it does not again accelerate in the new rotational field direction. This is mainly made automatically.

Counter-current operation induces pronounced braking reaction. The current impulse on switching over is considerably greater than starting through direct connection. The motor is generally braked in star connection in order to avoid a too great current.

Circuitry (See Fig. 2.10.8)

Circuitry description

In Fig. 2.10.8, protection K_1 switches on the three-phase motor. During switching off, K_2 connects the mains via two series resistors with two interchanged external conductors. The counter field brakes the rotors.

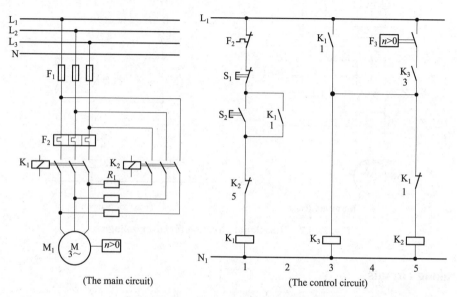

Fig. 2.10.8 Counter-current braking

K_2 falls off during motor standstill.

Actuating S_2 switches protection K_1 which holds itself in the current path "2" through a closer. K_2 is locked by the K_1 opener in the current path "5" whilst the closer in the current path "3" switches the locking relay K_3. Switching off by means of S_1, the K_1 opener closes the current path "5." K_2 is excited. Given standstill ($n = 0$) the closer of the automatic brake controller interrupts the F_3 current path "5." K_3 and K_2 drop out.

Direct current braking

Modes of operation

During this braking procedure the machine is disconnected from the mains and the stator winding is excited through direct current. Connection to the direct current source to the circuit is depicted in Fig. 2.10.9.

The stator establishes a constant magnetic field. Induction currents are yielded in the rotor winding. These induction currents give rise to a braking torque which facilitates impulse-free braking.

The asynchronous machine with direct current braking behaves in the same manner as an external pole synchronous generator.

Direct current braking is suitable for stopping all the categories of asynchronous machine drives. The dissipated heat converted through rotor circuit braking is much less than during counter-braking. The minimal exciting power and the admirably controlled speed of slip ring motors are further advantages of this circuitry.

Circuitry (See Fig.2.10.9)

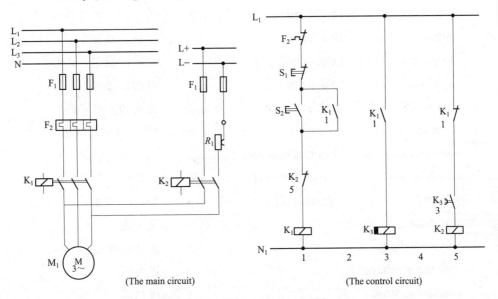

(The main circuit)　　　　　　　　　　(The control circuit)

Fig. 2.10.9　Direct current braking

Circuitry description

K_1 switches on the three-phase motor. On switching off, K_2 connects direct voltage to the stator winding. K_2 drops out after commensurate braking.

Actuating S_2 switches protection K_1 which holds itself via a closer in the current path "2." The K_1 closer in the current path "3" switches on the auxiliary contactor K_3 (release delay). K_1 openers in the current path "5" serve to lock K_2. K_1 drops out when S_1 switches off. Its opener locks the current path "5" (braking ensues through K_2) whilst its closer in the current path "3" switches K_3 off with delay.

The closer of K_3 in the current path "5" opens with delay whereby K_2 drops off.

TECHNICAL WORDS AND PHRASES

interlink	[ˌintə(ː)'liŋk]	vt.	连接，使结合
acceleration	[ækˌseləˈreiʃən]	n.	加速，增速
identical	[aiˈdentikəl]	adj.	同一的，同样的
procedure	[prəˈsiːdʒə]	n.	程序，手续，步骤

fuse	[fju:z]	n.	保险丝，熔丝
commensurate	[kə'menʃərit]	adj.	相称的，相当的
actuate	['æktjueit]	vt.	激励，驱使
adjustment	[ə'dʒʌstmənt]	n.	调整，调节，调节器
diminish	[di'miniʃ]	v.	（使）减少，（使）变小
illustrate	['iləstreit]	vt.	举例说明，图解
sufficient	[sə'fiʃənt]	adj.	充分的，足够的
curtail	[kə:'teil]	vt.	缩减，减少
designation	[,dezig'neiʃən]	n.	指示，指定，名称
assistance	[ə'sistəns]	n.	帮助，协助
substantial	[səb'stænʃəl]	adj.	充实的，丰富的
dissipate	['disipeit]	v.	驱散，（使）消散
counterclockwise	[,kauntə'klɔkwaiz]	adj.	反时针方向的
simultaneous	[,siməl'teinjəs]	adj.	同时的，同时发生的
standstill	['stændstil]	n.	停止，停顿
star-delta			星三角
stator winding			定子绕组
conductor voltage			线电压
conductor current			线电流
strand voltage			相电压
strand current			相电流
initial torque			启动转矩
external conductor			外部导线
neutral conductor			中性导线
thermal cut-out			热熔断路
main contactor			主触点
squirrel cage motor			鼠笼型电机
time relay			时间继电器
ohmic resistor			欧姆电阻器
series reactor			电抗器
starting torque			启动转矩，启动扭矩
rotating field			旋转磁场
slip ring			滑动环，集电环
counter-current braking			反接制动
direct current braking			能耗制动（直流电力制动）

braking torque 制动转矩
external pole synchronous generator 凸极式同步发电机

NOTES

1. The advantage of the star-delta connection for limiting the considerable starting current in an effective manner is, however, only possible through a further reduction in the already minimal initial torque.

   译文：星三角连接的优点在于它能够有效地抑制启动电流，然而该优点只有通过进一步减小启动转矩才可能实现。

   该句的主语为"The advantage of the star-delta connection for limiting the considerable starting current in an effective manner"，主语过长，为了平衡句子，翻译时将主语单独作为一句翻译。

2. A further possibility of diminishing stator voltage, thereby reducing motor current whilst starting, is to connect resistors in series to the stator windings.

   译文：此外减小启动时的定子电压，从而减小电机启动电流的方法还有：在定子绕组中串联电阻。

   该句主语部分为"A further possibility of diminishing stator voltage, thereby reducing motor current whilst starting"。"to connect resistors in series to the stator windings"为动词不定式，做表语。

3. With the help of the resistor R_v in a lead it becomes possible to adjust the possible starting torques between zero and the possible maximum value.

   译文：在定子的一个接线端中串入电阻 R_v 的情况下，我们就可在 0 和可能的最大值之间来调整启动转矩。

   "With the help of the resistor R_v in a lead"为英语中"介词with+复合结构"结构，也叫介词 with 的复合结构，该句中意为"在……情况下"。"it becomes possible to"为"It is+*adj.*+to do"的句型，意为"可以……"。

4. The torque and the rotor current can be aligned in the desired values during the starting operation with the assistance of the additional resistors which may be switched on via the slip rings of the rotor winding.

   译文：在启动期间，转子绕组的滑环将附加电阻接入，通过转子上的滑环来控制接入电阻的大小，从而让电机转矩和转子电流达到所要求的值。

   "with the assistance of the additional resistors which may be switched on via the slip rings of the rotor winding"为"介词with+复合结构"结构，也叫介词 with 的复合结构，表示伴随条件。

5. Starting can thus ensue with substantially less current than in the case of squirrel

cage motors whilst the initial torque attains substantial values because of the greater ohmic share in the rotor current.

译文：启动时的电流要比鼠笼型异步电机小很多，而启动转矩较大，因为转子电路中的电阻变大，导致转子电流变小。

该句由"whilst"连接两个并列句。

6. Switching on rotor starting resistors ensures that current heat losses through greater resistance generally arise outside the motor and, consequently, the motor is not excessively heated up.

译文：接入转子启动电阻使得电流产生的热损耗大部分消耗在电机外部的电阻上，从而电机不会产生过热。

该句中连词"consequently"连接两个句子，表示因果关系。前一个句子中"that"引导的是宾语从句，其主句的主语部分为"Switching on rotor starting resistors"，即动名词做主语；从句的主语部分为"current heat losses through greater resistance"。

EXERCISES

Ⅰ. **Complete the following sentences and translate them into Chinese.**

1. The considerable _____ is effectively restricted by switching the stator winding from the operational _____ connection to the _____ connection.

2. In a resistance stator _____ resistors are advantageous for lesser powered motors whilst _____ are more economical for higher powered motors.

3. Starting can _____ ensue with substantially less current than in the case of squirrel cage motors whilst the _____ attains substantial values because of the greater ohmic share in the rotor current.

4. Slip ring motors develop a pronounced _____ notwithstanding minimal current take-up. They can start up under _____.

5. The _____ during counter-current braking is based on the altered rotational _____. The motor tries to _____ in the other rotational direction.

Ⅱ. **Answer the following questions according to the text.**

1. In Fig. 2.44 what will happen when S_2 or S_3 is pressed?

2. Depict the operational principle of the circuitry in Fig. 2.41 and What's the function of resistor R_1?

3. When and why do we need to use star-delta starters? What's the advantage of the star-delta starter?

Supplementary Reading

Reading 10　How Relays Work

A relay is a simple electromechanical switch made up of an electromagnet and a set of contacts. Relays are found hidden in all sorts of devices. In fact, some of the first computers ever built used relays to implement Boolean gates.

In this article, we will see how relays work and a few of their applications.

Relay construction

Relays are amazingly simple devices. There are four parts in every relay:

- Electromagnets;
- Armatures that can be attracted by the electromagnet;
- Springs;
- A set of electrical contacts

Fig. 2.10.10 shows these four parts in action:

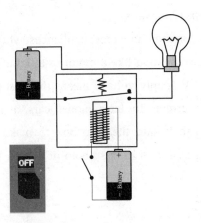

Fig. 2.10.10　How a relay works

In Fig. 2.10.10, you can see that a relay consists of two separate and completely independent circuits. The first is at the bottom and drives the electromagnet. In this circuit, a switch is controlling power to the electromagnet. When the switch is on, the electromagnet is on, and it attracts the armature (blue). The armature is acting as a switch in the second circuit. When the electromagnet is energized, the armature completes the second circuit and the light is on. When the electromagnet is not energized, the spring pulls the armature away and the circuit is not complete. In that case, the light is dark.

When you purchase relays, you generally have control over several variables:

- The voltage and the current that are needed to activate the armature;
- The maximum voltage and current that can run through the armature and the armature contacts;
- The number of armatures (generally one or two);
- The number of contacts for the armature (generally one or two—the relay shown here has two, one of which is unused);
- Whether the contact (if only one contact is provided) is normally open (NO) or normally closed (NC).

Relay applications

- In general, the point of a relay is to use a small amount of power in the electromagnet—coming, say, from a small dashboard switch or a low-power electronic circuit—to move an armature that is able to switch a much larger amount of power. For example, you might want the electromagnet to energize using 5 volts and 50 milliamps (250 milliwatts), while the armature can support 120 V AC at 2 amps (240 watts).
- Relays are quite common in home appliances where there is an electronic control turning on something like a motor or a light. They are also common in cars, where the 12 V supply voltage means that just about everything needs a large amount of current. In later model cars, manufacturers have started combining relay panels into the fuse box to make maintenance easier. For example, the six gray boxes in this photo of a Ford Windstar fuse box are all relays.

Chapter 3
Industrial Automation

Unit 11
PLC Systems

PLC Systems
翻译

NEMA, the National Electrical Manufacturers Association defines a programmable logic controller (PLC) as: A programmable controller is a digitally operating electronic apparatus which uses a programmable memory for the internal storage of instructions for implementing specific functions, such as logic, sequencing, timing, counting and arithmetic, to control through digital or analog input/output, various types of machines or process as shown in Fig. 3.11.1.

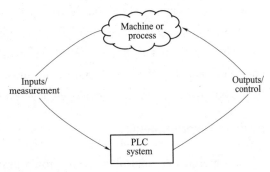

Fig. 3.11.1 The definition of PLC

Programmable logic controllers, programmable controllers, or PLCs are specialized industrial computers. The PLC accepts inputs from switches and sensors, evaluates these based on a program (logic), and changes the state of outputs to control a machine or process.

Initially, programmable logic controllers were used to replace traditional hard-wired relay logic; however, with its ever increasing functionality which is found in many more complex applications. PLCs are used in any industrial application where operating requirements are complex, constantly changing, or where high reliability is necessary.

Brief history of the PLC

The advent of the PLC began in the 1960's and 1970's to replace traditional "hard-wired" controls, and has since become the predominant choice for industrial controls. Before PLCs, much of machine control relied on contacts and relays providing hard-wired "logic" for machine controls. Changes to the logic were labor intensive and costly.

In 1968, GM's hydramatic division specified the design criteria for what would become the first programmable logic controller. They requested a solid-state system that would:
- Survive the industrial environment;
- Be easily programmed by plant engineers and technicians;
- Be easily reprogrammed and re-used.

The winning proposal came from Bedford Associate—which introduced the modular digital controller (MODICON). The MODICON is still a popular brand of PLC today, but is owned by Schneider Electric. Other prevalent PLC brands today are: Allen-Bradley, Siemens, Omron, and GE.

The automotive industry was a major early adopter of programmable logic controllers (PLCs). They wanted a programming method that could be easily understood by their existing control engineers and technicians. The result of this desire was a programming language called Relay Ladder Logic (or "ladder logic").

The layout of ladder logic is very similar to the diagrams for hard wired relay controls. Ladder logic is still one of the most popular "language" for programming PLCs, but many others have developed over the years.

Basic PLC components

Programmable controllers have grown throughout industrial control applications because of the ease they bring to creating a controller: ease of programming, ease of wiring, ease of installation, and ease of changing. PLCs span a wide range of sizes, but all contain six basic components as shown in Fig. 3.11.2:
- Processor or central processing unit (CPU);
- Rack or mounting;
- Input assembly;
- Output assembly;
- Power supply;
- Programming unit, device, or PC/software.

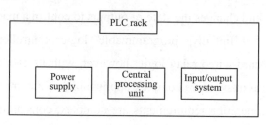

Fig. 3.11.2 Basic PLC components

We will start with explaining the physical components you see when looking at a PLC system—and then explore what goes on inside each part, and how the components relate to each other.

Rack assembly

Most medium to large PLC systems are assembled such that the individual components—CPU, Input/Output, Power Supply—are modules that are held together within a rack.

In smaller PLC systems—all of these components may be contained in a single housing or "brick"—these smaller systems are sometimes referred to as "bricks" or "shoebox" PLCs.

Power supply

The power supply provides power for the PLC system. The power supply provides internal DC current to operate the processor logic circuitry and input/output assemblies. Common power levels used are 24 V DC or 120 V AC.

Processors (CPUs)

The processor, also called central processing unit, or CPU, is the "brain" of the PLC. The size and type of CPU will determine things like: the programming functions available, the size of the application logic available, the amount of memory available, and the processing speed.

Input/output assembly

Inputs carry signals from the process into the controller. They can be input switches, pressure sensors, operator inputs, etc. These are like the senses and sensors of the PLC.

Outputs are the devices that the PLC uses to send changes out to the world. These are the actuator the PLC can change to adjust or control the process-motors, lights, relays, pumps, etc.

Many types of inputs and outputs can be connected to a PLC, and they can all be divided into two large groups—analog and digital. Digital inputs and outputs are those that operate due to a discrete or binary change—on/off, yes/no. Analog inputs and outputs change continuously over a variable range—pressure, temperature, and potentiometer.

Programming devices

The PLC is programmed using a specialty programmer or software on a computer that can load and change the logic inside. Most modern PLCs are programmed using software on a PC or laptop computer. Older systems used a custom programming device.

Basic operation of a PLC system

The operation of the PLC system shown in Fig. 3.11.3 is simple and straightforward. The process or CPU completes three processes: ① scans, or reads, from the input devices; ② executes or "solves" the program logic, and ③ updates, or writes, to the output devices.

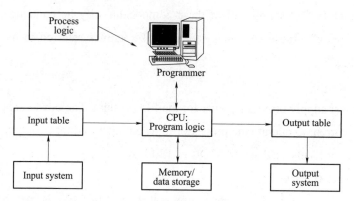

Fig. 3.11.3　The operation of a PLC system

PLC program

For the PLC to be useful, it must first have a program or logic for the CPU to execute. A system engineer or PLC programmer will first create the program logic in a programming device (these days it is usually software running on a personal computer). This logic can be written in Ladder Logic, Instruction List, Sequential Function Charts, or any of the IEC languages.

The programmer will then download the program to the PLC. This is usually done by temporarily connecting the programmer to the PLC. Once the program is installed or downloaded to the CPU, it is usually not necessary for the PC to remain connected.

Basic scan

Once the program is in the CPU—the PLC is then set to "run", and the PLC executes the application program repeatedly. In addition to executing the program, the CPU regularly reads the status of input devices, and sends data to the output device. The input system senses the status of the real world inputs (a switch, a level, etc.), translates them to values that can be used by the CPU, and writes those values to the input table. The application program is executed, and writes values to the output table. The output system then converts the output value to a real world change (A motor turns on, or a valve opens, etc.).

This process of reading inputs, executing logic, and writing outputs is called the PLC scan or sweep as shown in Fig. 3.11.4.

The CPU continuously reads inputs, solves logic, and writes outputs (There are other tasks the CPU does—which will be discussed later). It is important to understand the scan because it may dictate how a programmer structures logic.

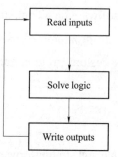

Fig. 3.11.4　The PLC scan

Memory

The control program or application program is stored in memory. As the PLC executes logic, it may also read and store values to memory. The values may also be used and referred to by the application program.

PLC input and output devices

The term I/O refers to Input/Output. I/O is information representing the data that are received from sensing devices and the commands that are sent to actuating and indicating devices. The I/O system is the collection of physical elements of the control system that either provides or uses I/O data. There are two major types of I/O:

- Digital—binary devices which must be in one of the only two states: on or off.
- Analog—continuous devices that sense and respond to a range of values.

Digital I/O

Digital input devices may be either on or off; they may not hold any other values. For example, digital position sensors do not sense how close an object is. They only tell if the object is within a range of positions. Common digital field input devices include pushbuttons, limit switches, etc. Common digital output devices include relays, motor starters, and solenoid valves.

Analog I/O

Analog input devices sense continuous parameters. The information that they provide is given as a continuous range of values, not just an on or off indicator. Common analog inputs are pressure, temperature, speed, etc. Analog output devices respond to a range of output values from the controller. Common analog output signals include motor speed, valve position, air pressure, etc.

I/O modules connect "real world" field devices to the controller. They convert the electrical signal used in the field device into the electronic signal that can be used by the control system.

PLC communications

To control a machine or process many times, multiple controllers or intelligent devices must work together to accomplish the task. In order to work together, these devices must communicate. In order to program a PLC, communications must take place—because the programming device (computer) must communicate with the PLC CPU in order to transfer the configuration and control logic before the PLC can even begin to run. For these reasons, it is important for anyone in automation to have a basic understanding of PLC communications. There are three basic levels/categories of communications that we are usually concerned with in industrial control: serial communications, industrial communications networks, and industrial I/O networks. The most basic form of communication is a direct, one way, connection between two devices where data is transmitted one bit at a time. We call this serial communication. An industrial network is a system of electronic devices that are connected in order to share information. The network can consist of PLC controllers, I/O devices, operator interfaces, HMI/SCADA computers, and many other elements. Each element is uniquely addressable—giving each component (controllers, I/O devices, operator interfaces, etc.) a unique name or label. Industrial networks provide bi-directional, real-time, (sometimes deterministic) communication. Each element has specific electronic components to allow the transfer of data between the elements, on a shared media, and according to a protocol.

TECHNICAL WORDS AND PHRASES

apparatus	[ˌæpəˈreitəs]	n.	仪器，装置，设备
arithmetic	[əˈriθmətik]	n.	算术，算法
switch	[switʃ]	n.	开关，电闸，转换
sensor	[ˈsensə]	n.	传感器
evaluate	[iˈvæljueit]	v.	评价，估计，求……的值
reliability	[riˌlaiəˈbiliti]	n.	可靠性
predominant	[priˈdɔminənt]	adj.	卓越的，支配的，主要的
brand	[brænd]	n.	商标，牌子
rack	[ræk]	n.	机架
potentiometer	[pəˌtenʃiˈɔmitə]	n.	电位计，分压计
execute	[ˈeksikju:t]	vt.	执行，实行
scan	[skæn]	n./v.	扫描
install	[inˈstɔ:l]	vt.	安装，安置
respond	[risˈpɔnd]	v.	响应
parameter	[pəˈræmitə]	n.	参数，参量
configuration	[kənˌfigjuˈreiʃən]	n.	构造，结构，配置，外形
unique	[ju:ˈni:k]	adj.	唯一的，独特的
discrete	[disˈkri:t]	adj.	不连续的，离散的

National Electrical Manufacturers Association(NEMA)

美国电气制造商协会

Unit 11　PLC Systems 123

hard-wired relay logic	硬件连接的继电器逻辑电路
hydramatic division	液压部门
Bedford Associate	贝德福德联盟
Schneider Electric	施耐德电气公司
Relay Ladder Logic /ladder logic	梯形图
pressure sensor	压力传感器
power supply	电源
programming unit	编程器
instruction list	指令表
laptop computer	膝上型计算机
sequential function chart	顺序功能图
indicating device	指示装置
limit switch	限位开关，极限开关
solenoid valve	电磁阀
serial communication	串行通信
industrial communications network	工业通信网络

NOTES

1. A programmable controller is a digitally operating electronic apparatus which uses a programmable memory for the internal storage of instructions for implementing specific functions, such as logic, sequencing, timing, counting and arithmetic, to control through digital or analog input/output, various types of machines or process.

   译文：可编程逻辑控制器是一种数字式的电子装置，采用可编程存储器在其内部储存指令。这些指令用来执行一些特定功能，如逻辑、排序、计时、计数与计算等，并通过数字或模拟的输入/输出模块，控制各种机械或生产过程。

   该句含有一个 which 引导的定语从句，修饰"a digitally operating electronic apparatus"。由于定语部分过长，因此翻译时往往译成后置的并列分句。

2. PLCs are used in any industrial application where operating requirements are complex, constantly changing, or where high reliability is necessary.

   译文：在控制要求复杂，控制任务变换频繁，且可靠性要求又高的工业应用中，可采用 PLC 来实现其控制任务。

   该句主句为"PLCs are used in any industrial application"，从句为两个"where"引导的并列定义从句。

3. We will start with explaining the physical components you see when looking at a PLC system—and then explore what goes on inside each part, and how the

components relate to each other.

译文：我们将从 PLC 系统外部的可见部件开始介绍，然后再介绍其内部的器件以及各个部件如何协同工作。

该句中 "and" 连接的是两个并列句："We will start with… at a PLC system" 和 "then explore what… each other"。第一句为复合句，其主句为 "We will start with explaining the physical components"，而 "you see when looking at a PLC system" 为定语从句，修饰 "the physical components"。该定语从句中又包含了一个 "when" 引导的状语从句。

4. The input system senses the status of the real world inputs (a switch, a level, etc.), translates them to values that can be used by the CPU, and writes those values to the input table.

译文：输入系统检测现实世界中的输入（开关、电平等）状态，并将它们转化为 CPU 能够读懂的数据，然后将这些数据写到输入表中。

该句为 3 个分句构成的并列句，由于在并列句中后边的分句可以省略与前边分句中相同的成分，因此后面两个分句的主语 "The input system" 被省略。

5. I/O is information representing the data that are received from sensing devices and the commands that are sent to actuating and indicating devices.

译文：I/O 是一种信息，表示来自传感器设备的数据和发送至执行装置和指示装置的命令。

该句为复合句，主句为 "I/O is information"。"representing the data… and the commands that…indicating devices" 为现在分词做定语，修饰 "information"。

EXERCISES

Ⅰ. **Translate the following words into English.**

1. 可编程控制器
2. 机架
3. 电源
4. 输入/输出模块
5. 电磁阀
6. 编程器
7. 限位开关
8. 指令表
9. 顺序功能图
10. 梯形图

Ⅱ. **Complete the following sentences.**

1. The PLC accepts inputs from _____ and _____, evaluates these based on a _____ (logic), and changes the state of _____ to control a machine or process.

2. Initially, programmable logic controllers were used to replace traditional _____;

however, with its ever increasing _____ it is found in many more complex applications.

3. The MODICON is still a popular _____ of PLC today, but is owned by _____. Other prevalent PLC brands today are: Allen-Bradley, _____, _____, and GE.

4. In order to program a PLC, _____ must take place—because the _____ (computer) must communicate with the PLC CPU in order to transfer the _____ and control logic before the PLC can even begin to run.

5. Digital inputs and outputs are those that operate due to a _____ or binary change—on/off, yes/no. Analog inputs and outputs change continuously over _____—pressure, temperature, _____.

III. Answer the following questions according to the text.

1. For what purpose did engineers design programmable logic controllers?
2. Please explain the process of PLC scan or sweep.
3. What resulted in the advent of the programming language "Relay Ladder Logic"?

Supplementary Reading

Reading 11 A Short History of Industrial Automation Growth

Trace the roots of all significant automation business segments and you'll find key people and innovations. Industrial instrumentation and controls have always been a hotbed of new products—improved sensors, amplifiers, displays, recorders, control elements, valves, actuators and other widgets and gismos. But the markets are relatively small, specialized and fragmented, and it's rare that any significant volume results directly from individual products.

Many automation companies were founded with innovative developments for niche applications. The target customers were usually local end-users who provided the opportunity to test new ideas, usually because of specific unmet needs. The successful startups expanded their products and markets beyond initially narrow applications and geographies, depending on the real value of the innovation, and also whether or not the founder was able to hire suitable management, sales & marketing leaders to grow the company beyond the initial entrepreneurial stages.

Since automation is such a fragmented business, all the larger (multi-billion $) companies are mostly a conglomeration of products and services; each product segment generates relatively small volume, but lumped together they form sizeable businesses.

Companies such as Ametek and Spectris have grown primarily through acquisition of small, innovative, niche product companies where growth is self-limited either through lack of capital for new products or global sales & market expansion. Indeed, these industrial mini-conglomerates thrive through astute and shrewd accumulation of innovative niche players. But few acquirers can come up with follow-through developments that match the original founder's innovations. And so the larger companies are usually satisfied with managed product extensions and expansions—with few, really innovative breakthroughs.

Major automation segments

Perhaps the exception to the small-company innovation rule was the distributed control system (DCS), a well-managed mix of several innovations developed in the 1970s by a team of engineers within Honeywell. This major industrial automation innovation achieved $100 M in sales in process control markets within just a couple of years. The segment has expanded to several billions of dollars, and has morphed into a variety of different shapes, sizes and form-factors for process, discrete and batch systems.

The other major automation product segment to achieve significance, also in the 1970s, was the programmable logic controller (PLC). This breakthrough innovation was the brainchild of inventor Dick Morley, who worked for a small development company, Bedford Associates, associated with Modicon (now part of Schneider). Also involved was Odo Struger of Allen-Bradley, now Rockwell Automation. Rockwell became the PLC leader in the US through good marketing and development of strong distribution channels—their Application Engineering Distributors (AED).

The first PLCs were developed for specific applications—reprogrammable test installations in the automobile manufacturing business, replacing hard-wired relay-logic which was hard to modify. The PLC market expanded rapidly in this key market to the extent that one Rockwell Distributor, McNaughton-McKay Electric, grew to well beyond $100 million through serving the automobile production business in just the Detroit area. Over the past 3 decades, PLCs have spread throughout industry and the PLC market segment that has grown to several billions of dollars worldwide.

For a couple of decades PLC applications remained focused around discrete automation markets, while DCS expanded primarily in process control systems. Then

PLCs expanded into control of remote I/O (input/output) systems with control and I/O clusters that could be easily connected as industrial networks. Soon personal computers became the easiest way to connect DCS, PLCs and remote I/O into the rapidly expanding hierarchy of factory and plant networks, fieldbus and the Internet.

Another major industrial automation segment is loosely termed "Supervisory Control and Data Acquisition" (SCADA). This loose conglomeration of products and innovations from several different sources remained fragmented between several markets and applications till networked PCs and Windows-based HMI software arrived in the late 1980s and 1990s.

Several innovative startups grew fairly rapidly, providing human-machine interface (HMI) software with connections to remote PLCs and industrial I/O. Wonderware (started by engineer Dennis Morin) was paced by Intellution (started by ex-Foxboro engineer Steve Rubin). There were several other startups in the same timeframe, but few achieved significance. It's interesting to note that the larger automation vendors did not take the lead in this new category; all significant growth came from innovative startups.

Although utilized across a broad array of market segments, the total available market for independent packaged software developments was limited, and the large process controls suppliers inevitably acquired the leaders. Wonderware was acquired by Invensys, which owned Foxboro; Emerson acquired Intellution as a key part of its DCS strategy, which developed into Delta V. Schneider recently acquired Citect, an innovative Australian company that had already branched out into broader software and system arenas. Iconics, another innovative software startup founded by another ex-Foxboro engineer Russ Agrusa, remains independent and hasn't grown on a broad front, remaining focused on targeted markets and customers. It will inevitably be acquired by one of the majors.

Sensors & actuators

Industrial control has sensors, actuators, and all the "stuff" in between. Rosemount started with special temperature sensors (RTDs) for aircraft and industrial applications and then grew rapidly with the development of its capacitive differential pressure sensors, rapidly overtaking the traditional instrumentation leaders—Foxboro, Taylor Instruments and Honeywell. The company was eventually acquired by Emerson—which also acquired other innovative sensor companies—Brooks (flow), Beckman (pH) and others.

At the other end of the automation business, Fisher Controls was started in Iowa by Bill Fisher, making innovative valves and actuators. This company was also acquired by Emerson—which now had both sensors and actuators. Interestingly, both Rosemount and Fisher tried to grow by branching out into DCS, but their offerings were relatively insignificant till Emerson put them together with PCs and Software (Intellution and other ingredients) to generate leadership with the combination that is now Emerson Process Systems.

Fragmented markets inhibit growth

In fragmented industrial markets, few companies achieve revenues of much beyond tens of millions of dollars. The problem is the variety of applications. There are millions of thermocouples used, but mostly specialized and related to specific industries and requirements. You won't find a $1 B thermocouple company—or even a sensor company that is quite approaching that size. European companies like Endress + Hauser and Pepperl + Fuchs look like they are approaching that threshold, but they are not quite making it.

At mid-size, there are the German "mittelstand" companies like Weidmuller and Phoenix, which primarily sell connectors and are approaching $1 B in total revenue. They have expanded into electronic instrumentation and controls, but have not succeeding in growing beyond about $50-100 million in this arena. And you may find other Europeans and Japanese, but they are all smaller players, looking for growth in a deceptively big market.

Growth plateaus

Many instrument companies start with a good idea. Once they expand beyond the natural volume of applications, they get topped out. There are very few requirements in automation for tens of millions of a product—even a measly million of anything. Growth in industrial automation takes time, money and marketing, which few people in the instrument business really have, or can afford. So, most automation companies seem to get acquired when they approach $100 million revenue.

The subject has been well documented in the Harvard Business Review and elsewhere. The engineer founder grows his company to $1 m, with 10–20 people, and then growth flattens. With a good, balanced team (including marketing, sales, manufacturing and finance), the startup grows to $10 M–20 M, reaching the 100-people barrier. Some try to cross the barrier to $100 m, and most get acquired in the process, as they run out of money and talent.

There are many examples:

- Rosemount came up with a differential pressure transducer which was significantly better than anything the leaders could offer. So, the company grew quickly and was bought by Emerson before it quite got to $100 M.
- Modicon (with Dick Morley involvement) came up with novel programmable controllers and was bought by Gould before it got to $100 M.
- With stubborn family ownership, Moore Products (based in Pennsylvania) went public and got to a couple of hundred million before it ran out of steam and was acquired by Siemens.
- Software leaders Wonderware and Intellution didn't get much past $50 M before they were acquired. And a whole bunch of other software companies now languish stubbornly around the $10-20 M mark.

There are many examples of good companies which have been around for several decades but have never quite achieved the $ 100 million benchmark. OPTO-22 started with Bill Engman who exited International Rectifier and made his own solid-state relays and then branched out into innovative I/O products with the founder's son now in charge. The other Moore—Moore Industries in California—is still headed up by the founder Len Moore, who insists that he enjoys what he's doing and continues to stimulate product innovations.

Then there are those companies that get stuck at the next plateau: $100 M to $1 B. The company may have gone "public" but is stuck in a niche that defies growth to the next level. Typically the founder is still around and has majority ownership—and so it stays independent.

Many significant automation companies grew steadily over a few decades—Fisher Controls, Fisher & Porter, Leeds & Northrup, Foxboro, Taylor Instruments, Bailey Controls. All of these were eventually acquired when they got beyond $ 100 M, but not quite $ 1 B.

There are, of course, interesting exceptions.

Innovative startups which remain independent

Omron in Japan is a standout. The company was founded in 1933 and has grown to be the largest industrial automation company in Japan. The unusual thing about Omron is that alone among any multi-billion corporations it devotes a significant amount of attention to its ethical, social and philosophical positions. This unusual ethos can be traced to the founder, an engineer Dr. Kazuma Tateisi, who has written a significant book—The Eternal Venture Spirit. His innovative yet practical entrepreneurial philosophy continues in the corporate culture of this significant company. The company continues to stimulate significant innovation and a plethora of new products, and has grown to several billion dollars worldwide, targeting a doubling in revenue by the end of this decade.

Another innovative startup National Instruments, headquartered in Austin, Texas, has about 4,000 employees, 2006 revenue of $660 M, trading on NASDAQ with market-cap of over $ 2 B. The company was co-founded in 1976 by Dr. James Truchard, while he was still at University of Texas, Austin. In 1986, Jim Truchard and Jeff Kodosky (who is also still at NI) invented LabVIEW graphical development software. The intuitive graphical environment of LabVIEW revolutionized the way engineers and scientists work, much like the spreadsheet providing a new way for financial professionals to do their jobs. The company is expected to grow well past the $ 1-billion benchmark and continue its independent growth and success.

Future growth in automation

Extrapolating automation history forward is an interesting challenge. In the past, growth inflection points have developed from new products and leadership (DCS, PLC, sensors, software). Today, growth is coming from global expansion and services, but that is only incremental, and not by any means a surge.

A new surge of growth will come through new technology (perhaps nanotech sensors, or wireless), production at the lowest cost for global distribution, and fast time-to-market (not impeded by standards committees and antiquated management conservatism). The managers, innovators and visionaries who recognize the possibilities will become the new leaders of tomorrow.

Unit 12 PLC Programming

Programming devices

PLCs can be reprogrammed through an appropriate programming device: Programming Console; PC; Hand Programmer.

Programming languages

IEC 61131-3 currently defines five programming languages for programmable control systems: FBD (Function block diagram), LD (Ladder diagram), ST (Structured text, similar to the Pascal programming language), IL (Instruction list, similar to assembly language) and SFC (Sequential function chart).

Introduction to ladder logic

Ladder logic uses graphic symbols similar to relay schematic circuit diagrams. Ladder diagram consists of two vertical lines representing the power rails. Circuits are connected as horizontal lines between these two verticals. Ladder diagram features are listed as follows: Power flows from left to right; Output on the right side cannot be connected directly with the left side; Contactor cannot be placed on the right of output; Each rung contains one output at least; Each output can be used only once in the program; A particular input and/or output can appear in more than one rung of a ladder; The inputs and/or outputs are all identified by their addresses, the notation used depending on the PLC manufacturer.

Introduction to statement list

Statement list is a programming language using mnemonic abbreviations of Boolean logic operations. Boolean operations work on combination of variables that are true or false. A statement is an instruction or directive for the PLC.

Statement List Operations: * Load (LD) instruction, And (A) instruction, Or (O) instruction, Output (=) instruction.

Function block diagrams

Function block is represented as a box with the function name written in. An example is shown in Fig. 3.12.1.

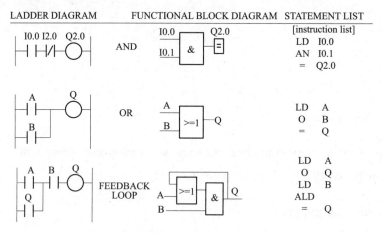

Fig. 3.12.1 A function block

PLC instructions

Functions and instructions

Relay-type (Basic) instructions: I, O, OSR, SET, RES, T, C

Data handling instructions: ZRST, DECO, ENCO, MEAN

Data move instructions: MOV, COP, FLL, TOD, FRD, DEG, RAD

Comparison instructions: EQU, NEQ, GEQ, GRT

Mathematical instructions: ADD, SUB, MUL, DIV

Continuous control instructions: (PID instructions)

Program flow control instructions: MCR (master control reset), JMP, LBL, JSR, SBR, RET, SUS, REF

Specific instructions: BSL, BSR (bit shift left/right), SQO, SQC, SQL

High speed counter instructions: HSC, HSL, RES, HSE

Communication instructions: MSQ, SVC

Internal relays

Auxiliary relays, markers, flags, coils, bit storage, used to hold data, and behave like relays, being able to be switched on or off and switch other devices on or off. They do not exist as real-world switching devices but are merely bits in the storage memory.

Retentive relays (battery-backed relays)

Such relays retain their state of activation, even when the power supply is off. They can be used in circuits to ensure a safe shutdown of plant in the event of a power failure and so enable it to restart in an appropriate manner.

Latch instructions (set and reset)

The set instruction causes the relay to self-hold, i.e. latch. It then remains in that condition until the reset instruction is received. The latch instruction is often called a SET or OTL (output latch). The unlatch instruction is often called a RES (reset), OTU (output unlatch) or RST (reset).

Timers

The timer is an instruction that awaits a set amount of time before doing something. Timers count fractions of seconds or seconds using the internal CPU clock. The time duration for which a timer has been set is termed the preset and is set in multiples of the time base used. Most manufacturers consider timers to behave like relays with coils which when energized result in the closure or opening of contacts after some preset time.

Counters

A counter is set to some preset value and, when this value of input pulses has been received, it will operate its contacts. The counter accumulated value ONLY changes at the off to on transition of the pulse input. Typically counters can count from 0 to 9999, −32,768 to +32,767 or 0 to 65535.

The normal counters are typically "software" counters—They don't physically exist in the PLC but rather they are simulated in software. A good rule of thumb is simply to always use the normal (software) counters unless the pulses you are counting will arrive faster than 2X the scan time.

Counter formats

Some manufacturers consider the counter as a relay and consist of two basic elements: One relay coil to count input pulses and the other to reset the counter, and the associated contacts of the counter being used in other rungs. Others (Siemens for example) treat the counter as an intermediate block in a rung from which signals emanate when the count is attained.

Data handling instructions

Timers, counters and individual relays are all concerned with the handling of individual bits, i.e. single on-off signal. PLC operations involve blocks of data representing a value, such blocks being termed words.

Data handling consists of operations involving moving or transferring numeric information stored in one memory word location to another word in a different location, comparing data values and carrying out simple arithmetic operations.

Master Control/ Master Control Reset (MC/MCR)

When large numbers of outputs have to be controlled, it is sometimes necessary for the whole sections of the program to be turned on or off when certain criteria are realized. This could be achieved by including an MCR instruction. An MCR instruction is an output instruction (Fig. 3.12.2).

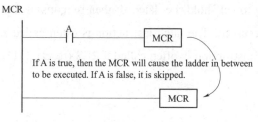

Fig. 3.12.2 MCR

The master control instruction typically is used in pairs with a master control reset. Different formats are used by different manufacturers:

MC/MCR (master control/master control reset), MCS/MCR (master control set/master control reset) or MCR (master control reset).

The zone being controlled begins with a rung that has the first MC instruction, whose status depends on its rung condition. This zone ends with a rung that has the second MCR instruction only.

When the rung with the first MCR instruction is true, the first MCR instruction is high, and the outputs of the rung in the controlled zone can be energized or de-energized according to their rung conditions. When this rung is false, all the outputs in the zone are de-energized, regardless of their rung conditions.

Timers should not be used inside the MC/MCR block because some manufacturers will reset them to zero when the block is false whereas other manufacturers will have them retain the current time state. Counters typically retain their current counted value.

RETURN / END

A return from subroutine instruction marks the end of subroutine instruction. When the rung condition of this instruction is true, it causes the PLC to resume execution in the calling program file at the rung following the jump to subroutine instruction in the calling program.

When a return from subroutine instruction is not programmed in a subroutine file, the END instruction automatically causes the PLC to move execution back to the rung following the jump to subroutine instruction. A jump to subroutine instruction can be used either in a main application program or a subroutine program to call another subroutine program.

Example

In Fig. 3.12.3 we want to fill the two tanks with water by a pump. The pump is operating manually by a push-button "Start." When the first tank becomes full, the circuit should automatically start to fill the second tank by closing the first valve, and opening the second valve. And when the second tank is full, the pump disconnects automatically and a "sign lamp" is turned on to show that the 2nd tank is full.

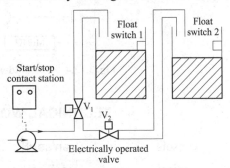

Fig. 3.12.3 An example

Solution

We need first to identify the inputs and outputs of the system, so we can set relations between the outside world and the inputs/outputs of the programmable logic controller.

Tab. 3.12.1 makes it clear: (remember NC: normally closed; NO: normally open), and Fig. 3.12.4 is the ladder diagram and instruction list for the system.

Tab. 3.12.1 I/O

Element	Symbol	Status	I/O	Number
Push Button OFF	OFF	NC	I	($I_{0.0}$)
Push Button ON	ON	NO	I	($I_{0.1}$)
Float Switch 1	FS_1	NO	I	($I_{0.2}$)
Float Switch 2	FS_2	NO	I	($I_{0.3}$)
Coil Valve 1	V_1	Normally OFF	O	($Q_{0.0}$)
Coil Valve 2	V_2	Normally OFF	O	($Q_{0.1}$)
Pump	P	Normally OFF	O	($Q_{0.2}$)
Internal Relay	M	Normally OFF	Memory	($M_{0.0}$)
Indictor Lamp	L	Normally OFF	O	($Q_{0.3}$)

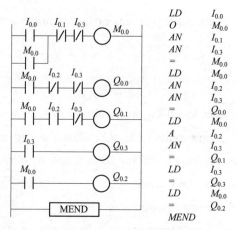

Fig. 3.12.4   The ladder diagram and instruction list

TECHNICAL WORDS AND PHRASES

console	[kən'səul]	n.	[计] 控制台
vertical	['və:tikəl]	adj.	垂直的，直立的
horizontal	[ˌhɔri'zɔntl]	adj.	地平线的，水平的
notation	[nəu'teiʃən]	n.	符号
shutdown	['ʃʌtdaun]	n.	关门，停工，停止
elapse	[i'læps]	v.	(时间)过去，消逝
pulse	[pʌls]	n.	脉冲
emanate	['eməneit]	v.	散发，发射，发出
subroutine	[ˌsʌbru:'ti:n]	n.	[计] 子程序
binary code			二进制编码
high level language			[计] 高级程序语言
function block diagram			功能图
structured text			结构化文本
instruction list			指令表
graphic symbol			图形符号
relay schematic circuit diagram			继电器电路图
Boolean logic			[数] 布尔逻辑
load (LD) instruction			装入指令
data handling instruction			数据处理指令
data move instruction			数据转移指令
comparison instruction			比较指令
mathematical instruction			数学运算指令

master control reset instruction	主控复位指令
bit shift instruction	位移指令
sequencer output	顺序输出
sequencer compare	顺序比较
SQL (sequencer load)	顺序装载
auxiliary relay	中间继电器，辅助继电器
latch instruction	锁存指令
time duration	周期
on-delay timer	通电延时定时器
off-delay timer	断电延时定时器
normally closed contact	常闭触点
normally open contact	常开触点

NOTES

1. used to hold data, and behave like relays, being able to be switched on or off and switch other devices on or off.

   译文：用来存储数据，类似于继电器，能够接通和关断，从而控制其他设备的通断。

   该句中 "used… data" 为过去分词做状语，表示一个同时发生的次要的或伴随的动作。"and behave like relays" 中的主语与前句的主语相同，均被省略。"being able to… off" 为现在分词做定语，但翻译时可译为并列句。

2. Most manufacturers consider timers to behave like relays with coils which when energized result in the closure or opening of contacts after some preset time.

   译文：大多数制造商把定时器看做带线圈的继电器，当线圈得电后其触点在设定时间后闭合或断开。

   该句中 "which when… time" 为 "coils" 的定语。从句中 "when energized" 为条件状语从句，"result… time" 为从句中的主句。

3. A good rule of thumb is simply to always use the normal (software) counters unless the pulses you are counting will arrive faster than 2X the scan time.

   译文：根据经验，一般情况下使用普通（软）计数器，除非你计数的脉冲数比 PLC 扫描次数的 2 倍还多。

   该句中 "unless" 引导的是条件状语从句。

4. Data handling consists of operations involving moving or transferring numeric information stored in one memory word location to another word in a different location, comparing data values and carrying out simple arithmetic operations.

译文：数据处理由一些操作构成，是将存在某一存储器内的数字信息传送到另一存储地址的字中，比较数值大小，再进行简单的数据运算。

"involving moving or transferring…arithmetic operations" 为 "operations" 的定语，该定语为 "involve doing…, doing… and doing…" 的结构，意为"包括做……，做……及做……"。

EXERCISES

Ⅰ. **Translate the following instructions into Chinese.**

1. data handling instruction
2. data move instruction
3. comparison instruction
4. mathematical instruction
5. high speed counter instruction
6. master control reset
7. relay-type instruction
8. latch instruction
9. normally closed contact
10. bit shift instruction

Ⅱ. **Select the right answer from the four choices.**

1. The format of programs in PLC systems is _____.
   A. machine   B. decimal code   C. binary code   D. ladder logic

2. Which of the following circuits is not right?

   A.　　　　B.　　　　C.　　　　D.

3. Which of the following statements about internal relays in the PLC is wrong?
   A. Auxiliary relays are internal relays.
   B. Internal relays cannot be seen in the real world.
   C. Internal relays exist in the real world.
   D. Internal relays are bits in the storage memory.

4. Which of the following is not On-Delay timer?
   A. TON.　　　B. TMRA.　　　C. TIM.　　　D. TMR.

5. Which of the following statements of counters is right?
   A. The counter accumulates any electrical input signal.
   B. The normal counters are "hardware" counters.
   C. When the pulses you are counting arrive faster than 2X the scan time, you should

use "software" counters.

D. All counters are considered as relays.

Supplementary Reading

Reading12 Process Control System with PLC

Introduction

Generally speaking, process control system is made up of a group of electronic devices and equipment that provide stability, accuracy and eliminate harmful transition statuses in production processes. Operating system can have different forms and implementations, from energy supply units to machines. As a result of fast progress in technology, many complex operational tasks have been solved by connecting programmable logic controllers and possibly a central computer. Beside connections with instruments like operating panels, motors, sensors, switches, valves and such, possibilities for communication among instruments are so great that they allow high level of exploitation and process coordination, as well as greater flexibility in realizing a process control system. Each component of a process control system plays an important role, regardless of its size. For example, without a sensor, PLC wouldn't know what exactly goes on in the process. In automated system, PLC controller is usually the central part of a process control system. With execution of a program stored in the program memory, PLC continuously monitors the status of the system through signals from input devices. Based on the logic implemented in the program, PLC determines which actions need to be executed with output instruments. To run more complex processes it is possible to connect more PLC controllers to a central computer. A real system could look like the one pictured below.

Conventional control panel

At the outset of industrial revolution, especially during the sixties and the seventies, relays were used to operate automated machines, and these were interconnected using wires inside the control panel. In some cases a control panel covered an entire wall. To discover an error in the system much time was needed especially with more complex process control systems. On top of everything, a lifetime of relay contacts was limited, so some relays had to be replaced. If replacement was required, machine had to be stopped and production too. Also, it could happen that there was not enough room for necessary changes. Control panel was used only for one particular process, and it wasn't easy to adapt to the requirements of a new system. As for maintenance, electricians had to be very skillful in finding errors. In short, conventional control panels proved to be very inflexible.

In this photo you can notice a large number of electrical wires, time relays, timers and other elements of automation typical for that period. Pictured control panel is not one of the more "complicated" ones, so you can imagine what complex ones looked like.

The most frequently mentioned disadvantages of a classic control panel are:
- Too much work required in connecting wires
- Difficulty with changes or replacements
- Difficulty in finding errors; requiring skillful work force
- When a problem occurs, hold-up time is indefinite, usually long

Control panel with a PLC controller

With invention of programmable controllers, much has changed in how a process control system is designed. Many advantages appeared. A typical example of control panel with a PLC controller is given in Fig.3.12.5.

The advantages of a control panel that is based on a PLC controller can be presented in the following basic points:

(1) Compared to a conventional process control system, the number of wires needed for connections is reduced by 80%.

(2) Consumption is greatly reduced because a PLC consumes less than a bunch of relays.

(3) Diagnostic functions of a PLC controller allow for fast and easy error detection.

(4) Change in operating sequence or application of a PLC controller to a different operating process can easily be accomplished by replacing a program through a console or using a PC software (not requiring changes in wiring, unless addition of some input or output device is required).

(5) Needs fewer spare parts.

(6) It is much cheaper compared to a conventional system, especially in cases where a large number of I/O instruments are needed and when operational functions are complex.

(7) Reliability of a PLC is greater than that of an electro-mechanical relay or a timer.

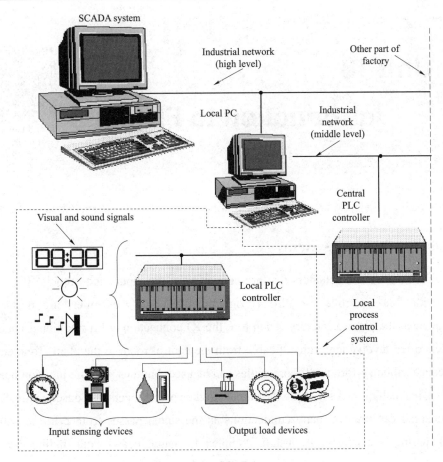

Fig.3.12.5　SCADA system

Unit 13
Introduction to Fieldbus

Introduction to Fieldbus 翻译

Traditionally wired systems

The sensors and actuators that are connected to the inputs and outputs (IO) of a Programmable Controller or PLC (Programmable Logic Controller) are normally mounted in the plant or factory. Therefore the IO connections of a traditional control system often involve long runs of cable from the control room to the plant. To attempt to reduce cabling effort, multi-core cables can be used, but these require junction boxes and/or marshalling racks to route the signals to the correct location. Consequently each IO channel can involve many connections as the signal passes from cable to cable. Such wiring is expensive to install, complex to maintain and fault-finding can be difficult.

Fieldbus

Fieldbus is an industrial network that is specifically designed for communication between PLCs or industrial controllers and the field-mounted sensors and actuators. Fieldbus is designed to replace the point-to-point wiring that connects each sensor and actuator to the controller I/O as shown in Fig. 3.13.1.

When the fieldbus is integrated into the sensor or actuator, the devices often provide additional capability such as remote device configuration and/or testing over the bus. Integrated devices can also provide diagnostic information back to the control room to help diagnose and locate device faults. Thus devices with integrated fieldbus are often more capable or "intelligent" than traditional actuators or sensors.

Remote IO stations can also be used with fieldbus wiring. Here the digital or analogue IO modules are mounted in the field, close to the sensors and actuators, and the data is communicated to the remote IO module via the fieldbus cable. However, when using remote IO, the field devices cannot use the bus to communicate additional data such as parameters or diagnostics. Here, we must use traditional (non-intelligent) actuators and sensors.

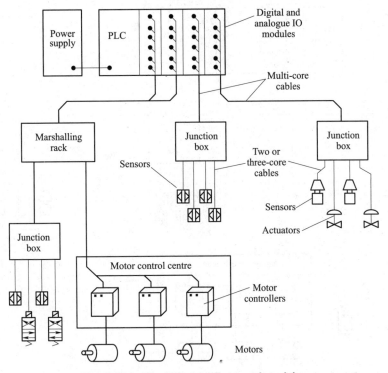

Fig. 3.13.1 Traditional point to point wiring

Fieldbus has many advantages over conventional point-to-point wiring:
- A significant reduction in installation costs (typically 20% to 40% savings) as shown in Fig. 3.13.2. This saving comes from reduced wiring, connections, junction boxes, marshalling cabinets, cable trays and supports, etc.
- System expansion and modification are simpler and less expensive since only the additional cable running from the existing network to the new device must be installed.
- Two-way communication means that additional information such as calibration and configuration data, diagnostic and test information, device documentation such as device tag numbers; serial numbers service history, etc. can be communicated over the network. Equipment maintenance and servicing become more centralized.
- Since communication is digital, accuracy is not affected by noise, interference or electrical loading effects, etc. This is a particular advantage in transmitting analogue values.
- Open standards mean that multi-vendor systems can be constructed. Product

certification ensures that communication will work between devices from different manufacturers.

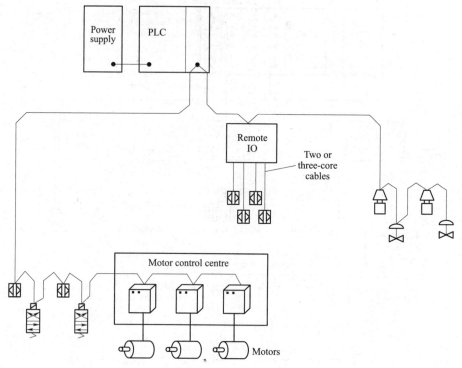

Fig. 3.13.2　Fieldbus wiring significantly reducing cables and connections

Types of fieldbus

There are many different fieldbus types available, most of which are defined by international standards and are supported by many different manufacturers. Specific fieldbus types are often designed for particular application areas or industries. For example, the requirements for the process industry are often quite different from those of part manufacturing or materials handling. What is suitable and cost effective for one application area is often not appropriate for another. Sometimes we need a simple low-cost fieldbus; other times we need extensive or flexible data capability. Some fieldbus systems need to be able to operate in potentially explosive atmospheres; others require extremely high reliability for safety-critical applications. Some fieldbus systems are designed to carry power to the field devices over the bus cable. This is often done using just two cable cores to carry power and data.

The different types of fieldbus are generally not compatible with each other. This means that devices on a network must all use the same type of fieldbus. However, this does not mean that different field buses cannot be used together in an application.

Gateways can be used to connect one type of network or fieldbus to another. These provide conversion from one technology to another and allow data to be passed between networks. Quite often an application will involve several different types of network.

Many people ask why we can't just have one type of network for all applications and levels. The answer is that there are many different requirements for communications in separate areas of the plant and at different levels in the hierarchy. Many different considerations must be taken into account: The required communication speed; data size and structure; environmental factors like explosion risk, wet or dirty conditions, ambient temperature variations, existence of electrical interference, etc. Some networking solutions are suitable only for clean and dry environments; others can be used in exposed locations. Cost, capability and robustness often vary greatly from one fieldbus to another.

By far the most common fieldbus is PROFIBUS, with well over 20 million devices installed around the world. PROFIBUS has solutions available for a wide range of applications including factory automation, process plant including explosive environments, high-speed motion control.

Another popular bus technology is actuator-sensor interface (AS-i), which is widely used in factory automation systems. AS-i is often used in conjunction with PROFIBUS for connecting simple binary (on-off) sensors and actuators to the PROFIBUS network using a gateway.

Ethernet and wireless networking is normally used at the office and plant level for plant management and organisational information across the whole company as shown in Fig. 3.13.3. Fieldbus and industrial Ethernet are used at the mid levels for control of plant units or cells for supervisory control and monitoring. Different fieldbus technologies are used at the lower sensor/actuator levels. Gateways provide an interface between the different network technologies and allow control and monitoring signals to pass up and down from one network to another.

Problems with fieldbus

All the above is really good news for the plant management, system designer, equipment installer, plant engineer and plant operator. Unfortunately there is a disadvantage when we use high-speed digital communications:

Fieldbus is much more sensitive to layout and wiring problems than traditional systems.

System designers must be aware of the rules for design and layout. They may be simple but expensive to correct pitfalls. It is essential that installers and maintenance technicians have a basic level of training covering the correct wiring techniques and basics for device and system testing. Commissioning and maintenance engineers need to be able to use network test tools such as a modern protocol analyser and high-speed oscilloscope to fault-find and health check the fieldbus network.

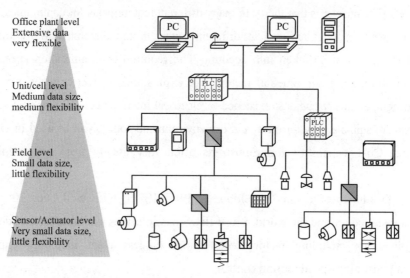

Fig. 3.13.3　The overall control system containing
Ethernet and wireless networking integrated with fieldbus

TECHNICAL WORDS AND PHRASES

fieldbus	[ˈfiːldbʌs]	n.	现场总线
actuator	[ˈæktjueitə]	n.	执行器，传动装置
cable	[ˈkeibl]	n.	电缆
multi-core	[ˈmʌltikɔː]	adj.	多芯的
install	[inˈstɔːl]	vt.	安装，安置
maintain	[menˈtein]	vt.	维护，维修
configuration	[kənˌfigjuˈreiʃən]	n.	构造，结构，配置
diagnostic	[ˌdaiəgˈnɔstik]	adj.	诊断的
locate	[ləuˈkeit]	vt.	查找……的地点，使……坐落于
expansion	[iksˈpænʃən]	n.	扩充，开展
modification	[ˌmɔdifiˈkeiʃən]	n.	更改，修改，修正
calibration	[ˌkæliˈbreiʃən]	n.	标度，刻度，校准
accuracy	[ˈækjurəsi]	n.	准确性，精确性
vendor	[ˈvendɔː]	n.	销售商

Unit 13　Introduction to Fieldbus

noise	[nɔiz]	n.	噪声
effective	[i'fektiv]	adj.	有效的
extensive	[iks'tensiv]	adj.	广大的，广阔的，广泛的
flexible	['fleksəbl]	adj.	易曲的，灵活的，能变形的
gateway	['geitwei]	n.	网关
ambient	['æmbiənt]	adj.	周围的，包围的
supervisory	[ˌsju:pə'vaizəri]	adj.	管理的，监督的
pitfall	['pitfɔ:l]	n.	缺陷
commissioning	[kə'miʃəniŋ]	n.	试运转，试车
oscilloscope	[ɔ'siləskəup]	n.	示波器
fault-finding		n.	故障排查
field-mounted		adj.	现场安装的
PROFIBUS		abbr.	过程控制现场总线
Ethernet		n.	以太网
cabling effort			电缆效应
junction box			[电] 接线盒，分线箱
marshalling rack			集线柜
I/O module			输入/输出模块
marshalling cabinet			集线盒
cable tray			线管
two-way communication			双向通信
serial number			序列号
electrical loading effect			电负载效应
potentially explosive atmosphere			易燃易爆环境
electrical interference			电干扰
actuator-sensor interface (AS-I)			执行器—传感器界面
plant unit			生产车间

NOTES

1. To attempt to reduce cabling effort, multi-core cables can be used, but these require junction boxes and/or marshalling racks to route the signals to the correct location.

   译文：为了减小电缆线的影响，可以使用多芯电缆，但是这需要分线盒或集线器来将信号送到正确的地点。

   该句中"multi-core cables can be used"虽然为被动语态，但翻译时应根据汉语的说话习惯译成主动句。

2. System expansion and modification are simpler and less expensive since only the additional cable running from the existing network to the new device must be installed.

译文：系统的扩展和修正更加容易而且花费更少，因为一个新设备加到已有的控制网络中时，只要在两者间另外安装一些电缆即可。

该句中"since"引导的是原因状语从句。从句的主语部分为"only the additional cable running from the existing network to the new device"，该部分包含了一个现在分词"running…"，做定语，修饰"the additional cable"。

3. The answer is that there are many different requirements for communications in separate areas of the plant and at different levels in the hierarchy.

译文：答案是在工厂的不同区域和不同的控制层其通信要求存在很大差异。

该句中"that"引导的是宾语从句，而从句中"in"引导的介词短语在翻译时应置于从句句首。

4. Fieldbus and industrial Ethernet are used at the mid levels for control of plant units or cells for supervisory control and monitoring.

译文：现场总线与工业以太网被使用在中间级，用来控制车间或监控室。

该句为"sth. be use at… for…"的结构，翻译时根据汉语的说话习惯将两个介词短语分开翻译。

5. It is essential that installers and maintenance technicians have a basic level of training covering the correct wiring techniques and basics for device and system testing.

译文：安装和维护人员必须就正确接线技术及设备和系统的测试方面进行基本的培训。

该句中"covering the correct wiring techniques and basics for device and system testing"为现在分词做定语，修饰"a basic level of training"。

EXERCISES

Ⅰ. **Translate the following words into Chinese.**

1. Fieldbus
2. junction box
3. potentially explosive atmosphere
4. compatible with
5. gateway
6. taken into account
7. actuator-sensor interface
8. robustness
9. control and monitoring signal
10. industrial Ethernet

II. **Mark the following statements with T(true) or F(false) according to the text.**
1. There are long runs of cable in traditional control systems. (　)
2. Traditional control systems often use multi-core cables to reduce cabling effects. (　)
3. When using remote I/O to connect actuators integrated with fieldbus, they can use the fieldbus to transfer diagnostic information. (　)
4. The different types of fieldbus cannot communicate with each other directly. (　)
5. Fieldbus can always carry power to the field devices over the bus cable. (　)

III. **Select the correct answer from the four choices.**
1. Fieldbus is used for communication between _____.
   A. the field-mounted sensors and actuators
   B. industrial controllers and field devices
   C. PLCs and industrial controllers
   D. field devices and actuators
2. Compared with traditional actuators or sensors, devices with integrated fieldbus can provide _____.
   A. device configuration information   B. device tag numbers
   C. serial numbers   D. all of the above
3. Gateways can be used to connect _____.
   A. PROFIBUS to actuator-sensor interface
   B. Ethernet to fieldbus
   C. one type of network or fieldbus to another
   D. all of the above
4. PROFIBUS is often used at the _____ level.
   A. office and plant   B. unit/cell   C. field   D. sensor/actuator
5. Which of the following is the disadvantage of fieldbus?
   A. There are too many types of fieldbus.
   B. Fieldbus is much more sensitive to layout and wiring problems.
   C. Fieldbus uses analogue signals to communicate.
   D. Fieldbus cannot be compatible with each other.

Supplementary Reading

Reading 13　Will Industrial Ethernet Render Fieldbus Systems Obsolete?

Although it is universally accepted that Industrial Ethernet is transforming automation and process technology, this does not imply that it is the only feasible option, as Martin Müller, marketing manager of the Business Unit "Automation Systems" of Phoenix Contact, points out. Numerous exhibitors taking part in INTERKAMA+, one of the leading international trade shows that make up HANNOVER MESSE (Hannover Fair) April 24–28, 2006, are staging an information-packed event that examines the possibilities and limitations of Ethernet in industrial applications. This themed event will be backed up by the special presentations "Wireless Automation" and "Secure Automation."

Users should not expect all the automation systems to be based on the same language. Developments in the field of networking technology, bus systems and the whole area of control, monitoring and sensor technology are moving forward at such a fast pace and the world-wide supply market is simply too diverse for this to happen in the near future.

As Martin Müller explains, there is not even a uniform protocol for Industrial Ethernet, as can be seen by the use of the abbreviations "http" and "ftp." This diversity extends to the communication systems—especially field bus systems—and will also impact on nascent wireless technologies, which are highlighted in the very topical special presentation "Wireless Automation" within HANNOVER MESSE 2006.

Modern process and automation technologies place quite disparate demands on communication and bus systems, and also on sensor technology and transmission. For this reason Martin Müller expects heterogeneous systems architecture to remain the norm. Naturally, this also reflects the interests and marketing policies of the major developers of proprietary protocols, for whom a "pedigree" or single universal system of networking would be disadvantageous.

The fast rate of development allows no leeway for the creation of new norms and standards. Furthermore, as the technology is being constantly upgraded, any standards quickly become outdated. In addition to Office Ethernet, a wide array of new systems and components have joined the arsenal of industrial automation in the last few years, including USB, Firewire, Bluetooth and other established technologies. HANNOVER MESSE 2006 will provide a showcase for virtually all these new technologies.

On the positive side, whenever Industrial Ethernet is successfully introduced as a central communication system, it does improve overall performance and interoperability, facilitating the use of disparate intelligent technologies. For example, it permits the transmission of sensor data to a PLC. In this scenario, every equipment manufacturer will do his utmost to exploit the specific benefits he provides—including the system of protection and the operating conditions.

It is when large amounts of data need to be communicated that the benefits of

Industrial Ethernet systems compared with field bus systems become most apparent. As Martin Müller says: "On the one hand we have fieldbus, which is based on machine/sensor concepts. Performance is limited because these systems were developed decades ago, primarily to connect numerous sensors. Thus practically all fieldbus systems, including the Interbus system from Phoenix Contact, have always been further developed. In a sense, familiarity made them more popular." Consequently, fieldbus systems were constantly being adapted for a broader spectrum of functions.

The current trend favours networking concepts originally developed for commercial applications involving the transmission of large amounts of data. These systems are now challenging field bus systems. According to Martin Müller: "Industrial Ethernet becomes interesting in applications which demand the transfer of large quantities of data and/or when there is a flow of data to office and administrative applications."

In his opinion, it would make sense to relieve fieldbus systems of the additional functions they have been saddled with and use Industrial Ethernet instead. This would facilitate the achievement of clear structures and make it easier for engineers to access information from the production process as many are well acquainted with Ethernet technology.

Many users question whether Ethernet, which was originally for administrative and office applications, is really suited to industrial applications. This fear can easily be allayed. During the last few years many new products have emerged on the market—for example, the IP 65 and IP 67 versions of the Ethernet connector.

What about real-time use?

Many of the systems currently being offered meet this requirement without additional hardware or software. However, this is not the case if Industrial Ethernet is open to all technologies or machines—for example, master-slave machines, where a sensor responds only if the master communicates with it. According to Müller, automation experts are not too keen on this kind of set-up due to the reliance on proprietary protocols which could exclude the use of standard PCs. This is one of the difficulties that Ethernet encounters with respect to real-time capability and the processing of TPC/IP services. Real-time means, for instance, micro-second or milli-second communication with sensors with unlimited determinants.

A further difficulty that needs to be addressed is the performance of Ethernet in highly complex entire systems. In this case efficient Ethernet communication could prove problematic. Whereas the parties in Interbus subsystems require neither an IP address nor a DIP switch, users of Ethernet need an MAC address, an IP address and a name, which is clearly more complicated. Müller believes that this alone means that in future "a kind of peaceful coexistence between fieldbus systems and Industrial Ethernet" is the most likely scenario.

This article was written and provided by HANNOVER MESSE.

About HANNOVER MESSE

The world's leading exhibition of industrial technology took place from 24 to 28 April in Hannover. The program for 2006 consisted of the following flagship trade shows: INTERKAMA+, Factory Automation, Industrial Building Automation, Energy, Pipeline Technology, Subcontracting, Digital Factory, Industrial Facility Management & Services, MicroTechnology and Research & Technology. The featured Partner Country at HANNOVER MESSE 2006 was India, one of the world's fastest-growing markets.

Unit 14

Why HMIs Are Everywhere

Why HMIs Are Everywhere
翻译

Displays, touchscreens, terminals—those human-machine interfaces are quite literally everywhere. Little more than pushbuttons and switches a mere decade ago, these devices have grown in sophistication, bringing management and operations the control and information they need.

The near ubiquitous spread of HMIs throughout industry is due to the fact that they help companies make better business decisions by delivering, managing, and presenting information—in real time—in a visually compelling and actionable format. Incorporating HMIs into applications has been proven to increase productivity, lower costs, improve quality, and reduce material waste. HMIs help companies become more profitable by positioning them for change.

Bringing information everywhere

Three developments, in particular, have influenced industry's growing dependence on HMIs, according to Gary Nelson, product marketing manager for InTouch industrial computers, DA servers, and toolkits for Wonderware:
- Improvements in HMI software;
- Ability of HMIs to visualize data more competently and bring information together where it matters most;
- Increased and improved integration and connectivity technologies.

"Companies are demanding tools that improve their business process," says Nelson, "and HMIs help them do that by measuring the effectiveness of their processes and their machines. An HMI doesn't just present data on a machine. It presents information in different forms to different people at different levels of an organization. Plant floor data don't stay at the plant floor level anymore, and the HMI is the key to moving that data."

Burgeoning use of HMIs is fueled by their transition from pure visualization tools to tools that help manage the manufacturing process. In the eyes of Bruce Fuller, director of product management, control and visualization business for Rockwell Automation, "There has been a huge shift over the past decade in what people expect from HMI interfaces and software." Fuller sees HMI software functionality being pushed into a wider variety of embedded devices as customers demand more functionality and capability on the machine as well as at the operator interface (Fig. 3.14.1).

Fig. 3.14.1 Increased capabilities at lower costs that are encouraging manufacturers to place HMIs at more locations, and to move into applications they hadn't considered before. (Source: AutomationDirect)

HMI and PC merge

The rising importance of HMIs is strongly affected by their growing ties to the PC world. As Prasad Pai, HMI/SCADA—iFix product manager at GE Fanuc, puts it, "HMIs are fast becoming an extension of PCs and of the IT department. They've had to become IT-friendly."

Greg Philbrook, HMI product manager for Automation Direct, concurs, "The standard HMI is nothing more than an industrial PC at a lower price. PC features—including trending, logging, Web, and email capabilities—are being incorporated into HMIs. Higher processor speeds are enabling animation, and drops in costs are allowing the lower end of the market to move into applications they hadn't considered before."

"HMIs used to be dumb terminals," says Ted Thayer, Bosch Rexroth's PLC and HMI product manager. "Now they've become industrial PCs running Microsoft Windows operating systems. Technological advancements available at lower costs have opened a lot of doors. Improved system integration allows any good HMI system to talk to many product lines, encouraging companies to increase the HMIs

Unit 14   Why HMIs Are Everywhere   155

they use."

"But it's not just more interfaces or more information that underlie recent HMI proliferation," adds Jay Coughlin, manager of HMI Business USA at Siemens Energy & Automation. "It is more useful information. These systems let you store data, then simplify those data in dashboards so that those who may be unfamiliar with, say, the inner workings of a machine, but who do know the ins and outs of making quality products, can see data in a format they understand."

Industry- and application-specific

HMIs are incorporating more sophisticated software, enhanced graphics, tools such as wizards and informational portals, and capabilities that range from mobile and portable to wireless. Features that give users more reasons to apply an increasing number of HMIs include:

- Specialized software. Industry-specific software—such as application packages for water and wastewater plants and packaging industry operations—provides objects, modules, and sample screens specific to that industry. This allows, for example, easier and more efficient monitoring of fluid flow rates and pressures, or provides built-in work-in-process steps for bottling operations. "Users can overlay industry packs on top of the system platform because they are easy to integrate," says Wonderware's Nelson, "making available more specialized information."
- Enhanced graphics and wizards. Striving to help users streamline screen development, some vendors are adding animation and harnessing the power of wizards to make it simpler to build visualization screens by prompting users through the process. For example, "we've recently introduced a water productivity solution that uses updated graphics and wizards to help configure some of the more common tools found in water and wastewater management operations," says GE Fanuc's Cerrato.
- Wireless and mobile capabilities. Mobility also adds to the attraction of HMIs. "Mobile panels give operators a way to move around a workstation," says Siemens' Coughlin.

Also, price decreases are opening the way for placing HMIs on small systems, such as packaging machines. "Units with screens 3- or 4-in in size with very high resolutions can be used in portable applications such as remote well stations or mounted on vehicles," adds AutomationDirect's Philbrook. "These developments are allowing HMIs to go almost anywhere."

Improvements in HMI hardware and software help businesses measure the effectiveness of their processes and their machines, and share information beyond the plant floor. Industrially hardened equipment coupled with sophisticated programs brings more intelligence to the device, while interconnectivity furthers corporate bottom-to-top reporting, analysis, and data warehousing. (Sources: Bosch Rexroth and Wonderware)

Although interest in wireless systems has not been as great as some had anticipated, most believe acceptance will come, making HMIs even more valuable. Bosch-Rexroth's Thayer admits he's comfortable with wireless, but that the typical customer has not shown a lot of interest in it yet. "But," he says, "wireless will come, largely because it lowers cost. It eliminates cabling that deteriorates, breaks down, or gets cut."

Industry-specific software packages help add detailed precision to specialized applications. This screen shows a backwash filter sequence for a water and wastewater management application built with a wizard designed to simplify visualization-screen development. (Source: GE Fanuc)

HMI as a controller

"In the 1990s, HMIs changed how blue-collar workers did their jobs," says Wonderware's Nelson. "Today, they are changing how the boardroom does its job as well."

Bosch Rexroth's Thayer foresees a time when HMIs will perform control to such an extent that a PLC is almost unnecessary. "Today, we can actually embed the PLC control logic engine inside the HMI in its own hard real-time system," he says. "An operator might run PLCs, control the line, and do database transactions from one station. It will make it a lot easier to tie systems together and lead to more simplified system architectures."

"The use of HMIs is limited only by the amount of information an operator can effectively use," says Rockwell Automation's Fuller. "Advancements will continue to reduce development time and troubleshooting efforts. That's where the next round of big changes will come. The differentiator, however, lies not in the hardware, but in the software and the kind of information it allows you to present and use on that display. As people want more and more information right where they are, they will need additional HMIs."

Unit 14 Why HMIs Are Everywhere

TECHNICAL WORDS AND PHRASES

touchscreen	[ˈtʌtʃskriːn]	n.	触摸屏
sophistication	[səˌfistiˈkeiʃən]	n.	成熟
ubiquitous	[juːˈbikwitəs]	adj.	到处存在的，(同时)普遍存在的
visualize	[ˈvizjuəlaiz]	vt.	形象化，可视化
burgeon	[ˈbəːdʒ(ə)n]	v.	发芽，生长
merge	[məːdʒ]	v.	合并，并入
logging	[ˈlɔgiŋ]	n.	登录
proliferation	[prəuˌlifəˈreiʃən]	n.	增殖，扩散，衍生物
dashboard	[ˈdæʃˌbɔːd]	n.	仪表板
enhance	[inˈhɑːns]	v.	提高，增强
graphics	[ˈgræfiks]	n.	图形
wizard	[ˈwizəd]	n.	向导
portal	[ˈpɔːt(ə)l]	n.	大门，入口
platform	[ˈplætfɔːm]	n.	平台
strive	[straiv]	v.	努力，奋斗，力争
vendor	[ˈvendɔː]	n.	卖主
harness	[ˈhɑːnis]	v.	统治，管理
anticipate	[ænˈtisipeit]	v.	预期，期望
deteriorate	[diˈtiəriəreit]	v.	(使)恶化
boardroom	[ˈbɔːdruːm]	n.	会议室，交换场所
architecture	[ˈɑːkitektʃə]	n.	体系，机构
troubleshoot	[ˈtrʌblʃuːt]	n./v.	检修，故障排除
human-machine interface			人机界面
product marketing manager			市场拓展经理
operating system			操作系统
product line			生产线
water and wastewater plant			污水处理厂
packaging industry			包装工业

NOTES

1. Little more than pushbuttons and switches a mere decade ago, these devices have grown in sophistication, bringing management and operations the control and information they need.

译文：就像10年前的按钮和开关，这些设备不断发展成熟，人机界面对所需要的控制和信息进行管理和操作。

"Little more than"为"和……无差别"、"一样"的意思。该句的主干为"devices have grown"。"bringing... they need"为现在分词结构，做"devices"的定语从句。该从句又包含一个定语从句"they need"，修饰"the control and information"。

2. Fuller sees HMI software functionality being pushed into a wider variety of embedded devices as customers demand more functionality and capability on the machine as well as at the operator interface.

译文：Fuller认为由于顾客要求人机界面不但具备操作界面的功能，还希望它的功能能进一步增强，因此人机界面正被纳入嵌入式设备这一大范畴。

该句中"as"引导的是原因状语从句，主句部分为"Fuller sees... devices"。该句为"see sb. doing sth."的结构，原因状语从句为"customers... interface"。

3. Higher processor speeds are enabling animation, and drops in costs are allowing the lower end of the market to move into applications they hadn't considered before.

译文：更高的处理速度使得动画成为可能，而且成本的下降使得低端市场具有它们以前从未想过的应用功能。

该句主语为"Higher processor speeds"，带有两个由"and"引导的并列句。这两个并列从句为因果关系。

4. These systems let you store data, then simplify those data in dashboards so that those who may be unfamiliar with, say, the inner workings of a machine, but who do know the ins and outs of making quality products, can see data in a format they understand.

译文：这些人机界面系统可让你在界面上存储信息，简化信息，从而可让那些对机器内部工作方式不熟悉但又知道高质量产品生产细节的人能读懂数据。

该句中"so that"引导的是目的状语从句，主句为"These systems... dashboards"，从句为"those... can see data in a format they understand"。从句部分的主干为"those can see data"，其中主语"those"有两个由"who"引导的定语从句，宾语"data"由一个定语从句"they understand"修饰。

5. Striving to help users streamline screen development, some vendors are adding animation and harnessing the power of wizards to make it simpler to build visualization screens by prompting users through the process.

译文：为了帮助用户更顺利地开发监控界面，一些生产商增加了动画和向导功能，从而更加容易建立可视化屏幕。

该句包含现在分词做目的状语从句，从句的逻辑主语与主句主语一致，都为"some vendors"。

EXERCISES

I. Translate the following words into Chinese.

1. terminal
2. integration
3. visualization
4. diagnostic
5. maintenance worker
6. real-time system
7. database transaction
8. workstation
9. human-machine interface
10. troubleshoot

II. Mark the following statements with T(true) or F(false) according to the text.

1. Human-machine interfaces are similar to pushbuttons and switches. (   )
2. Improvements in HMI software have influenced industry's growing dependence on HMIs. (   )
3. An HMI just presents data on a machine. (   )
4. HMIs are fast becoming a combination of PCs and of the IT department. (   )
5. Now HMIs are dumb terminals. (   )

III. Complete the following sentences.

1. Displays, _____, terminals—those _____ are quite literally everywhere.
2. Incorporating HMIs into _____ has been proven to increase _____, lower costs, improve quality, and reduce _____.
3. _____ use of HMIs is fueled by their transition from pure _____ tools to tools that help manage the _____ process.
4. Striving to help users streamline _____ development, some vendors are adding _____ and harnessing the power of _____ to make it simpler to build visualization screens by prompting users through the process.
5. Wireless will come, largely because it _____. It eliminates cabling that _____, breaks down, or gets cut.

Supplementary Reading

Reading 14   HMI Software Products

Control Engineering subscribers, using a list provided, identified the following as leading suppliers of HMI software: Rockwell Software, Wonderware, Siemens Energy & Automation, GE Fanuc Automation, AutomationDirect, Honeywell, ABB, National

Instruments, Emerson Process Management, Maple Systems, Opto 22, and Iconics. Examples of the latest products are provided below, with additional details online. Complete study results are available in the Control Engineering Resource Center at www.resource.controleng.com. To find other suppliers, search www.cesuppliersearch.com. To find system integrators with related expertise, go to www.controleng.com/integrators.

Open windows to enterprises

FactoryTalk View suite of HMI software solutions from Rockwell Software is supported by the company's Integrated Architecture for tight integration into its Logix Control Platform, third-party, and legacy systems and easy access to critical production data. FactoryTalk View features a common development platform and application—and system—wide tag reuse to help engineers, programmers, and support personnel speed HMI application development, configuration, and training time. Software comes in two editions: FactoryTalk View Machine Edition and FactoryTalk View Site Edition. Machine Edition supports open and embedded operation interface solutions for monitoring and controlling individual machines and small processes. Platforms include Microsoft Windows CE, 2000, and XP.

Rockwell software

Engineering, migration

InTouch HMI software version 9.5 from Wonderware, a unit of Invensys Inc., includes new features. New operational capabilities support intelligent alarm techniques, dynamic operator guidance, runtime language switching, and virtually unlimited scalability. New engineering productivity capabilities significantly decrease the cost and time associated with application creation, modification, deployment, and maintenance. Included are enhancements to SmartSymbol change propagation, pan-and-zoom capabilities in development, and one-click I/O backup configuration. Applications using prior versions of InTouch software can be easily migrated. InTouch 9.5 uses industry standards-based Archestra technology.

Wonderware, a unit of Invensys Systems Inc.

Easy setup, wizards

Simatic WinCC flexible 2007 software from Siemens Energy & Automation continues to emphasize ease of configuration and use as its primary benefit to users. Reducing configuration time saves money and ease of configuration reduces issues associated with start-ups and engineering modifications. Tools and wizards simplify such HMI tasks as importing and exporting configuration data. Templates are easily applicable throughout a project; multiple recipe options provide maximum flexibility. It has been expanded by incorporating soft control based on the new MP277 hardware platform. The system also provides validation support at the engineering and runtime stages and tracks manufacturing processes using audit trails.

Siemens energy & automation

Tough monitoring, controls

Proficy HMI/SCADA—Cimplicity 7.0, the latest edition of GE Fanuc Automation's supervisory monitoring and control software, is designed to handle complex, multi-user applications on multi-tasking operating systems for processes in many industries. The system helps companies improve business performance through integration with other products in the Proficy family. It provides seamless management and tracking of software changes at the component and application levels and tracks specific change histories within the development environment. Enhancements include improved OPC connectivity and configuration, security with password rules, and flexibility through right-mouse-button menu actions.

GE fanuc automation

Open connectivity HMI

LookoutDirect PC-based HMI software from AutomationDirect has 500 I/O point capacity and is based on National Instruments' Lookout object-based automation software to make it suitable for small to medium HMI applications. LookoutDirect has drivers for top 10 PLC/RTU products and AutomationDirect's DirectLogic driver. Easy-to-use configuration package requires no programming or scripting. Object-oriented, event-driven architecture provides a graphical interface to the process. Graphical representations of devices are easy to create and link to PLCs for real-time data acquisition, graphical animation, alarm generation, report printing, and network connection to a business system. Prices start at $995.

AutomationDirect

Intuitive HMI uses Web

Experion Station, part of Honeywell's Experion Process Knowledge System (PKS), is said to be a powerful, robust HMI that provides an intuitive, safe operating environment. HMIWeb technology, a Web-based architecture, offers one infrastructure across the enterprise to ensure seamless, third-party Web-based integration. Alarm and event design follows Abnormal Situation Management (ASM) Consortium and British Engineering Equipment and Materials Users Association (EEMUA) Publication 191 guidelines. Configurable, pull-down menus and toolbars allow easy navigation and fast data access. Features include live video integration, ActiveX support, scripting, and launching applications. Mobile Station provides a control environment for field operators.

Honeywell

Connect workstations

System 800 xA Operations from ABB accesses enterprise-wide data and interacts with multiple applications from any connected workstation in the plant or office. It harnesses the company's Process Portal, an intuitive system interface, to provide a single window for navigating, accessing, and viewing plant information in real time to facilitate business decisions and actions to maximize productivity. System 800 xA gathers information from multiple plant sources and transforms it into relevant information for a diverse set of users. Contextual navigation presents the production facility in one window and cuts data overload.

ABB

HMI for graphical LabView

NI TPC-2012 12-in touch panel computer from National Instruments works with its LabView 8.20 Touch Panel Module to provide another option for deploying the LabView graphical development environment on Microsoft Windows CE HMI devices for machine control, embedded control, and distributed data acquisition systems. LabView offers a single graphical development environment in which to create touch panel applications in the same environment used for logic programming. Users can develop control algorithms, embed logic on FPGAs, build the accompanying HMI, and then deploy to the TPC-2012, all using LabView 8.20.

National instruments

Machinery health software

AMS Suite: Machinery Health Manager, version 5.0, from Emerson Process Management offers users of CSI vibration data collectors continuous online monitoring and infrared (IR) thermography technology with a new asset-centric interface for easy navigation. New time-saving features allow users to analyze more equipment in less time. Users can quickly identify a machine for evaluation, and then decide what database tools to use for analysis, plotting, and reporting. New version reportedly makes it easier than ever to analyze and communicate data from the field. Software lets users customize each module to fit their preferences within the Microsoft Windows environment.

Unit 15
8051 Microcontroller Architecture

8051 Microcontroller Architecture 翻译

As seen in Fig. 3.15.1, the 8051 microcontroller is nothing impressive in appearance.
- 4 kb of ROM is not much at all.
- 128 kB of RAM (including SFRs) satisfies the user's basic needs.
- 4 ports having in total of 32 input/output lines are in most cases sufficient to make all necessary connections to peripheral environment.

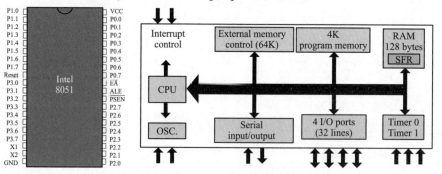

Fig. 3.15.1 Configuration of 8051

The whole configuration is obviously thought of as to satisfy the needs of most programmers working on the development of automation devices. One of its advantages is that nothing is missing and nothing is too much. In other words, it is created exactly in accordance to the average user's taste and needs. Other advantages are RAM organization, the operation of Central Processor Unit (CPU) and ports which completely use all recourses and enable further upgrade.

Input/output ports (I/O ports)

All 8051 microcontrollers have 4 I/O ports each comprising 8 bits which can be configured as inputs or outputs. Accordingly, in total of 32 input/output pins enabling the microcontroller to be connected to peripheral devices are available for use.

Port 0

The P0 port shown in Fig. 3.15.2 is characterized by two functions. If external memory is used, then the lower address byte (addresses A_0-A_7) is applied on it. Otherwise, all bits of this port are configured as inputs/outputs.

The other function is expressed when it is configured as an output. Unlike other ports consisting of pins with built-in pull-up resistor connected by its end to 5 V power supply, pins of this port have this resistor left out. This apparently small difference has its consequences:

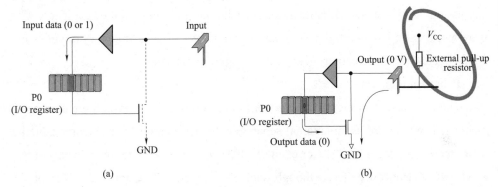

Fig. 3.15.2 P0 port

(a) Input; (b) Output

If any pin of this port is configured as an input in Fig. 3.15.2(a), then it acts as if it "floats." Such an input has unlimited input resistance and indetermined potential.

When the pin is configured as an output in Fig. 3.15.2(b), it acts as an "open drain." By applying logic 0 to a port bit, the appropriate pin will be connected to ground (0 V). By applying logic 1, the external output will keep on "floating." In order to apply logic 1 (5 V) on this output pin, it is necessary to build in an external pull-up resistor.

Port 1

P1 is a true I/O port, because it doesn't have any alternative functions as is the case with P0, but can be configured as general I/O only. It has a pull-up resistor built-in and is completely compatible with TTL circuits.

Port 2

P2 acts similarly to P0 when external memory is used. Pins of this port occupy addresses intended for external memory chip. This time it is about the higher address byte with addresses A_8-A_{15}. When no memory is added, this port can be used as a general input/output port showing features similar to P1.

Port 3

All port pins can be used as general I/O, but they also have an alternative function. In order to use these alternative functions, a logic one (1) must be applied to appropriate bit of the P3 register. In terms of hardware, this port is similar to P0, with the difference that its pins have a pull-up resistor built-in.

Memory organization

The 8051 has two types of memory and these are Program Memory and Data Memory. Program Memory (ROM) is used to permanently save the program being executed, while Data Memory (RAM) is used for temporarily storing data and intermediate results created and used during the operation of the microcontroller.

All 8051 microcontrollers have a 16-bit addressing bus and are capable of addressing 64 kb memory. It is neither a mistake nor a big ambition of engineers who were working on basic core development. It is a matter of smart memory organization which makes these microcontrollers a real "programmers' goody."

Program memory

The first models of the 8051 microcontroller family did not have internal program memory. It was added as an external separate chip. These models are recognizable by their label beginning with 803 (for example 8031 or 8032). All later models have a few Kbyte ROM embedded. Even though such an amount of memory is sufficient for writing most of the programs, there are situations when it is necessary to use additional memory as well. A typical example is so called lookup tables. They are used in cases when equations describing some processes are too complicated or when there is no time for solving them. In such cases all necessary estimates and approximates are executed in advance and the final results are put in the tables (similar to logarithmic tables).

How the microcontroller handles external memory depends on the EA pin logic state as shown in Fig. 3.15.3.

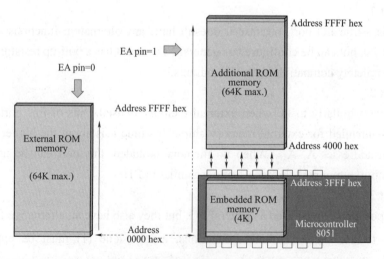

Fig. 3.15.3 The mode of microcontroller handling external memory

EA=0. In this case, the microcontroller completely ignores internal program memory and executes only the program stored in external memory.

EA=1. In this case, the microcontroller executes first the program from built-in ROM, then the program stored in external memory.

In both cases, P0 and P2 are not available for use since being used for data and address transmission. Besides, the ALE and PSEN pins are also used.

Data memory

As already mentioned, data memory is used for temporarily storing data and intermediate results created and used during the operation of the microcontroller. Besides, RAM memory built in the 8051 family includes many registers such as hardware counters and timers, input/output ports, serial data buffers, etc. The previous models had 256 RAM locations, while for the later models this number was incremented by additional 128 registers. However, the first 256 memory locations (addresses 0-FFh) are the heart of memory common to all the models belonging to the 8051 family. Locations available to the user occupy memory space with addresses 0–7 Fh, i.e. first 128 registers. This part of RAM is divided into several blocks.

The first block consists of 4 banks each including 8 registers denoted by R_0–R_7. Prior to accessing any of these registers, it is necessary to select the bank containing it. The next memory block (address 20 h–2 Fh) is bit-addressable, which means that each bit has its own address (0–7 Fh). Since there are 16 such registers, this block contains in total of 128 bits with separate addresses. The third group of registers occupies addresses 2 Fh–7 Fh, i.e. 80 locations, and does not have any special functions or features.

Additional RAM

In order to satisfy the programmers' constant hunger for Data Memory, the manufacturers decided to embed an additional memory block of 128 locations into the latest versions of the 8051 microcontrollers as shown in Fig. 3.15.4. However, it's not as simple as it seems to be. The problem is that electronics performing addressing has 1 byte (8 bits) on disposal and is capable of reaching only the first 256 locations, therefore. In order to keep already existing 8-bit architecture and compatibility with other existing models a small trick was done.

What does it mean? It means that an additional memory block shares the same addresses with locations intended for the SFRs (80 h–FFh). In order to differentiate between these two physically separated memory spaces, different ways of addressing are used. The SFRs memory locations are accessed by direct addressing, while additional RAM memory locations are accessed by indirect addressing.

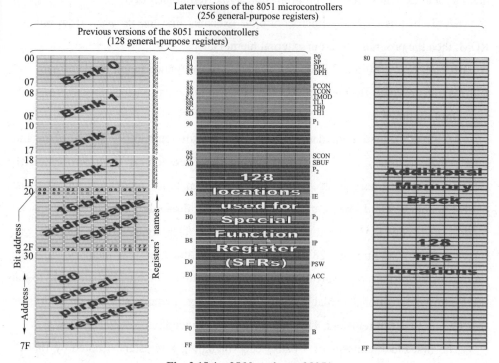

Fig. 3.15.4 256 locations of 8051

Memory expansion

In case memory (RAM or ROM) built in the microcontroller is not sufficient, it is possible to add two external memory chips with capacity of 64 kb each. P_2 and P_3 I/O ports are used for their addressing and data transmission.

Special function registers (SFRs)

Special function registers (SFRs) shown in Fig. 3.15.5 are a sort of control table used for running and monitoring the operation of the microcontroller. Each of these registers as well as each bit they include, has its name, address in the scope of RAM and precisely defined purpose such as timer control, interrupt control, serial communication control, etc. Even though there are 128 memory locations intended to be occupied by them, the basic core, shared by all the types of 8051 microcontrollers, has only 21 such registers. The rest of locations are intentionally left unoccupied in order to enable the manufacturers to further develop microcontrollers keeping them compatible with the previous versions. It also enables programs written a long time ago for microcontrollers which are out of production now to be used today.

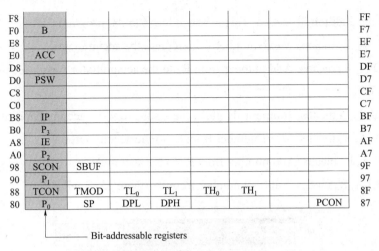

Fig. 3.15.5 Special function registers

"A" registers (Accumulators)

The "A" register is a general-purpose register used for storing intermediate results obtained during operation. Prior to executing an instruction upon any number or operand it is necessary to store it in the accumulator first. All results obtained from arithmetical operations performed by the ALU are stored in the accumulator. Data to be moved from one register to another must go through the accumulator. In other words, the "A" register is the most commonly used register and it is impossible to imagine a microcontroller without it. More than half instructions used by the 8051 microcontroller use somehow the accumulator.

"B" registers

Multiplication and division can be performed only upon numbers stored in the "A" and "B" registers. All other instructions in the program can use this register as a spare accumulator (A).

"R" registers (R_0-R_7)

This is a common name for 8 general-purpose registers (R_0, R_1, and R_2...R_7). Even though they are not true SFRs, they deserve to be discussed here because of their purpose. They occupy 4 banks within RAM as shown in Fig. 3.15.6. Similar to the accumulator, they are used for temporary storing variables and intermediate results during operation. Which one of these banks is to be active depends on two bits of the PSW Register. Active bank is a bank the registers of which are currently used.

The following example best illustrates the purpose of these registers. Suppose it is necessary to perform some arithmetical operations upon numbers previously stored in the "R" registers: (R_1+R_2)−(R_3+R_4). Obviously, a register for temporarily storing the results of the addition is needed. This is how it looks in the program:

MOV A, R_3 means: Move number from R_3 into the accumulator.

ADD A, R_4 means: Add number from R_4 to the accumulator (result remains in the accumulator).

MOV R_5, A means: Temporarily move the result from the accumulator into R_5.

MOV A, R_1 means: Move number from R_1 to the accumulator.

ADD A, R_2 means: Add number from R_2 to the accumulator.

SUBB A, R_5 means: Subtract number from R_5 (there are R_3+R_4).

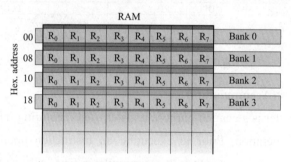

Fig. 3.15.6 "R" Registers

Program status word (PSW) registers

The PSW register shown in Fig. 3.15.7 is one of the most important SFRs. It contains several status bits that reflect the current state of the CPU. Besides, this register contains Carry bit, Auxiliary Carry, two register bank select bits, Overflow flag, parity bit and user-definable status flag.

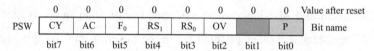

Fig. 3.15.7 A program status word (PSW) register

Data pointer registers (DPTRs)

The DPTR register is not a true one because it doesn't physically exist. It consists of two separate registers: DPH (Data Pointer High) and DPL (Data Pointer Low). For this reason it may be treated as a 16-bit register or as two independent 8-bit registers. Their 16 bits are primarily used for external memory addressing. Besides, the DPTR register is usually used for storing data and intermediate results.

Stack pointer (SP) registers

A value stored in the stack pointer (Fig. 3.15.8) points to the first free stack address and permits stack availability. Stack pushes increment the value in the stack pointer by 1. Likewise, stack pops decrement its value by 1. Upon any reset and power-on, the value 70 is stored in the stack pointer, which means that the space of RAM reserved for the stack starts at this location. If another value is written to this register, the entire stack is moved to the new memory location.

Fig. 3.15.8 A stack pointer (SP) register

TECHNICAL WORDS AND PHRASES

architecture	['ɑːkitektʃə]	n.	结构，建筑，建筑学
microcontroller	[ˌmaikrəkən'trəulə]	n.	微处理器
sufficient	[sə'fiʃənt]	adj.	充分的，足够的
peripheral	[pə'rifərəl]	adj.	外围的
configuration	[kənˌfigju'reiʃən]	n.	构造，结构，配置，外形
function	['fʌŋkʃən]	n.	官能，功能，作用
byte	[bait]	n.	（二进制的）字节，位组
bit	[bit]	n.	[计]位，比特
alternative	[ɔːl'təːnətiv]	adj.	选择性的，二中择一的
register	['redʒistə]	n.	寄存器
counter	['kauntə]	n.	计数器
timer	['taimə]	n.	定时器
interrupt	[ˌintə'rʌpt]	n.	中断
accumulator	[ə'kjuːmjuleitə]	n.	累加器，加法器
multiplication	[ˌmʌltipli'keiʃən]	n.	[数]乘法，增加
division	[di'viʒən]	n.	[数学]除法
spare	[spɛə]	adj.	备用的
illustrate	['iləstreit]	vt.	举例说明，图解，加插图于，阐明
addition	[ə'diʃən]	n.	加，加起来，加法
reset	['riːset]	v.	复位
power-on			重启
ROM		abbr.	[计]只读存储器
RAM		abbr.	[计]随机存取内存，随机存储器
SFR		abbr.	特殊功能寄存器
ALU		abbr.	算术逻辑部件
PSW		abbr.	程序状态字

DPTR	abbr.	数据指针寄存器
carry bit		进位，移位
built-in		内置的
peripheral device		外围设备
external memory		外存储器，外部存储器
pull-up resistor		上拉电阻
input resistance		输入电阻
open drain		开漏
program memory		程序存储器
data memory		数据存储器
intermediate result		中间结果
lookup table		查找表
direct addressing		直接寻址
indirect addressing		间接寻址
serial communication		串行通讯
arithmetical operation		数学运算
auxiliary carry		辅助进位标志位
overflow flag		溢出标志位
parity bit		奇偶标志位
user-definable status flag		用户标志位
data pointer high		数据指针高位
data pointer low		数据指针低位
stack pointer (SP) register		堆栈指针寄存器
stack push		入栈
stack pop		出栈

NOTES

1. 4 ports having in total of 32 input/output lines are in most cases sufficient to make all necessary connections to peripheral environment.

   译文：4个端口一共有32条输入/输出通道，在大多数情况下这些通道足够用来与外围的设备建立必要的连接。

   该句结构为：主语"4 ports having in total of 32 input/output lines"+谓语"are"+表语"sufficient"+补语"to make all necessary connections to peripheral environment"。

2. Unlike other ports consisting of pins with built-in pull-up resistor connected by its end to 5 V power supply, pins of this port have this resistor left out.

译文：其他端口的引脚通过内置上拉电阻接到 5 V 电源，与其不同的是，该口的引脚须外接这个上拉电阻。

该句为 "unlike A，B do..." 句型，其中 A 与 B 是同类事物，表示 "与 A 不同，B..."。A 为 "other ports"；"consisting of pins with... 5 V power supply" 为现在分词结构，做 A 的定语；B 为 "pins of this port"。

3. Program Memory (ROM) is used to permanently save the program being executed, while Data Memory (RAM) is used for temporarily storing data and intermediate results created and used during the operation of the microcontroller.

译文：程序存储器（ROM）用来永久地存储所要执行的程序，而数据存储器用来临时地存放微处理器运行过程中使用和产生的数据及中间结果。

"while" 在此连接两个并列句，表示对比或转折，意为 "然而"。第一个分句中 "being executed" 为现在分词做定语，修饰 "program"。第二个分句中 "created and used... microcontroller" 为过去分词做定语，修饰 "data and intermediate results"。

4. They are used in cases when equations describing some processes are too complicated or when there is no time for solving them.

译文：当描述过程的方程过于复杂或没时间来解它们的时候，就要使用外部存储器。

该句中 "when" 引导的从句为定语从句，等于 "in which"。

5. Upon any reset and power-on, the value 70 is stored in the stack pointer, which means that the space of RAM reserved for the stack starts at this location.

译文：在微处理器复位或重启后，栈指针的值为 70。也就是说，RAM 中栈的开始区域为 "70"。

"upon" 在此表示 "在……后立即" 的意思。该句中 "which" 引导一个非限定性定语从句，该从句中又含一个 "that" 引导的宾语从句，而该宾语从句中的 "reserved for the stack" 为过去分词做定语。

EXERCISES

Ⅰ. **Write out the complete forms of the following abbreviations and translate them into Chinese.**

1. ACC
2. ALU
3. ROM
4. RAM
5. SFR
6. PSW
7. CPU
8. SP
9. I/O
10. DPTR

Ⅱ. **Complete the following sentences with the following words. Change their forms if necessary.**

alternate, configuration, intended, ignores, stored, executes, perform

1. All 8051 microcontrollers have 4 I/O ports each comprising 8 bits which can be _____ as inputs or outputs.
2. P_1 is a true I/O port, because it doesn't have any _____ functions as is the case with P_0.
3. Pins of this port occupy addresses _____ for external memory chip.
4. When EA=0, the microcontroller completely _____ internal program memory and _____ only the program _____ in external memory.
5. All results obtained from arithmetical operations _____ by the ALU are stored in the accumulator.

III. Answer the following questions according to the text.

1. What's the difference between Program Memory and Date Memory?
2. Why are the ways of addressing between SFRs memory locations and RAM memory locations different?
3. When we use external memory chips, which ports should be used for addressing and data transmission?

Supplementary Reading

Reading 15 8051 Microcontroller Architecture (2)

Counters and timers

As you already know, the microcontroller oscillator uses quartz crystal for its operation. As the frequency of this oscillator is precisely defined and very stable, pulses it generates are always of the same width, which makes them ideal for time measurement. Such crystals are also used in quartz watches. In order to measure time between two events it is sufficient to count up pulses coming from this oscillator. That is exactly what the timer does. If the timer is properly programmed, the value stored in its register will be incremented (or decremented) with each coming pulse, i.e. once per each machine cycle. A single machine-cycle instruction lasts for 12 quartz oscillator periods, which means that by embedding quartz with oscillator frequency of 12 MHz, a number stored in the timer register will be changed million times per second, i.e. each microsecond.

The 8051 microcontroller has 2 timers/counters called T_0 and T_1. As their names suggest, their main purpose is to measure time and count external events. Besides, they

Unit 15 8051 Microcontroller Architecture 175

can be used for generating clock pulses to be used in serial communication, so called Baud Rate.

Timer T_0

As seen in Fig. 3.15.9, the timer T_0 consists of two registers—TH_0 and TL_0 representing a low and a high byte of one 16-digit binary number.

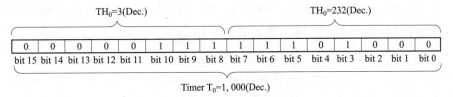

Fig. 3.15.9 The timer T_0

Accordingly, if the content of the timer T_0 is equal to 0 ($T_0=0$), then both registers it consists of will contain 0. As seen in Fig. 3.15.9, if the timer contains, for example, number 1,000 (decimal), then the TH_0 register (high byte) will contain the number 3, while the TL_0 register (low byte) will contain decimal number 232.

Formula used to calculate values in these two registers is very simple:

$$TH_0 \times 256 + TL_0 = T$$

Matching the previous example it would be as follows:

$$3 \times 256 + 232 = 1{,}000$$

Since the timer T_0 is virtually 16-bit register, the largest value it can store is 65,535. In case of exceeding this value, the timer will be automatically cleared and counting starts from 0. This condition is called an overflow. Two registers TMOD and TCON are closely connected to this timer and control its operation.

TMOD registers (Timer modes)

The TMOD register shown in Fig. 3.15.10 selects the operational mode of the timers T_0 and T_1. As seen in Fig.3.15.10, the low 4 bits (bit0-bit3) refer to the timer 0, while the high 4 bits (bit4-bit7) refer to the timer 1. There are 4 operational modes and each of them is described herein.

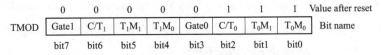

Fig. 3.15.10 The TMOD register

Bits of this register have the following function:

- Gate1/0 enables and disables Timer 1/0 by means of a signal brought to the $INT_{1/0}$ pin:

- ○ **1**—Timer 1/0 operates only if the INT_1 bit is set.
- ○ **0**—Timer 1/0 operates regardless of the logic state of the INT_1 bit.
- $C/T_{1/0}$ selects pulses to be counted up by the timer/counter 1/0:
  - ○ **1**—Timer counts pulses brought to the $T_{1/0}$ pin.
  - ○ **0**—Timer counts pulses from internal oscillator.
- $T_{1/0}$ M1, $T_{1/0}$ M_0 These two bits select the operational mode of the Timer 1/0.

Timer 0 in mode 0 (13-bit timer) (Fig. 3.15.11(a))

This is one of the rarities being kept only for the purpose of compatibility with the previous versions of microcontrollers. This mode configures timer 0 as a 13-bit timer which consists of all 8 bits of TH_0 and the lower 5 bits of TL_0. As a result, the Timer 0 uses only 13 of 16 bits. How does it operate? Each coming pulse causes the lower register bits to change their states. After receiving 32 pulses, this register is loaded and automatically cleared, while the higher byte (TH_0) is incremented by 1. This process is repeated until registers count up 8192 pulses. After that, both registers are cleared and counting starts from 0.

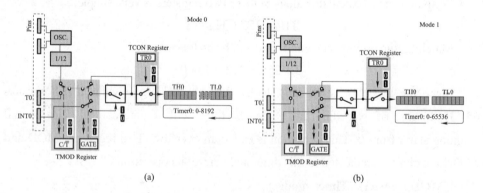

Fig. 3.15.11　Timer 0 in mode 0 and mode 1

(a) Timer 0 in mode 0; (b) Timer 0 in mode 1

Timer 0 in mode 1 (16-bit timer) (Fig. 3.15.11(b))

Mode 1 configures timer 0 as a 16-bit timer comprising all the bits of both registers TH_0 and TL_0. That's the reason why this is one of the most commonly used modes. Timer operates in the same way as in mode 0, with difference that the registers count up to 65,536 as allowable by the 16 bits.

Timer 0 in mode 2 (Auto-reload timer) (Fig. 3.15.12(a))

Mode 2 configures timer 0 as an 8-bit timer. Actually, timer 0 uses only one 8-bit register for counting and never counts from 0, but from an arbitrary value (0–255) stored in another (TH_0) register.

The following example shows the advantages of this mode. Suppose it is necessary to constantly count up 55 pulses generated by the clock.

If mode 1 or mode 0 is used, it is necessary to write the number 200 to the timer registers and constantly check whether an overflow has occurred, i.e. whether they reached the value 255. When it happens, it is necessary to rewrite the number 200 and repeat the whole procedure. The same procedure is automatically performed by the microcontroller if set in mode 2. In fact, only the TL_0 register operates as a timer, while another (TH_0) register stores the value from which the counting starts. When the TL_0 register is loaded, instead of being cleared, the contents of TH_0 will be reloaded to it. Referring to the previous example, in order to register each 55th pulse, the best solution is to write the number 200 to the TH_0 register and configure the timer to operate in mode 2.

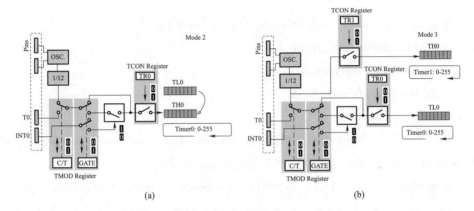

Fig. 3.15.12   Timer 0 in mode 2 and mode 3

(a) Timer 0 in mode 2; (b) Timer 0 in mode 3

Timer 0 in Mode 3 (Split timer) (Fig. 3.15.12(b))

Mode 3 configures timer 0 so that registers TL_0 and TH_0 operate as separate 8-bit timers. In other words, the 16-bit timer consisting of two registers TH_0 and TL_0 is split into two independent 8-bit timers. This mode is provided for applications requiring an additional 8-bit timer or counter. The TL_0 timer turns into timer 0, while the TH_0 timer turns into timer 1. In addition, all the control bits of 16-bit timer 1 (consisting of the TH1 and TL1 registers), now control the 8-bit timer 1. Even though the 16-bit timer 1 can still be configured to operate in any of modes (mode 1, 2 or 3), it is no longer possible to disable it as there is no control bit to do it. Thus, its operation is restricted when timer 0 is in mode 3.

The only application of this mode is when two timers are used and the 16-bit timer

1 the operation of which is out of control is used as a baud rate generator.

Timer control (TCON) registers

The TCON register shown in Fig. 3.15.13 is also one of the registers whose bits are directly in control of timer operation. Only 4 bits of this register are used for this purpose, while the rest of them are used for interrupt control (to be discussed later).

	0	0	0	0	0	0	0	0	Value after reset
TCON	TF_1	TR_1	TF_0	TR_0	IE_1	IT_1	IE_0	IT_0	Bit name
	bit7	bit6	bit5	bit4	bit3	bit2	bit1	bit0	

Fig. 3.15.13   The timer control (TCON) register

- TF_1 bit is automatically set on the timer 1 overflow.
- TR_1 bit enables the timer 1.
  - 1—Timer 1 is enabled.
  - 0—Timer 1 is disabled.
- TF_0 bit is automatically set on the timer 0 overflow.
- TR_0 bit enables the timer 0.
  - 1—Timer 0 is enabled.
  - 0—Timer 0 is disabled.

How to use the timer 0

In order to use timer 0, it is first necessary to select it and configure the mode of its operation. Bits of the TMOD register are in control of it:

Referring to Fig. 3.15.14, the timer 0 operates in mode 1 and counts pulses generated by internal clock the frequency of which is equal to 1/12 the quartz frequency.

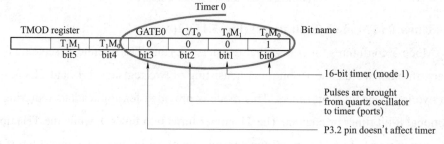

Fig. 3.15.14   The TMOD register

Turn on the timer:

As seen in Fig. 3.15.15 the TR_0 bit is set and the timer starts operation. If the quartz crystal with frequency of 12 MHz is embedded, then its contents will be incremented every microsecond. After 65,536 microseconds, the both registers the timer consists of will be loaded. The microcontroller automatically clears them and the timer keeps on repeating procedure from the beginning until the TR_0 bit value is logic zero (0).

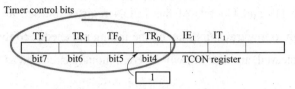

Fig. 3.15.15 The TCON register

How to "read" a timer?

Depending on application, it is necessary either to read a number stored in the timer registers or to register the moment they have been cleared.

—It is extremely simple to read a timer by using only one register configured in mode 2 or mode 3. It is sufficient to read its state at any moment. That's all!

—It is somehow complicated to read a timer configured to operate in mode 2. Suppose the lower byte is read first (TL_0), then the higher byte (TH_0). The result is:

$$TH_0 = 15 \quad TL_0 = 255$$

Everything seems to be OK, but the current state of the register at the moment of reading was:

$$TH_0 = 14 \quad TL_0 = 255$$

In case of negligence, such an error in counting (255 pulses) may occur for not so obvious but quite logical reason. The lower byte is correctly read (255), but at the moment the program counter was about to read the higher byte TH_0, an overflow occurred and the contents of both registers have been changed (TH_0: 14→15, TL_0: 255→0). This problem has a simple solution. The higher byte should be read first, then the lower byte and once again the higher byte. If the number stored in the higher byte is different, then this sequence should be repeated. It's about a short loop consisting of only 3 instructions in the program.

There is another solution as well. It is sufficient to simply turn the timer off while reading is going on (the TR_0 bit of the TCON register should be cleared), and turn it on again after reading is finished.

8051 microcontroller interrupts

There are five interrupt sources for the 8051, which means that they can recognize 5 different events that can interrupt regular program execution. Each interrupt can be enabled or disabled by setting the bits of the IE register. Likewise, the whole interrupt system can be disabled by clearing the EA bit of the same register. Refer to Fig. 3.15.16.

Now, it is necessary to explain a few details referring to external interrupts—INT_0 and INT_1. If the IT_0 and IT_1 bits of the TCON register are set, an interrupt will be generated on high to low transition, i.e. on the falling pulse edge (only in that moment). If these bits are cleared, an interrupt will be continuously executed as far as the pins are held low.

IE registers (interrupt enable shown in Fig. 3.15.17)
- EA—global interrupt enable/disable:
  - 0—disables all interrupt requests.
  - 1—enables all individual interrupt requests.

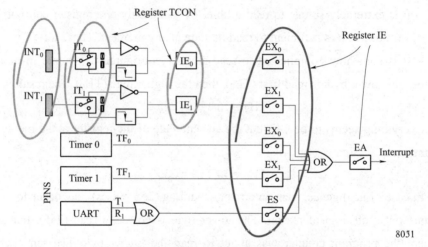

Fig. 3.15.16 8051 microcontroller interrupts

	bit7	bit6	bit5	bit4	bit3	bit2	bit1	bit0	
Value after reset	0	X	0	0	0	0	0	0	
IE	EA		ET_2	ES	ET_1	EX_1	ET_0	EX_0	Bit name

Fig. 3.15.17 The IE register (interrupt enable)

- ES—enables or disables serial interrupt:
  - 0—UART system cannot generate an interrupt.
  - 1—UART system enables an interrupt.
- ET_1—bit enables or disables timer 1 interrupt:
  - 0—Timer 1 cannot generate an interrupt.
  - 1—Timer 1 enables an interrupt.
- EX_1—bit enables or disables external 1 interrupt:
  - 0—change of the pin INT_0 logic state cannot generate an interrupt.
  - 1—enables an external interrupt on the pin INT_0 state change.
- ET_0—bit enables or disables timer 0 interrupt:
  - 0—Timer 0 cannot generate an interrupt.

- o 1—enables timer 0 interrupt.
- EX₀—bit enables or disables external 0 interrupt:
  - o 0—change of the INT_1 pin logic state cannot generate an interrupt.
  - o 1—enables an external interrupt on the pin INT_1 state change.

Interrupt priorities

It is not possible to foresee when an interrupt request will arrive. If several interrupts are enabled, it may happen that while one of them is in progress, another one is requested. In order that the microcontroller knows whether to continue operation or meet a new interrupt request, there is a priority list instructing it what to do.

The priority list offers 3 levels of interrupt priority:

(1) Reset! The absolute master. When a reset request arrives, everything is stopped and the microcontroller restarts.

(2) Interrupt priority 1 can be disabled by Reset only.

(3) Interrupt priority 0 can be disabled by both Reset and interrupt priority 1.

The IP Register (Interrupt Priority Register) specifies which one of existing interrupt sources has higher and which one has lower priority. Interrupt priority is usually specified at the beginning of the program. According to that, there are several possibilities:

- If an interrupt of higher priority arrives while an interrupt is in progress, it will be immediately stopped and the higher priority interrupt will be executed first.
- If two interrupt requests, at different priority levels, arrive at the same time, then the higher priority interrupt is serviced first.
- If both the interrupt requests, at the same priority level, occur one after another, the one which came later has to wait until routine being in progress ends.
- If two interrupt requests of equal priority arrive at the same time, then the interrupt to be serviced is selected according to the following priority list:

(1) External interrupt INT_0.

(2) Timer 0 interrupt.

(3) External Interrupt INT_1.

(4) Timer 1 interrupt.

(5) Serial communication interrupt.

IP (interrupt priorities) registers

The IP register bits specify the priority level of each interrupt (high or low priority) as shown in Fig. 3.15.18.

IP	X	X	0	0	0	0	0	0	Value after reset
			PT_2	PS	PT_1	PX_1	PT_0	PX_0	Bit name
	bit7	bit6	bit5	bit4	bit3	bit2	bit1	bit0	

Fig. 3.15.18　The IP register

- PS—Serial Port interrupt priority bit.
  - Priority 0.
  - Priority 1.
- PT_1—Timer 1 interrupt priority.
  - Priority 0.
  - Priority 1.
- PX_1—External interrupt INT_1 priority.
  - Priority 0.
  - Priority 1.
- PT_0—Timer 0 interrupt priority.
  - Priority 0.
  - Priority 1.
- PX_0—External interrupt INT_0 priority.
  - Priority 0.
  - Priority 1.

Handling interrupts

When an interrupt request arrives the following occurs:

(1) Instruction in progress is ended.

(2) The address of the next instruction to execute is pushed on the stack.

(3) Depending on which interrupt is requested, one of 5 vectors (addresses) is written to the program counter in accordance to Tab. 3.15.1.

(4) Interrupt source and vector.

Tab. 3.15.1　The interrupt source and its corresponding address

Interrupt Source	Vector (address)
IE0	3 h
TF_0	B h
TF_1	1 B h
RI, TI	23 h
All addresses are in hexadecimal format	

(5) These addresses store appropriate subroutines processing interrupts. Instead of

them, there are usually jump instructions specifying locations on which these subroutines reside.

(6) When an interrupt routine is executed, the address of the next instruction to execute is popped from the stack to the program counter and interrupted program resumes operation from where it left off.

Reset

Reset occurs when the RS pin is supplied with a positive pulse in duration of at least 2 machine cycles (24 clock cycles of crystal oscillator). After that, the microcontroller generates an internal reset signal which clears all SFRs, except SBUF registers, Stack Pointer and ports (the state of the first two ports is not defined, while the FF value is written to the ports configuring all their pins as inputs). Depending on the surrounding and purpose of the device, the RS pin is usually connected to a power-on reset push button or circuit or to both of them. Fig. 3.15.19 illustrates one of the simplest circuits providing safe power-on reset.

Basically, everything is very simple: After turning the power on, the electrical capacitor is being charged for several milliseconds through a resistor connected to the ground. The pin is driven high during

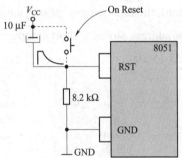

Fig. 3.15.19 The safe power-on reset circuit

this process. When the capacitor is charged, the power supply voltage is already stable and the pin remains connected to the ground, thus providing normal operation of the microcontroller. Pressing the reset button causes the capacitor to be temporarily discharged and the microcontroller is reset. When released, the whole process is repeated…

Through the program step by step…

Microcontrollers normally operate at a very high speed. The use of 12 MHz quartz crystal enables 1,000,000 instructions to be executed per second. Basically, there is no need for a higher operating rate. In case it is needed, it is easy to be built in a crystal for high frequency. The problem arises when it is necessary to slow down the operation of the microcontroller. For example, during testing in real environment when it is necessary to execute several instructions step by step in order to check I/O pins' logic state.

The interrupt system of the 8051 microcontroller practically stops the operation of the microcontroller and enables instructions to be executed one after another by pressing the button. Two interrupt features enable that:

- Interrupt request is ignored if an interrupt of the same priority level is in progress.
- Upon interrupt routine execution, a new interrupt is not executed until at least one instruction from the main program is executed.

In order to use this in practice, the following steps should be done:

(1) External interrupt sensitive to the signal level should be enabled (for example INT_0).

(2) Three following instructions should be inserted into the program (at the 03hex. address):

What is going on? As soon as the P3.2 pin is cleared (for example, by pressing the button), the microcontroller will stop program execution and jump to the 03hex address. This address stores a short interrupt routine consisting of 3 instructions as shown in Fig. 3.15.20.

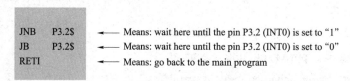

Fig. 3.15.20 Interrupt routine

The first instruction is executed until the push button is realised (logic one (1) on the P3.2 pin). The second instruction is executed until the push button is pressed again. Immediately after that, the RETI instruction is executed and the processor resumes operation of the main program. Upon execution of any program instruction, the interrupt INT_0 is generated and the whole procedure is repeated (The push button is still pressed). In other words, one button press—one instruction.

Unit 16
How to Start Working with a Microcontroller

How to Start Working with a Microcontroller 翻译

How to start working

A microcontroller is a good-natured "genie in the bottle" and no extra knowledge is required to use it.

In order to create a device controlled by the microcontroller, it is necessary to provide the simplest PC, program for compiling and simple device to transfer the code from PC to the chip itself.

Even though the whole process is quite logical, there are often some queries, not because it is complicated, but for numerous variations. Let's take a look.

Writing program in assembly language

In order to write a program for the microcontroller, a specialized program in the Windows environment may be used. It may, but it does not have to... When using such a software, there are numerous tools which facilitate the operation (simulator tool comes first), which is an obvious advantage. But there is also another way to write a program. Basically, text is the only thing that matters. Any program for text processing can be used for this purpose. The point is to write all instructions in such an order that they should be executed by the microcontroller, observe the rules of the assembly language and write instructions exactly as they are defined. In other words, you just have to follow the program idea. That's all!

```
RESET   VECTOR
        CSEG    AT      0
        JMP     XRESET          ; Reset vector
        CSEG
        ORG     100 H
```

```
XRESET:    ORL     WMCON, #PERIOD    ; Define Watch-dog period
           ORL     WMCON, #WDTEN     ; Watch-dog timer is enabled
```

To enable the compiler to operate successfully, it is necessary that a document containing this program has the extension, .asm in its name, for example, Program.asm.

When a specialized program (mplab) is used, this extension will be automatically added. If any other program for text processing (Notepad) is used, then the document should be saved and renamed. For example: Program.txt → Program.asm. This procedure is not necessarily performed. The document may be saved in the original format while its text may be copied to the programmer for further use.

Compiling a program

The microcontroller "does not understand" assembly language as such. That is the reason why it is necessary to compile the program into machine language. It is more than simple when a specialized program (mplab) is used because a compiler is part of the software. Just one click on the appropriate icon solves the problem and a new document with ".hex" extension appears. It is actually the same program, only compiled into machine language which the microcontroller perfectly understands. Such documentation is commonly named "hex code" and seemingly represents a meaningless sequence of numbers in hexadecimal number system.

03000000020100FA1001000075813F

ADAF6DD00000001FF255AFED8FE

D9FA

In the event that other software for program writing in assembly language is used, a special software for compiling the program must be installed and used as follows—set up the compiler, open the document with ".asm" extension and compile. The result is the same—a new document with extension ".hex." The only problem now is that it is stored in your PC.

Programming a microcontroller

In order to transfer a "hex code" to the microcontroller, it is necessary to provide a cable for serial communication and a special device, called programmer, with software. There are several ways to do it.

A large number of programs and electronic circuits having this purpose can be found on the Internet. Do as follows: Open hex code document, set a few parameters and click the icon for compiling. After a while, a sequence of zeros and ones will be programmed into the microcontroller through the serial connection cable and programmer hardware. What's left is to place the programmed chip into the target device. In the event that it is necessary to make some changes in the program, the previous procedure may be repeated an unlimited number of times (Fig. 3.16.1).

The end or...

This section briefly describes the use of MPLAB and programmer software developed by Mikroelektronika. Everything is very simple...

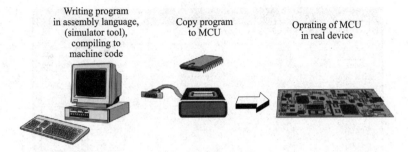

Fig. 3.16.1

Start the program Mikroelektronika Asm51 Console. The window appears...

...Open a new document: File→New. Write your program or copy text...

...Save and name your document: File→Save As... (Document name is limited to 8 characters!)

Finally, to compile program into HEX code select: Project→Build or click the "play" icon. If everything works properly, the computer will respond with a short report.

The program is written and successfully compiled. All that's left is to dump the program to the microcontroller. For this purpose it is necessary to have software that takes the written and compiled program and passes it to the microcontroller.

Start the program 8051 Flash_setup.exe...

Program installation is performed as usual—just click Next, Accept, Next... and finally Finish!

The program has been installed and ready for use. The settings are easily performed so that there is no need for additional explanations (the type of the microcontroller, frequency and clock oscillator, etc.).

- Connect the PC and programmer via a USB cable;
- Load the HEX code using command: File→Load HEX; and
- Click the "Write" push button and wait.

That's all! The microcontroller is programmed and everything is ready for operation. If you are not satisfied, make some changes in the program and repeat the procedure as shown in Fig. 3.16.2. Until when? Until you feel satisfied...

Development systems

A device which in the testing program phase can simulate any environment is called a development system. Apart from the programmer, the power supply unit and the microcontroller's socket, the development system contains elements for input pin activation and output pin monitoring. The simplest version has every pin connected to

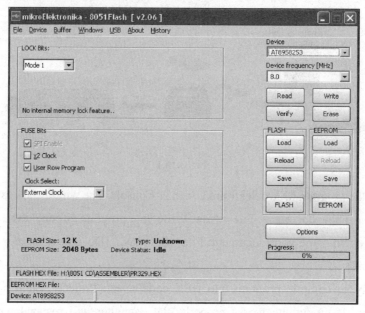

Fig. 3.16.2　The window used to make some changes in the program

one push button and one LED as well. A high quality version has LED displays, LCD displays, temperature sensors and all other elements which can be supplied with the target device. These peripherals can be connected to the MCU via miniature jumpers. In this way, the whole program may be tested in practice during its development stage, because the microcontroller doesn't know or care whether its input is activated by a push button or a sensor built in a real device.

Easy8051A development system

The Easy8051A development system shown in Fig. 3.16.3 is a high-quality development system used for programming 8051 compatible microcontrollers manufactured by Atmel. In addition to chip programming, this system enables all the parts of the program to be tested as it contains most components which are normally built in real devices.

The Easy8051A development system consists of:
- Sockets for placing microcontrollers in (14, 16, 20 and 40-pin packages);
- Connector for external power supply (DC 12 V);

Unit 16 How to Start Working with a Microcontroller

- USB programmer;
- Power supply selector (external or via USB cable);
- 8 MHz quartz crystal oscillator;
- 32 LEDs for output pin state indication;
- 32 push buttons for input pin activation;
- Four 7-segment LED displays in multiplex mode;
- Graphic LCD display;
- Alphanumeric LCD display (4- or 8-bit mode);
- Connector and driver for serial communication RS232;
- Digital thermometer DS1820;
- 12-bit A/D converter (MCP3204);
- 12-bit D/A converter (MCP4921);
- Reference voltage source 4.096 V (MCP1541).
- Multiple-pin connectors for direct access to I/O ports.

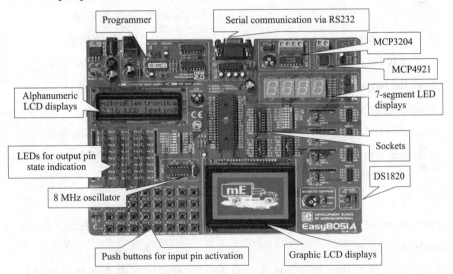

Fig. 3.16.3 The Easy8051A development system

TECHNICAL WORDS AND PHRASES

compile	[kəm'pail]	vt.	编译，编辑，汇编
variation	[ˌvɛəriˈeiʃən]	n.	变异，变种
observe	[əbˈzəːv]	vt.	遵守
extension	[iksˈtenʃən]	n.	扩展名
notepad	[ˈnəutpæd]	n.	记事本
procedure	[prəˈsiːdʒə]	n.	程序，手续

format	[ˈfɔːmæt]	n.	版式，形式，格式
hexadecimal	[heksəˈdesim(ə)l]	n.	十六进制
parameter	[pəˈræmitə]	n.	参数，参量
console	[kənˈsəul]	n.	[计] 控制台
installation	[ˌinstəˈleiʃən]	n.	[计] 安装，装置
frequency	[ˈfriːkwənsi]	n.	频率，周率，发生次数
oscillator	[ˈɔsileitə]	n.	振荡器
activation	[ˌæktiˈveiʃən]	n.	活化，激活
socket	[ˈsɔkit]	n.	插座
miniature	[ˈminjətʃə]	n.	缩小的模型
jumper	[ˈdʒʌmpə]	n.	[电学] 跳线，跨接线
alphanumeric	[ælfənjuːˈmerik]	adj.	字母与数字混合编排的
MCU		abbr.	微处理机控制单元
LED		abbr.	发光二极管
LCD		abbr.	液晶显示屏
A/D converter			模/数转换器
assembly language			[计] 汇编语言
machine language			[计] 机器语言
development system			开发系统
quartz crystal oscillator			石英晶体振荡器
reference voltage source			参考电压源

NOTES

1. A microcontroller is a good-natured "genie in the bottle" and no extra knowledge is required to use it.

   译文：微处理器的一大优点就是"起点低"，使用它不需要其他额外的知识。"genie in the bottle" 在此应译为"起点低"。

2. The point is to write all instructions in such an order that they should be executed by the microcontroller, observe the rules of assembly language and write instructions exactly as they are defined.

   译文：关键是所有的指令需按它们在微处理器中执行的顺序来书写，遵循汇编语言的规则并且严格按照指令的定义来写指令。

   该句采用了"be+动词不定式"结构，不定式做表语，表示主语和表语在概念上是等同的。"to"后加了3个并列的"do"，即"write"、"observe"和"write"，其中第一个表语中含有一个定语从句"they should be executed by the microcontroller",修饰"order"。

3. It is more than simple when a specialized program (mplab) is used because a compiler is part of the software.

译文：当使用专业的编程软件（如 mplab）时这个过程就非常简单了，因为编译器是该软件的一个部分（功能）。

词句中"more than + 形容词"意为"很"或"非常"的意思；该句为"when"引导的条件状语从句。

4. In the event that other software for program writing in assembly language is used, a special software for compiling the program must be installed and used as follows—set up the compiler, open the document with ".asm" extension and compile.

译文：如果使用了其他用汇编语言来编程的软件，就必须安装一种专门用来编译程序的软件进行如下操作——打开编译器，打开扩展名为".asm"的文件，然后编译它。

"In the event that"表示"如果"、"在……情况下"的意思。该句虽然为被动语态，但应该翻译成主动句。

5. The Easy8051A development system shown in Fig. 3.16.3 is a high-quality development system used for programming 8051 compatible microcontrollers manufactured by Atmel.

译文：图 3.16.3 所示的 Easy8051A 开发系统是一个高级版的开发系统，可对由 Atmel 制造的与 8051 兼容的微处理器进行编程。

该句结构为：主语"The Easy8051A development system shown in Fig. 3.16.3"+谓语"is"+表语"a high-quality development system"+表语的定语"used for programming 8051 compatible microcontrollers manufactured by Atmel"。表语的定语中的"manufactured by Atmel"，即过去分词做定语，修饰"microcontrollers"。

EXERCISES

Ⅰ. Translate the following words into English.

1. 汇编语言
2. 仿真工具
3. 扩展文件
4. 编译器
5. 十六进制
6. 参数
7. 跳线
8. 石英晶体振荡器
9. 开发系统
10. 数字温度计

II. **Mark the following statements with T(true) or F(false) according to the text.**

1. The knowledge about microcontrollers is hard to learn, because it needs a lot of fundamentals. (   )
2. In order to write a program for the microcontroller, we must use a specialized program. (   )
3. If the program is downloaded to the microcontroller, we cannot modify it. (   )
4. The development system is a device which in the testing program phase can simulate any environment. (   )
5. The Easy8051A development system is used for programming 8051 microcontrollers only. (   )

III. **Answer the following questions according to the text.**

1. Please briefly describe the procedure of creating a device controlled by the microcontroller.
2. Why must we compile the assembly language into hex code?
3. What's the purpose of the microcontroller development system?

Supplementary Reading

Reading 16 The 8051 Instruction Set

Introduction

Writing program for the microcontroller mainly consists of giving instructions (commands) in the order in which they should be executed later in order to carry out the specific task. As electronics cannot "understand" what, for example, instruction "if the push button is pressed—turn the light on" means, then a certain number of more simple and precisely defined orders that decoder can recognize must be used. All commands are known as INSTRUCTION SET. All microcontrollers compatible with the 8051 have in total of 255 instructions, i.e. 255 different words available for program writing.

At first sight, it is imposing the number of odd signs that must be known by heart. However, It is not as complicated as it looks like. Many instructions are considered to be "different," even though they perform the same operation, so there are only 111 truly different commands. For example: ADD A, R0, ADD A, R_1... ADD A, R_7 are instructions that perform the same operation (addition of the accumulator and register) but since there are 8 such registers, each instruction is counted separately! Taking into account that all instructions perform only 53 operations (addition, subtraction, copy, etc.) and most of them are rarely used in practice, there are actually 20-30 shortened forms needed to be known, which is acceptable.

Types of instructions

Depending on the operation they perform, all instructions are divided into several groups:

- Arithmetic instructions;
- Branch instructions;
- Data transfer instructions;
- Logical instructions;
- Logical instructions with bits.

The first part of each instruction, called MNEMONIC, refers to the operation an instruction performs (copying, addition, logical operation, etc.). Mnemonics are commonly shortened forms of the names of operations being executed. For example:

INC R1—Means: Increment R1 (increment register R1)

Another part of instruction, called OPERAND, is separated from mnemonics at least by one empty space and defines data being processed by instructions. Some instructions have no operand, and some have one, two or three. If there is more than one operand in instruction, they are separated by comma. For example:

RET—(Return from sub-routine)—No operand.

ADD A, R3—(Add R3 and accumulator)—Two operands.

CJNE A, #20, LOOP—(Compare accumulator with 20. If they are not equal, jump to address specified as LOOP)—Three operands.

The operands listed below are written in shortened forms having the following meaning:

A—Accumulator.

Rn—Rn is one of R registers (R_0–R_7) in the currently active bank in RAM.

Rx—Rx is any register in RAM with 8-bit address. It can be a general-purpose register or SFR register (I/O port, control register etc.).

@Ri—Ri is R0 or R1 register in the currently active bank. It contains registers.

address—The instruction is referring to.

#X—X is any 8-bit number (0-255).

#X16—X is any 16-bit number (0-65535).

adr16—16-bit address is specified.

adr11—11-bit address is specified.

rel—The address of a close memory location is specified (-128 do +127 relative to the current one).

bit—Bit address is specified.

C—Carry bit in the status register (register PSW).

Arithmetic instructions

These instructions perform several basic operations (addition, subtraction, division, multiplication, etc.). After execution, the result is stored in the first operand. For example:

ADD A, Rn—Instruction adds the number in the accumulator and the number in register Rn (R0–R7). After addition, the result is stored in the accumulator.

SUBB A,Rx

Description: Instruction performs subtract operation: A-Rx including the Carry bit as well which acts as borrow. If the higher bit is subtracted from the lower bit then the Carry bit is set. As it is direct addressing, Rx can be some of SFRs or general-purpose register with address 0–7 Fh. (0–127 dec.). The result is stored in the accumulator.

DEC Rx—Description: Instruction decrements value of the register Rx by 1. As it is direct addressing, Rx must be within the first 255 locations of RAM. If there is a 0 in the register, the result will be FFh.

Branch instructions

There are two kinds of these instructions:

(1) Unconditional jump instructions: After their execution, a jump to a new location from where the program continues execution is executed. For example:

ACALL adr11—Call subroutine located at address within 2 K byte Program Memory space.

RET—Return from subroutine.

(2) Conditional jump instructions: if some condition is met, a jump is executed. Otherwise, the program normally proceeds with the next instruction. For example:

JBC bit, rel—Description: This instruction first checks if the bit is set. If it is set, a jump to the specified address is executed and afterwards the bit is cleared. Otherwise, the program proceeds with the first next instruction. This is a short jump instruction, which means that the address of a new location must be relatively near the current position in the program (−129 to + 127 locations relative to the first following instruction).

Data transfer instructions

These instructions move the content of one register to another one. The register whose content is moved remains unchanged. If they have the suffix "X" (MOVX), the data are exchanged with external memory. For example:

MOV A,@Ri—Description: Instruction moves the Rx register to the accumulator. Rx register address is stored in the Ri register (R0 or R1). After instruction execution, the result is stored in the accumulator. The Rx Register is not affected.

XCH A, Rx—Description: Instruction sets the contents of the accumulator into the register Rx. At the same time, the content of the Rx register is set into the accumulator. As it is direct addressing, the register Rx can be some of SFRs or general-purpose registers with address 0–7 Fh (0–127 dec.).

Logical instructions

These instructions perform logical operations between corresponding bits of two registers. After execution, the result is stored in the first operand.

ADD A, Rx—Description: Instruction adds the accumulator and Rx register. As it is direct addressing, Rx can be some of SFRs or general-purpose registers with address 0-7 Fh. The result is stored in the accumulator.

ORL A, #X—Description: Instruction performs logical-OR operation between the accumulator and number X. The result of this logical operation is stored in the accumulator.

CLR A / C—Description: Clear accumulator/ Carry bit.

Logical operations on bits

Similar to logical instructions, these instructions perform logical operations. The difference is that these operations are performed on single bits.

ANL C, bit—Description: Instruction performs logical-AND operation between the addressed bit and Carry bit.

Chapter 4
Principles of
Automatic Control

Unit 17
Introduction to Control

Introduction to Control 翻译

The subject of automatic control is enormous, covering the control of variables such as temperature, pressure, flow, level, and speed.

Need for automatic control

There are three major reasons why process plants or buildings require automatic control:

(1) Safety—The plant or process must be safe to operate. The more complex or dangerous the plant or process is, the greater the need for automatic control and safeguard protocol will be.

(2) Stability—The plant or processes should work steadily, predictably and repeatably, without fluctuations or unplanned shutdowns.

(3) Accuracy—This is a primary requirement in factories and buildings to prevent spoilage, increase quality and production rates, and maintain comfort. These are the fundamentals of economic efficiency.

Other desirable benefits such as economy, speed, and reliability are also important, but it is against the three major parameters of safety, stability and accuracy that each control application will be measured.

Automatic control terminology

Specific terms are used within the control industry, primarily to avoid confusion. The same words and phrases come together in all aspects of control, and when used correctly, their meanings are universal.

The simple manual system described in Example 4.17.1 and illustrated in Fig. 4.17.1 is used to introduce some standard terms used in control engineering.

Example 4.17.1 A simple analogy of a control system

In the example shown in Fig. 4.17.1, the operator manually varies the flow of water by opening or closing an inlet valve to ensure that:

- The water level is not too high; or it will run to waste via the overflow.

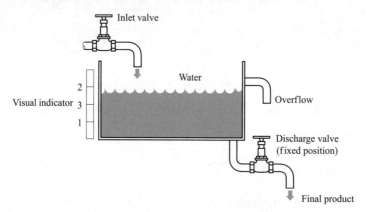

Fig. 4.17.1 Manual control of a simple process

- The water level is not too low; or it will not cover the bottom of the tank.

The outcome of this is that the water runs out of the tank at a rate within a required range. If the water runs out at too high or too low a rate, the process it is feeding cannot operate properly.

At an initial stage, the outlet valve in the discharge pipe is fixed at a certain position.

The operator has marked three lines on the side of the tank to enable him to manipulate the water supply via the inlet valve. The 3 levels represent:

(1) The lowest allowable water level to ensure the bottom of the tank is covered.

(2) The highest allowable water level to ensure there is no discharge through the overflow.

(3) The ideal level is between 1 and 2.

The Example (Figure 4.17.1) demonstrates that:

(1) The operator is aiming to maintain the water in the vessel between levels 1 and 2. The water level is called the Controlled Condition.

(2) The controlled condition is achieved by controlling the flow of water through the valve in the inlet pipe. The flow is known as the Manipulated Variable, and the valve is referred to as the Controlled Device.

(3) The water itself is known as the Control Agent.

(4) By controlling the flow of water into the tank, the level of water in the tank is altered. The change in water level is known as the Controlled Variable.

(5) Once the water is in the tank, it is known as the Controlled Medium.

(6) The level of water trying to be maintained on the visual indicator is known as the Set Value (also known as the Set Point).

(7) The water level can be maintained at any point between 1 and 2 on the visual indicator and still meet the control parameters such that the bottom of the tank is covered and there is no overflow. Any value within this range is known as the Desired Value.

(8) Assume the level is strictly maintained at any point between 1 and 2. This is the water level at steady state conditions, referred to as the Control Value or Actual Value.

> Note: With reference to (7) and (8) above, the ideal level of water to be maintained was at point 3. But if the actual level is at any point between 1 and 2, then that is still satisfactory. The difference between the Set Point and the Actual Value is known as Deviation.

(9) If the inlet valve is closed to a new position, the water level will drop and the deviation will change. A sustained deviation is known as Offset.

Example 4.17.2 Elements of automatic control (Fig. 4.17.2)

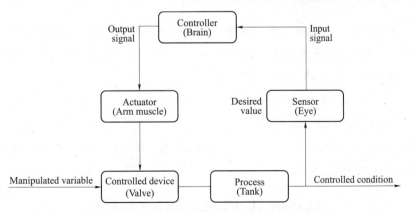

Fig. 4.17.2 Elements of automatic control

(1) The operator's eye detects the movement of the water level against the marked scale indicator. His eye could be thought of as a Sensor.

(2) The eye (sensor) signals this information back to the brain, which notices a deviation. The brain could be thought of as a Controller.

(3) The brain (controller) acts to send a signal to the arm muscle and hand, which could be thought of as an Actuator.

(4) The arm muscle and hand (actuator) turn the valve, which could be thought of as a Controlled Device.

It is worth repeating these points in a slightly different way to reinforce Example 4.17.2.

In simple terms the operator's aim in Example 4.17.1 is to hold the water within the tank at a pre-defined level. Level 3 can be considered to be his target or Set Point.

The operator physically manipulates the level by adjusting the inlet valve (the control device). Within this operation it is necessary to take the operator's competence and concentration into account. Because of this, it is unlikely that the water level will be exactly at Level 3 at all times. Generally, it will be at a point above or below Level 3. The position or level at any particular moment is termed the Control Value or Actual Value.

The amount of error or difference between the Set Point and the Actual Value is termed deviation. When a deviation is constant, or in a steady state, it is termed Sustained Deviation or Offset.

Although the operator is manipulating the water level, the final aim is to generate a proper outcome, in this case, a required flow of water from the tank.

Assessing safety, stability and accuracy

It can be assumed that a process typical of that in Example 4.17.1 contains neither valuable nor harmful ingredients. Therefore, overflow or water starvation will be safe, but not economic or productive.

In terms of stability, the operator would be able to handle this process providing he pays full and constant attention.

Accuracy is not a feature of this process because the operator can only respond to a visible and recognizable error.

TECHNICAL WORDS AND PHRASES

variable [ˈvɛəriəbl] n. 变量

Unit 17　Introduction to Control

safeguard	[ˈseifɡɑːd]	n.	防护措施，保护，防护
stability	[stəˈbiliti]	n.	稳定（性），稳固
steadily	[ˈstedili]	adv.	稳定地，有规则地
fluctuation	[ˌflʌktjuˈeiʃən]	n.	波动，起伏
accuracy	[ˈækjurəsi]	n.	精确（性），准确（性）
spoilage	[ˈspɔilidʒ]	n.	腐败，损坏，毁坏
manually	[ˈmænjuəli]	adv.	手工地，手动地
overflow	[ˌəuvəˈfləu]	n.	溢出，溢出物
outcome	[ˈautkʌm]	n.	结果
manipulate	[məˈnipjuleit]	v.	（熟练地）操作，使用（机器等）
demonstrate	[ˈdemənstreit]	n.	说明，演示
deviation	[ˌdiːviˈeiʃən]	n.	背离，偏离
sustained	[səsˈteind]	adj.	持续不变的，相同的
offset	[ˈɔfset]	n.	偏移量
actuator	[ˈæktjueitə]	n.	执行器，执行机构
competence	[ˈkɔmpitəns]	n.	能力，技能，称职
concentration	[ˌkɔnsənˈtreiʃən]	n.	专心，专注，集中，集结

automatic control			自动控制
process plant			工艺装置，制炼厂
control engineering			控制工程
manual system			人工系统，手工系统
inlet valve			进水阀，进气阀，入口阀
outlet valve			排气阀，出水阀，出口阀
manipulated variable			被控变量，调节量，操纵量
controlled condition			受控状态，受控条件
controlled device			受控装置
control agent			调节介质，控制介质
controlled variable			控制变量，受控变量
controlled medium			控制介质，受控媒介
set value			设定值
desired value			预定值，期待值
actual value			实际值
set point			设定点

NOTES

1. The subject of automatic control is enormous, covering the control of variables such as temperature, pressure, flow, level, and speed.

   译文：自动控制的主题是庞大的，涵盖了对许多变量的控制，如温度、压力、流量、水平和速度。

   现在分词 covering 做状语，意思是"涵盖"，such as 的意思是"例如"、"诸如"。

2. Other desirable benefits such as economy, speed, and reliability are also important, but it is against the three major parameters of safety, stability and accuracy that each control application will be measured.

   译文：诸如经济性、速度和可靠性等其他可获得的益处同样也很重要，但是控制方面的每个应用都要以安全性、稳定性和精确性这3个主要因素来衡量。

   该句由两个并列转折分句组成，后一个分句是由 that 引导的限制性定语从句，修饰"the three major parameters of safety, stability and accuracy"。

3. Specific terms are used within the control industry, primarily to avoid confusion. The same words and phrases come together in all aspects of control, and when used correctly, their meanings are universal.

   译文：在控制工业界用到了一些专门术语，主要是避免混淆。同样的语言和表达一同构成了控制的所有方面，当正确使用时，它们的含义具有普遍性。

   谓语为被动时，经常可译成主动句，把主语译成宾语，构成无主语的动宾结构。

4. Although the operator is manipulating the water level, the final aim is to generate a proper outcome, in this case, a required flow of water from the tank.

   译文：尽管操作员熟练控制着水位，但是其最终目标是获得一个正确的结果，也就是从水箱中流出的期望的水流。

EXERCISES

Ⅰ. Translate the following words into English.

1. 稳定性
2. 准确性
3. 偏离量
4. 补偿
5. 执行机构
6. 控制工程
7. 设定值
8. 实际值

Ⅱ. Complete the following sentences.

1. The plant or process must be safe to operate. _____ the plant or

process, _____ for automatic control and safeguard protocol.

2. _____ is a primary requirement in factories and buildings to prevent spoilage, increase quality and production rates, and maintain comfort. These are _____.

3. Other desirable benefits such as _____, _____, and _____ are also important, but it is against the three major parameters of _____, _____ and _____ that each control application will be measured.

4. _____ are used within the control industry, primarily to avoid confusion. The same _____ come together in all aspects of control, and when used correctly, their meanings are universal.

III. Answer the following questions according to the text.

1. After reading the text, can you tell me why plants or buildings require automatic control?
2. Can you simply analyze the principle of the control system described in Example 4.17.1 and illustrated in Figure 4.17.1 in your own words?

Supplementary Reading

Reading 17   Elements of a Temperature Control System

Example 4.17.1 depicted a simple manual level control system. This can be compared with a simple temperature control example as shown in Example 4.17.3 (manually controlled) and Fig. 4.17.3. All the previous factors and definitions apply.

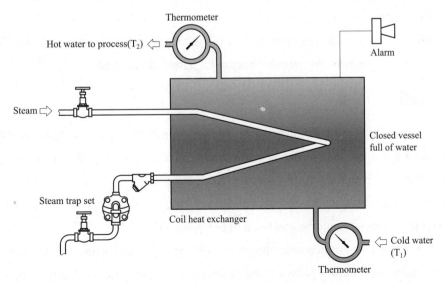

Fig. 4.17.3   A simple manual temperature control

Example 4.17.3 Depicting a simple manual temperature control system

The task is to admit sufficient steam (the heating medium) to heat the incoming water from a temperature of T_1; ensuring that hot water leaves the tank at a required temperature of T_2.

Assessing safety, stability and accuracy

Whilst manual operation could probably control the water level in Example 4.17.1, the manual control of temperature is inherently more difficult in Example 4.17.3 for various reasons.

If the flow of water varies, conditions will tend to change rapidly due to the large amount of heat held in the steam. The operator's response in changing the position of the steam valve may simply not be quick enough. Even after the valve is closed, the coil will still contain a quantity of residual steam, which will continue to give up its heat by condensing.

Anticipating change

Experience will help, but in general, the operator will not be able to anticipate change. He must observe change before making a decision and performing an action.

This and other factors, such as the inconvenience and cost of a human operator permanently on duty, potential operator error, variations in process needs, accuracy, rapid changes in conditions and the involvement of several processes, all lead to the need for automatic control.

With regards to safety, an audible alarm has been introduced in Example 4.17.3 to warn us of overtemperature—another reason for automatic control.

Automatic control

A controlled condition might be temperature, pressure, humidity, level, or flow. This means that the measuring element could be a temperature sensor, a pressure transducer or transmitter, a level detector, a humidity sensor or a flow sensor.

The manipulated variable could be steam, water, air, electricity, oil or gas, whilst the controlled device could be a valve, damper, pump or fan.

For the purposes of demonstrating the basic principles, this artical will concentrate on valves as the controlled device and temperature as the controlled condition, with temperature sensors as the measuring element.

Unit 18
Transfer Functions

Transfer Functions 翻译

A Transfer Function is the ratio of the output of a system to the input of a system, in the Laplace domain considering its initial conditions to be zero. If we have an input function of $X(s)$, and an output function $Y(s)$, we define the transfer function $H(s)$ to be:

$$H(s) = \frac{Y(s)}{X(s)}$$

Readers who have read the Circuit Theory book will recognize the transfer function as being the Laplace Transform of a circuit's impulse response.

Impulse response

For comparison, we will consider the time-domain equivalent to the above input/output relationship. In the time domain, we generally denote the input to a system as $x(t)$, and the output of the system as $y(t)$. The relationship between the input and the output is denoted as the impulse response, $h(t)$.

We define the impulse response as being the relationship between the system output and its input. We can use the following equation to define the impulse response:

$$h(t) = \frac{y(t)}{x(t)}$$

Impulse function

It would be handy at this point to define precisely what an "impulse" is. The Impulse Function, denoted with $\delta(t)$ is a special function defined piece-wise as follows:

$$\delta(t) = \begin{cases} 0 & t > 0 \\ undefined & t = 0 \\ 0 & t < 0 \end{cases}$$

The impulse function is also known as the delta function because it's denoted with the Greek lower-case letter δ. The delta function is typically graphed as an arrow towards infinity, as shown below (Fig. 4.18.1).

It is drawn as an arrow because it is difficult to show a single point at infinity in any other graphing method. Notice how the arrow only exists at location 0, and does not exist for any other time t. The delta function works with regular time shifts just like any other function. For instance, we can graph the function $\delta(t-N)$ by shifting the function $\delta(t)$ to the right, as such (Fig. 4.18.2)

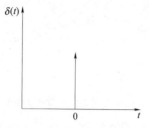

Fig. 4.18.1   The delta function   Fig. 4.18.2   The function $\delta(t-N)$

An examination of the impulse function will show that it is related to the unit-step function as follows:

$$\delta(t) = \frac{du(t)}{dt}$$

and

$$u(t) = \int \delta(t)dt$$

The impulse function is not defined at point $t=0$, but the impulse response must always satisfy the following condition, or else it is not a true impulse function:

$$\int_{-\infty}^{+\infty} \delta(t)dt = 1$$

The response of a system to an impulse input is called the impulse response. Now, to get the Laplace Transform of the impulse function, we take the derivative of the unit step function, which means we multiply the transform of the unit step function by s:

$$L[u(t)] = U(s) = \frac{1}{s}$$

$$L[\delta(t)] = sU(s) = \frac{s}{s} = 1$$

Step response

Similarly to the impulse response, the step response of a system is the output of the system when a unit step function is used as the input. The step response is a common analysis tool used to determine certain metrics about a system. Typically, when a new system is designed, the step response of the system is the first characteristic of the system to be analyzed.

Convolution

However, the impulse response cannot be used to find the system output from the system input in the same manner as the transfer function. If we have the system input and the impulse response of the system, we can calculate the system output using the convolution operation as such:

$$y(t) = h(t) * x(t)$$

Where "*" (asterisk) denotes the convolution operation. Convolution is a complicated combination of multiplication, integration and time-shifting. We can define the convolution between two functions, $a(t)$ and $b(t)$, as the following:

$$(a*b)(t) = (b*a)(t) = \int_{-\infty}^{+\infty} a(\tau)b(t-\tau)d\tau$$

This operation can be difficult to perform. Therefore, many people prefer to use the Laplace Transform (or another transform) to convert the convolution operation into a multiplication operation, through the Convolution Theorem.

Time-invariant system response

If the system in question is time-invariant, then the general description of the system can be replaced by a convolution integral of the system's impulse response and the system input. We can call this the convolution description of a system, and define it as below:

$$y(t) = x(t) * h(t) = \int_{-\infty}^{+\infty} a(\tau)b(t-\tau)d\tau$$

Convolution theorem

This method of solving for the output of a system is quite tedious, and in fact it can waste a large amount of time if you want to solve a system for a variety of input signals. Luckily, the Laplace Transform has a special property, called the Convolution Theorem, which makes the operation of convolution easier.

The Convolution Theorem can be expressed using the following equations:

$$L[f(t) * g(t)] = F(s)G(s)$$
$$L[f(t)g(t)] = F(s) * G(s)$$

This also serves as a good example of the property of Duality.

Using the transfer function

The transfer function fully describes a control system. The order, type and frequency response can all be taken from this specific function. Nyquist and Bode plots can be drawn from the open loop transfer function. These plots show the stability of the system when the loop is closed. Using the denominator of the transfer function, called the characteristic equation the roots of the system can be derived.

For all these reasons and more, the transfer function is an important aspect of classical control systems. Let's start out with the definition:

If the complex Laplace variable is s, then we generally denote the transfer function of a system as either $G(s)$ or $H(s)$. If the system input is $X(s)$, and the system output is $Y(s)$, then the transfer function can be defined as such:

$$H(s) = \frac{Y(s)}{X(s)}$$

If we know the input to a given system, and we have the transfer function of the system, we can solve for the system output by multiplying:

$$Y(s) = H(s)X(s)$$

Frequency response

The frequency response is similar to the transfer function, except that it is the relationship between the system output and input in the complex Fourier Domain, not the Laplace Domain. We can obtain the frequency response from the transfer function, by using the following change of variables:

$$s = j\omega$$

Because the frequency response and the transfer function are so closely related, typically only one is ever calculated, and the other is gained by simple variable substitution. However, despite the close relationship between the two representations, they are both useful individually, and are each used for different purposes.

TECHNICAL WORDS AND PHRASES

Laplace	[lɑːˈplɑːs]	n.	拉普拉斯
equivalent	[iˈkwivələnt]	adj.	相等的，相当的
relationship	[riˈleiʃənʃip]	n.	关系，关联性
denote	[diˈnəut]	v.	为……的符号，指示，指出
derivative	[diˈrivətiv]	n.	导数，派生物，引出物

multiply	[ˈmʌltiplai]	v.	乘,（使）相乘,（使）增加
verify	[ˈverifai]	v.	证实,核实,证明
metrics	[ˈmetriks]	n.	度量,韵律学,作诗法
convolution	[ˌkɔnvəˈljuːʃən]	n.	卷积,回旋
multiplication	[ˌmʌltipliˈkeiʃən]	n.	乘法,增殖,乘
integration	[ˌintiˈgreiʃən]	n.	综合,集成,积分
tedious	[ˈtiːdiəs]	adj.	乏味的,单调的
duality	[djuːˈæliti]	n.	二元性,对偶性
substitution	[ˌsʌbstiˈtjuːʃən]	n.	替代,替换,代入
specification	[ˌspesifiˈkeiʃən]	n.	规格
representation	[ˌreprizenˈteiʃən]	n.	表现,表示,代理
individual	[ˌindiˈvidjuəl]	adj.	个别的,单独的,个人的
purpose	[ˈpəːpəs]	n.	目的,作用,用途,效果
transfer function			传递函数
Laplace domain			拉普拉斯域
circuit theory			电路理论
Laplace Transform			拉普拉斯变换
impulse response			脉冲响应
time domain			时域
impulse function			脉冲函数
unit-step function			单位阶跃函数
step response			阶跃响应
convolution operation			卷积运算
time-shifting			时间平移
convolution theorem			卷积理论
time-invariant			时不变
Nyquist plot			奈奎斯特图
Bode plot			波特图
characteristic equation			特征方程
frequency response			频率响应
Fourier domain			傅里叶域

NOTES

1. A Transfer Function is the ratio of the output of a system to the input of a system, in the Laplace domain considering its initial conditions to be zero.

译文：传递函数是在拉普拉斯变换域内初值为零时系统的输出与输入之比值。

现在分词"considering"做状语，意思是"考虑"。

2. We take the derivative of the unit step function, which means we multiply the transform of the unit step function by *s*.

译文：我们对单位阶跃函数进行微分，这就意味着要将单位阶跃函数的拉氏变换乘以 *s*。

句中"which"引导的是非限制性定语从句。

3. Therefore, many people prefer to use the Laplace Transform (or another transform) to convert the convolution operation into a multiplication operation, through the Convolution Theorem.

译文：因此许多人更喜欢利用拉普拉斯变换，根据卷积定理将卷积运算转换成乘法运算。

"convert...into..."意思是"把……转换成……"，"Convolution Theorem"意思是"卷积定理"。

4. The frequency response is similar to the transfer function, except that it is the relationship between the system output and input in the complex Fourier Domain, not the Laplace Domain.

译文：频率响应与传递函数类似，除了是在复数傅里叶域中考虑输出与输入之间的关系，而不是拉普拉斯域内。

"except that"后加从句，表示"只是"。

EXERCISES

Ⅰ. **Translate the following words into English.**

1. 导数
2. 乘
3. 卷积
4. 替代
5. 个人的
6. 脉冲响应
7. 阶跃响应
8. 卷积理论

Ⅱ. **Complete the following sentences.**

1. Readers who have read the _____ book will recognize the transfer function as being the Laplace Transform of a circuit's _____.
2. The _____ is also known as the delta function because it's denoted with _____ δ.
3. However, the _____ cannot be used to find the system output from the system input in the same manner as the _____.

4. Because the _____ and the transfer function are so closely related, typically only one is ever calculated, and the other is gained by _____.

III. Answer the following questions according to the text.

1. After reading the text, can you tell me what Impulse Function is and how to describe it mathematically?
2. Many people prefer to use the Laplace Transform (or another transform) to convert the convolution operation into a multiplication operation, through the Convolution Theorem. Can you tell us why?

Supplementary Reading

Reading 18 Frequency Response

Frequency response is the measure of any system's output spectrum in response to an input signal. In the audible range it is usually referred to in connection with electronic amplifiers, microphones and loudspeakers. Radio spectrum frequency response can refer to measurements of coaxial cables, category cables, video switchers and wireless communications devices. Subsonic frequency response measurements can include earthquakes and electroencephalography.

Frequency response requirements differ depending on the application. In high fidelity audio, an amplifier requires a frequency response of at least 20–20,000 Hz, with a tolerance as tight as ±0.1 dB in the mid-range frequencies around 1,000 Hz, however, in telephony, a frequency response of 400–4,000 Hz, with a tolerance of ±1 dB is sufficient for intelligibility of speech.

Frequency response curves are often used to indicate the accuracy of electronic components or systems. When a system or component reproduces all desired input signals with no emphasis or attenuation of a particular frequency band, the system or component is said to be "flat," or to have a flat frequency response curve.

The frequency response is typically characterized by the magnitude of the system's response, measured in decibels (dB), and the phase, measured in radians, versus frequency. The frequency response of a system can be measured by applying a test signal, for example:

- Applying an impulse to the system and measuring its response.
- Sweeping a constant-amplitude pure tone through the bandwidth of interest and measuring the output level and phase shift relative to the input.

- Applying a signal with a wide frequency spectrum (for example, digitally-generated maximum length sequence noise, or analog filtered white noise equivalent, like pink noise), and calculating the impulse response by deconvolution of this input signal and the output signal of the system.

These typical response measurements can be plotted in two ways: by plotting the magnitude and phase measurements to obtain a Bode plot or by plotting the imaginary part of the frequency response against the real part of the frequency response to obtain a Nyquist plot.

Once a frequency response has been measured (e.g., as an impulse response), providing the system is linear and time-invariant, its characteristic can be approximated with arbitrary accuracy by a digital filter. Similarly, if a system is demonstrated to have a poor frequency response, a digital or analog filter can be applied to the signals prior to their reproduction to compensate for these deficiencies.

Frequency response measurements can be used directly to quantify system performance and design control systems. However, frequency response analysis is not suggested if the system has slow dynamics.

Unit 19
Modes of Control

Modes of Control 翻译

An automatic temperature control might consist of a valve, actuator, controller and sensor detecting the space temperature in a room. The control system is said to be "in balance" when the space temperature sensor does not register more or less temperature than that required by the control system. What happens to the control valve when the space sensor registers a change in temperature (a temperature deviation) depends on the type of control system used. The relationship between the movement of the valve and the change of temperature in the controlled medium is known as the mode of control or control action.

There are two basic modes of control:
- On/Off—The valve is either fully open or fully closed, with no intermediate state.
- Continuous—The valve can move between fully open or fully closed, or be held at any intermediate position.

On/off control

Occasionally known as two-step or two-position control, it is the most basic control mode. Considering the tank of water shown in Fig. 4.19.1, the objective is to heat the water in the tank using the energy given off a simple steam coil. In the flow pipe to the coil, a two-port valve and actuator is fitted, complete with a thermostat, placed in the water in the tank.

The thermostat is set to 60 ℃, which is the required temperature of the water in the tank. Logic dictates that if the switching point were actually at 60 ℃, the system would never operate properly, because the valve would not know whether to be open or closed at 60 ℃. From then on it could open and shut rapidly, causing wear.

For this reason, the thermostat would have an upper and lower switching point. This is essential to prevent over-rapid cycling. In this case the upper switching point might be 61 ℃ (the point at which the thermostat tells the valve to shut) and the lower switching point might be 59 ℃ (the point when the valve is told to open). Thus there is an in-built switching difference in the thermostat of ±1 ℃ about the 60 ℃ set point.

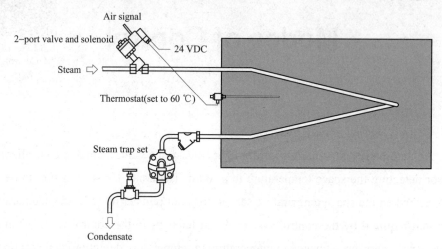

Fig. 4.19.1　The on/off temperature control of water in a tank

This 2 ℃ (±1 ℃) is known as the switching differential (This will vary between thermostats). A diagram of the switching action of the thermostat would look like the graph shown in Fig. 4.19.2. The temperature of the tank contents will fall to 59 ℃ before the valve is asked to open and will rise to 61 ℃ before the valve is instructed to close.

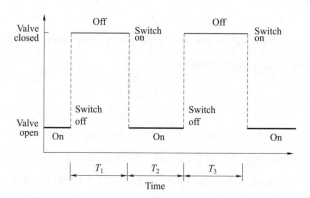

Fig. 4.19.2　The on/off switching action of the thermostat

Fig. 4.19.2 shows straight switching lines but the effect on heat transfer from coil to water will not be immediate. It will take time for the steam in the coil to affect the temperature of the water in the tank. Not only that, but the water in the tank will rise above the 61 ℃ upper limit and fall below the 59 ℃ lower limit. This can be explained by cross referencing Fig. 4.19.2 and 4.19.3.

At point A (59 ℃, Fig. 4.19.3) the thermostat switches on, directing the valve wide open. It takes time for the transfer of heat from the coil to affect the water temperature, as shown by the graph of the water temperature in Figure 4.19.3. At point B (61 ℃) the thermostat switches off and allows the valve to shut. However the coil is still full of steam, which continues to condense and give up its heat. Hence the water temperature continues to rise above the upper switching temperature, and "overshoots" at C, before eventually falling.

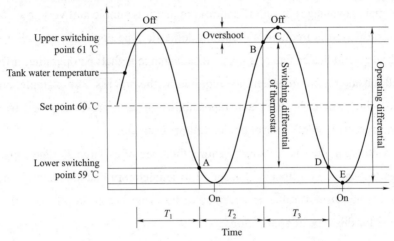

Fig. 4.19.3 The water temperature versus time curve

From this point onwards, the water temperature in the tank continues to fall until, at point D (59 ℃), the thermostat tells the valve to open. Steam is admitted through the coil but again, it takes time to have an effect and the water temperature continues to fall for a while, reaching its trough of undershoot at point E.

The difference between the peak and the trough is known as the operating differential. The switching differential of the thermostat depends on the type of the thermostat used. The operating differential depends on the characteristics of the application such as the tank, its contents, the heat transfer characteristics of the coil, the rate at which heat is transferred to the thermostat, and so on.

Essentially, with on/off control, there are upper and lower switching limits and the valve is either fully open or fully closed—there is no intermediate state.

However, controllers are available that provide a proportioning time control, in which it is possible to alter the ratio of the "on" time to the "off" time to control the controlled condition. This proportioning action occurs within a selected bandwidth around the set point; the set point being the bandwidth midpoint.

If the controlled condition is outside the bandwidth, the output signal from the controller is either fully on or fully off, acting as an on/off device. If the controlled condition is within the bandwidth, the controller output is turned on and off relative to the deviation between the value of the controlled condition and the set point.

With the controlled condition being at a set point, the ratio of "on" time to "off" time is 1:1, that is, the "on" time equals the "off" time. If the controlled condition is below the set point, the "on" time will be longer than the "off" time, whilst if above the set point, the "off" time will be longer.

The main advantages of on/off control are that it is simple and very low cost. This is the reason why it is frequently found on domestic type applications such as central heating boilers and heater fans. Its major disadvantage is that the operating differential might fall outside the control tolerance required by the process. For example, on a food production line, where the taste and repeatability of taste are determined by precise temperature control, on/off control could well be unsuitable.

By contrast, in the case of space heating there are often large storage capacities (a large area to heat or cool that will respond to temperature change slowly) and slight variation in the desired value is acceptable. In many cases on/off control is quite appropriate for this type of application.

If on/off control is unsuitable because more accurate temperature control is required, the next option will be continuous control.

Continuous control

Continuous control is often called modulating control. It means that the valve is capable of moving continually to change the degree of valve opening or closing. It does not just move to either fully open or fully close, as with on-off control.

There are three basic control actions that are often applied to continuous control:

- Proportional (P);
- Integral (I);
- Derivative (D).

It is also necessary to consider these in combination such as P + I, P + D, P + I + D. Although it is possible to combine the different actions, and all help to produce the required response, it is important to remember that both the integral and derivative actions are usually corrective functions of a basic proportional control action.

TECHNICAL WORDS AND PHRASES

valve	[vælv]	n.	阀，真空管
intermediate	[ˌintəˈmiːdjət]	adj.	中间的，中级的
continuous	[kənˈtinjuəs]	adj.	连续的，没有中断的

occasionally	[ə'keiʒənəli]	adv.	有时候，偶尔
objective	[əb'dʒektiv]	n.	目标，目的
thermostat	['θə:məstæt]	n.	恒温（调节）器
dictate	[dik'teit]	v.	指示，指定，指令
upper	['ʌpə]	adj.	上的，上面的，较高的
condense	[kən'dens]	v.	缩合，凝聚，压缩
overshoot	[ˌəuvə'ʃu:t]	n.&v.	超过，超调量，超调
bandwidth	['bændwidθ]	n.	带宽，频宽，误差
combination	[ˌkɔmbi'neiʃən]	n.	合作，结合，组合
on/off control			开/关控制
continuous control			连续控制
in balance			平衡
control action			控制作用，控制动作
two-step control			双级控制
two-position control			双位调节，双位控制
in-built			内置的，固定的，嵌入的
give up			放弃，认输，猜不出
operating differential			运行误差
by contrast			相比之下
modulating control			调幅控制，调节控制

NOTES

1. An automatic temperature control might consist of a valve, actuator, controller and sensor detecting the space temperature in a room.

   译文：一个自动温度控制系统可能是由阀、执行器、控制器和用来检测房间内温度的传感器组成的。

   "consist of" 在句子中虽然从句型上看是主动语态，但在翻译的时候一般翻译成被动语态。

2. With the controlled condition being at a set point, the ratio of "on" time to "off" time is 1:1, that is, the "on" time equals the "off" time.

   译文：如果控制状态处于设定点，"开" 时间与 "关" 时间的比值为 1:1。也就是说，"开" 时间等于 "关" 时间。

   句中 "that is" 翻译成 "也就是说"。

3. The main advantages of on/off control are that it is simple and very low cost. This is the reason why it is frequently found on domestic type applications such as central

heating boilers and heater fans.

译文：开/关控制的主要优点是简单和成本低，这就是为什么其频繁地出现在一些典型家庭应用中，如中央暖气系统和加热炉。

第一句中"that"引导的是表语从句，第二句中"why"引导的是定语从句。

4. Although it is possible to combine the different actions, and all help to produce the required response, it is important to remember that both the integral and derivative actions are usually corrective functions of a basic proportional control action.

译文：尽管有可能组合得到不同的功能，所有的都是为了产生期望的响应，然而重要的是要记住积分和微分两者作用通常要与基本的比例控制作用相关。

EXERCISES

Ⅰ. **Translate the following words into English.**

1. 连续的
2. 恒温器
3. 超调量
4. 频宽
5. 连续控制
6. 双级控制
7. 运行误差
8. 调幅控制

Ⅱ. **Complete the following sentences.**

1. An automatic temperature control might consist of a _____, _____, _____ and sensor detecting the space temperature in a room.
2. Occasionally known as _____ or _____, on/off control is the most basic control mode.
3. The difference between the peak and the trough is known as the _____.
4. If the controlled condition is outside the _____, the output signal from the controller is either fully on or fully off, acting as _____.

Ⅲ. **Translate the following sentences into Chinese.**

1. The control system is said to be "in balance" when the space temperature sensor does not register more or less temperature than that required by the control system.
2. The operating differential depends on the characteristics of the application such as the tank, its contents, the heat transfer characteristics of the coil, the rate at which heat is transferred to the thermostat, and so on.
3. However, controllers are available that provide a proportioning time control, in which it is possible to alter the ratio of the "on" time to the "off" time to control the controlled condition.

4. For example, on a food production line, where the taste and repeatability of taste are determined by precise temperature control, on/off control could well be unsuitable.

Supplementary Reading

Reading 19   Robust Control

Robust control is a branch of control theory that explicitly deals with uncertainty in its approach to controller design. Robust control methods are designed to function properly so long as uncertain parameters or disturbances are within some (typically compact) set. Robust methods aim to achieve robust performance and/or stability in the presence of bounded modelling errors.

The early methods of Bode and others were fairly robust; the state-space methods invented in the 1960s and 1970s were sometimes found to lack robustness, prompting research to improve them. This was the start of the theory of Robust Control, which took shape in the 1980s and 1990s and is still active today.

In contrast with an adaptive control policy, a robust control policy is static; rather than adapting to measurements of variations, the controller is designed to work assuming that certain variables will be unknown but, for example, bounded.

When is a control method said to be robust

Informally, a controller designed for a particular set of parameters is said to be robust if it would also work well under a different set of assumptions. High-gain feedback is a simple example of a robust control method; with sufficiently high gain, the effect of any parameter variations will be negligible. High-gain feedback is the principle that allows simplified models of operational amplifiers and emitter-degenerated bipolar transistors to be used in a variety of different settings. This idea was already well understood by Bode and Black in 1927.

The modern theory of robust control

The theory of robust control began in the late 1970s and early 1980s and soon developed a number of techniques for dealing with bounded system uncertainty.

Probably the most important example of a robust control technique is H-infinity loop-shaping, which was developed by Duncan McFarlane and Keith Glover of Cambridge University; this method minimizes the sensitivity of a system over its frequency spectrum, and this guarantees that the system will not greatly deviate from expected trajectories when disturbances enter the system.

Another example is LQG/LTR, which was developed to overcome the robustness problems of LQG control.

Unit 20

Control Loops

Control Loops 翻译

Open loop control systems

Open loop control simply means there is no direct feedback from the controlled condition; in other words, no information is sent back from the process or system under control to advise the controller that corrective action is required. The heating system shown in Fig. 4.20.1 demonstrates this by using a sensor outside of the room being heated. The system shown in Fig. 4.20.1 is not an example of a practical heating control system; it is simply being used to depict the principle of open loop control.

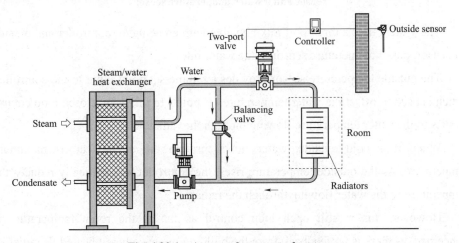

Fig. 4.20.1 An open loop control system

The system consists of a proportional controller with an outside sensor sensing ambient air temperature. The controller might be set with a fairly large proportional band, such that at an ambient temperature of −1 ℃ the valve is full open, and at an ambient of 19 ℃ the valve is fully closed. As the ambient temperature will have an effect on the heat loss from the building, it is hoped that the room temperature will be controlled.

However, there is no feedback regarding the room temperature and heating due to other factors. In mild weather, although the flow of water is being controlled, other factors, such as high solar gain, might cause the room to overheat. In other words, open control tends only to provide a coarse control of the application. Fig. 4.20.2 depicts a slightly more sophisticated control system with two sensors.

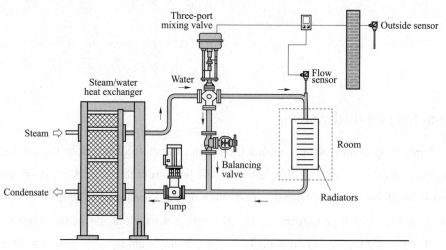

Fig. 4.20.2   An open loop control system with an outside temperature sensor and a water temperature sensor

The system uses a three-port mixing valve with an actuator, controller and outside air sensor, plus a temperature sensor in the water line.

The outside temperature sensor provides a remote set point input to the controller, which is used to offset the water temperature set point. In this way, closed loop control applies to the water temperature flowing through the radiators.

When it is cold outside, water flows through the radiator at its maximum temperature. As the outside temperature rises, the controller automatically reduces the temperature of the water flowing through the radiators.

However, this is still open loop control as far as the room temperature is concerned, as there is no feedback from the building or space being heated. If radiators are oversized or design errors have occurred, overheating will still occur.

Closed loop control

Quite simply, closed loop control requires feedback; information is sent back directly from the process or system. Using the simple heating system shown in Fig. 4.20.3, the addition of an internal space temperature sensor will detect the room temperature and provide closed loop control with respect to the room.

In Fig. 4.20.3, the valve and actuator are controlled via a space temperature sensor in the room, providing feedback from the actual room temperature.

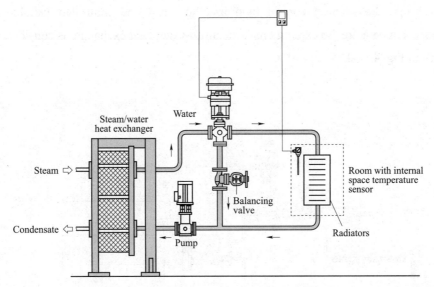

Fig. 4.20.3   A closed loop control system with a sensor for internal space temperature

Disturbance

Disturbance factors usually exist, which enter the process or system to upset the value of the controlled medium. These disturbance factors can be caused by changes in load or by outside influence.

For example, if in a simple heating system, a room was suddenly filled with people, this would constitute a disturbance factor, since it would affect the temperature of the room and the amount of heat required to maintain the desired space temperature.

Feedback control

This is another type of closed loop control. Feedback control takes account of disturbance factors and feeds this information back to the controller, to allow corrective action to be taken. For example, if a large number of people enter a room, the space temperature will increase, which will then cause the control system to reduce the heat input to the room.

Feed-forward control

With feed-forward control, the effects of any disturbance are anticipated and allowed for before the event actually takes place.

Single loop control

This is the simplest control loop involving just one controlled variable, for instance, temperature. To explain this, a steam-to-water heat exchanger is considered as shown in Fig. 4.20.4.

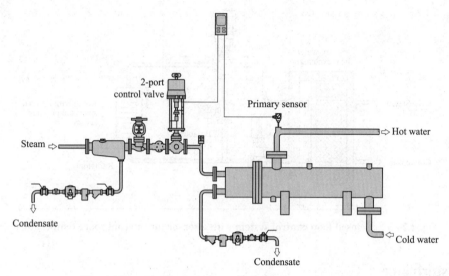

Fig. 4.20.4　The single loop control on a heating calorifier

The only one variable controlled in Fig. 4.20.4 is the temperature of the water leaving the heat exchanger. This is achieved by controlling the 2-port steam valve supplying steam to the heat exchanger. The primary sensor may be a thermocouple or PT100 platinum resistance thermometer sensing the water temperature.

The controller compares the signal from the sensor with the set point on the controller. If there is a difference, the controller sends a signal to the actuator of the valve, which in turn moves the valve to a new position. The controller may also include an output indicator, which shows the percentage of valve opening.

Single control loops provide the vast majority of control for heating systems and industrial processes.

Other terms used for single control loops include:
- Set value control;
- Single closed loop control;
- Feedback control;
- Multi-loop control.

The following example considers an application for a slow moving timber-based product, which must be controlled to a specific humidity level (Fig. 4.20.5 and

Fig. 4.20.6).

In Fig. 4.20.5, the single humidity sensor at the end of the conveyor controls the amount of heat added by the furnace. But if the water spray rate changes due to, for instance, fluctuations in the water supply pressure, it may take perhaps 10 minutes before the product reaches the far end of the conveyor and the humidity sensor reacts. This will cause variations in product quality.

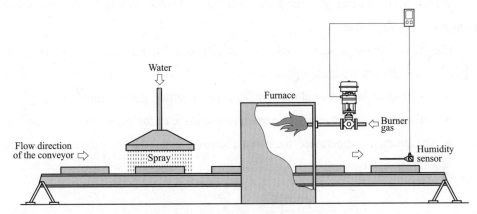

Fig. 4.20.5   The single humidity sensor

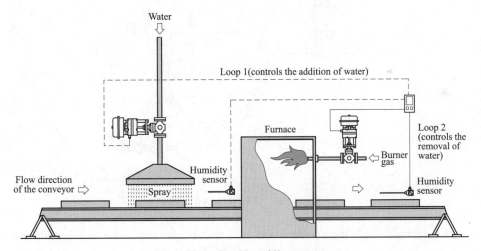

Fig. 4.20.6   Dual humidity sensors

To improve the control, a second humidity sensor on another control loop can be installed immediately after the water spray, as shown in Fig. 4.20.6. This humidity sensor provides a remote set point input to the controller which is used to offset the local set point. The local set point is set at the required humidity after the furnace. This, in a simple form, illustrates multi-loop control.

This humidity control system consists of two control loops:
- Loop 1 controls the addition of water.

- Loop 2 controls the removal of water.

Within this process, factors will influence both loops. Some factors such as water pressure will affect both loops. Loop 1 will try to correct for this, but any resulted error will have an impact on Loop 2.

Cascade control

Where two independent variables need to be controlled with one valve, a cascade control system may be used.

Fig. 4.20.7 shows a steam jacketed vessel full of liquid product. The essential aspects of the process are quite rigorous:

- The product in the vessel must be heated to a certain temperature.
- The steam must not exceed a certain temperature or the product may be spoiled.
- The product temperature must not increase faster than a certain rate or the product may be spoiled.

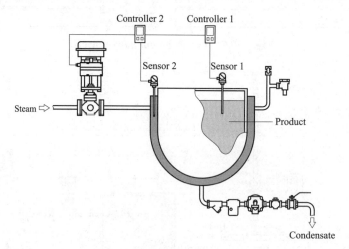

Fig. 4.20.7 The jacketed vessel

If a normal, single loop control was used with the sensor in the liquid, at the start of the process the sensor would detect a low temperature, and the controller would signal the valve to move to the fully open position. This would result in a problem caused by an excessive steam temperature in the jacket.

The solution is to use a cascade control using two controllers and two sensors:

- A slave controller (Controller 2) and sensor monitoring the steam temperature in the jacket, and outputting a signal to the control valve.
- A master controller (Controller 1) and sensor monitoring the product

temperature with the controller output directed to the slave controller.

The output signal from the master controller is used to vary the set point in the slave controller, ensuring that the steam temperature is not exceeded.

An example of cascade control applied to a process vessel

The liquid temperature is to be heated from 15 ℃ to 80 ℃ and maintained at 80 ℃ for two hours. The steam temperature cannot exceed 120 ℃ under any circumstance.

The product temperature must not increase faster than 1 ℃/minute.

The master controller can be ramped so that the rate of increase in water temperature is not higher than that specified.

The master controller is set in reverse acting mode, so that its output signal to the slave controller is 20 mA at low temperature and 4 mA at high temperature.

The remote set point on the slave controller is set so that its output signal to the valve is 4 mA when the steam temperature is 80 ℃ and 20 mA when the steam temperature is 120 ℃.

In this way, the temperature of the steam cannot be higher than that tolerated by the system, and the steam pressure in the jacket cannot be higher than the saturation pressure at 120 ℃.

TECHNICAL WORDS AND PHRASES

corrective	[kəˈrektiv]	adj.	有改正作用的，矫正的
demonstrate	[ˈdemənstreit]	v.	说明，演示，论证
depict	[diˈpikt]	v.	描绘，描画，描述
proportional	[prəˈpɔːʃənəl]	adj.	比例的，成比例的
ambient	[ˈæmbiənt]	adj.	周围的，包围着的
coarse	[kɔːs]	adj.	粗糙的，粗野的
sophisticated	[səˈfistikeitid]	adj.	老练的，精密的，高雅的
disturbance	[disˈtəːbəns]	n.	打扰，扰乱，困扰
anticipate	[ænˈtisipeit]	v.	预感，期望
exchanger	[iksˈtʃeindʒə]	n.	交换器
platinum	[ˈplætinəm]	n.	铂，白金
percentage	[pəˈsentidʒ]	n.	百分比，百分率，比例
conveyor	[kənˈveiə]	n.	输送机，传送机，传送带
rigorous	[ˈrigərəs]	adj.	严密的，缜密的，严格的
circumstance	[ˈsəːkəmstəns]	n.	环境，条件，情况

control loop	控制回路
open loop control	开环回路控制
consist of	由……组成，包含
closed loop control	闭环回路控制
with respect to	关于，就……而言
feedback control	反馈控制
feed-forward control	前馈控制
take place	发生，产生
single loop control	单回路控制
set value control	给定值控制
single closed loop control	单闭回路控制
multi-loop control	多回路控制
cascade control	串级控制

NOTES

1. Open loop control simply means there is no direct feedback from the controlled condition; in other words, no information is sent back from the process or system under control to advise the controller that corrective action is required.

   译文：简单地说，开环控制表示没有来自控制状态处的直接反馈。换句话说，被控过程或系统没有反馈回信息给控制器，以指引控制器做出所期望的纠正行为。

   "in other words" 意思是 "换句话说"。

2. However, this is still open loop control as far as the room temperature is concerned, as there is no feedback from the building or space being heated.

   译文：然而，就房间温度来讲，该系统依然是开环控制，因为没有来自房间或供暖空间的反馈。

   "as far as sth. is concerned" 意思是 "就……而言"。句中的第三个 "as" 引导的是原因状语从句。

3. The output signal from the master controller is used to vary the set point in the slave controller, ensuring that the steam temperature is not exceeded.

   译文：来自主控制器的输出信号用来改变从属控制器的设定点，保证蒸汽温度不过量。

   现在分词 "ensuring" 做状语。"that" 引导了一个宾语从句。

4. The master controller is set in reverse acting mode, so that its output signal to the slave controller is 20 mA at low temperature and 4 mA at high temperature.

   译文：主控制器设置成反向行动模式，所以它对从属控制器的输出信号在低温时为 20 毫安，而在高温时为 4 毫安。

EXERCISES

Ⅰ. Translate the following words into English.
1. 演示
2. 老练的
3. 干扰
4. 开环回路控制
5. 闭环回路控制
6. 单回路控制
7. 多回路控制
8. 串级控制

Ⅱ. Complete the following sentences.
1. Quite simply, closed loop control requires _____; information is sent back direct from _____.
2. _____ are factors, which enter the process or system to upset the value of the _____.
3. Feedback control _____ disturbance factors and feeds this information back to the controller, to allow _____ to be taken.
4. Where two independent variables need to be controlled with one valve, a _____ system may be used.

Ⅲ. Answer the following questions according to the text.
1. What is the difference between the open loop control system and the closed loop control system?
2. What is cascade control? Why do we use it?

Supplementary Reading

Reading 20　Main Control Strategies

Every control system must guarantee first the stability of the closed-loop behavior. For linear systems, this can be obtained by directly placing the poles. Non-linear control systems use specific theories (normally based on Aleksandr Lyapunov's Theory) to ensure stability without regard to the inner dynamics of the system. The possibility to fulfill different specifications varies from the model considered and the control strategy chosen. Here a summary list of the main control techniques is shown:

Adaptive control

Adaptive control uses on-line identification of the process parameters, or modification of controller gains, thereby obtaining strong robustness properties. Adaptive control was applied for the first time in the aerospace industry in the 1950s, and has found particular success in that field.

Hierarchical control

A hierarchical control system is a type of control system in which a set of devices and governing software are arranged in a hierarchical tree. When the links in the tree are implemented by a computer network, then that hierarchical control system is also a form of networked control system.

Intelligent control

Intelligent control uses various AI computing approaches like neural networks, Bayesian probability, fuzzy logic, machine learning, evolutionary computation and genetic algorithms to control a dynamic system.

Optimal control

Optimal control is a particular control technique in which the control signal optimizes a certain "cost index": For example, in the case of a satellite, the jet thrust needed brings it to the desired trajectory that consumes the least amount of fuel. Two optimal control design methods have been widely used in industrial applications, as it has been shown they can guarantee closed-loop stability. These are Model Predictive Control (MPC) and Linear-Quadratic-Gaussian control (LQG). First of all, we should more explicitly take into account constraints on the signals in the system, which is an important feature in many industrial processes. However, the "optimal control" structure in MPC is only a means to achieve such a result that it does not optimize a true performance index of the closed-loop control system. Together with PID controllers, MPC systems are the most widely used control technique in process control.

Robust control

Robust control deals explicitly with uncertainty in its approach to controller design. Controllers designed using robust control methods tend to be able to cope with small differences between the true system and the nominal model used for design. The early methods of Bode and others were fairly robust; the state-space methods invented in 1960s and 1970s were sometimes found to lack robustness. A modern example of a robust control technique is H-infinity loop-shaping developed by Duncan McFarlane and Keith Glover of Cambridge University, the United Kingdom. Robust methods aim to achieve robust performance and/or stability in the presence of small modeling errors.

Stochastic control

Stochastic control deals with control design with uncertainty in the model. In typical stochastic control problems, it is assumed that there exist random noise and disturbances in the model and the controller, and the control design must take into account these random deviations.

Unit 21
PID Controller

PID Controller
翻译

The PID control scheme is named after its three correcting terms, whose sum constitutes the manipulated variable (*MV*). Hence:

$$MV(t) = P_{out} + I_{out} + D_{out}$$

where P_{out}, I_{out}, and D_{out} are the contributions to the output from the PID controller from each of the three terms, as defined below.

Proportional terms

The proportional term makes a change to the output that is proportional to the current error value. The proportional response can be adjusted by multiplying the error by a constant K_p, called the proportional gain.

The proportional term is given by:

$$P_{out} = K_p e(t)$$

where

- P_{out} : Proportional output;
- K_p : Proportional gain, a tuning parameter;
- e : Error;
- t : Time or instantaneous time (the present).

A high proportional gain results in a large change in the output for a given change in the error. If the proportional gain is too high, the system can become unstable. In contrast, a small gain results in a small output response to a large input error. If the proportional gain is too low, the control action may be too small when responding to the system disturbance.

In the absence of disturbance, pure proportional control will not settle at its target value, but will retain a steady state error that is a function of the proportional gain and the process gain. Despite the steady-state offset, both tuning theory and industrial practice indicate that it is the proportional term that should contribute the bulk of the output change.

Integral terms

The contribution from the integral term is proportional to both the magnitude of the error and the duration of the error. Summing the instantaneous error over time (integrating the error) gives the accumulated offset that should have been corrected previously. The accumulated error is then multiplied by the integral gain and added to the controller output. The magnitude of the contribution of the integral term to the overall control action is determined by the integral gain K_i.

The integral term is given by:

$$I_{out} = K_i \int_0^t e(t)dt$$

where

- I_{out}: Integral output;
- K_i: Integral gain, a tuning parameter;
- e: Error = $SP-PV$;
- t: Time in the past contributing to the integral response.

The integral term (when added to the proportional term) accelerates the movement of the process towards setpoint and eliminates the residual steady-state error that occurs with a proportional only controller. However, since the integral term is responding to accumulated errors from the past, it can cause the present value to overshoot the setpoint value (cross over the setpoint and then create a deviation in the other direction).

Derivative terms

The rate of change of the process error is calculated by determining the slope of the error over time (i.e. its first derivative with respect to time) and multiplying this rate of change by the derivative gain K_d. The magnitude of the contribution of the derivative term to the overall control action is termed the derivative gain K_d.

The derivative term is given by:

$$D_{out} = K_d \frac{de}{dt}$$

where

- D_{out}: Derivative output;
- K_d: Derivative gain, a tuning parameter;
- e: Error = $SP-PV$;
- t: Time or instantaneous time (the present).

The derivative term slows the rate of change of the controller output and this effect is most noticeably close to the controller setpoint. Hence, derivative control is used to reduce the magnitude of the overshoot produced by the integral component and improve the combined controller-process stability. However, differentiation of a signal amplifies noise and thus this term in the controller is highly sensitive to noise in the error term, and can cause a process to become unstable if the noise and the derivative gain are sufficiently large.

Summary

The outputs from the three terms, the proportional, the integral and the derivative terms are summed to calculate the output of the PID controller. Defining $u(t)$ as the controller output, the final form of the PID algorithm is:

$$u(t) = MV(t) = K_p e(t) + K_i \int_0^t e(t)\mathrm{d}t + K_d \frac{\mathrm{d}e}{\mathrm{d}t}$$

and the tuning parameters are:

(1) K_p: Proportional gain—Larger K_p typically means faster response since the larger the error is, the larger the proportional term compensation will be. An excessively large proportional gain will lead to process instability and oscillation.

(2) K_i: Integral gain—Larger K_i implies steady state errors are eliminated quicker. The trade-off is larger overshoot: Any negative error integrated during transient response must be integrated away by positive error before we reach a steady state.

(3) K_d: Derivative gain—larger K_d decreases overshoot, but slows down transient response and may lead to instability due to signal noise amplification in the differentiation of the error.

TECHNICAL WORDS AND PHRASES

scheme	[skiːm]	n.	策划，图谋，计划，方案
constitute	['kɔnstitjut]	v.	构成，组成，建立
contribution	[ˌkɔntri'bjuːʃən]	n.	捐助物，贡献
response	[ri'spɔns]	n.	反应，响应
adjust	[ə'dʒʌst]	n.	调整，校正
instantaneous	[ˌinstən'teinjəs]	adj.	瞬间发生的，即刻的
respond	[ri'spɔnd]	v.	回答，回报，响应
settle	['setl]	v.	安排，安放，安家，定居
bulk	[bʌlk]	v.&n.	变得越来越大；大小，体积
magnitude	['mægnitjuːd]	n.	幅度，幅值，巨大，重要性
duration	[djuə'reiʃən]	n.	持续，持续的时间，期间

Unit 21 PID Controller

accumulate	[əˈkjuːmjuleit]	v.	堆积，积累
overall	[ˈəuvərɔːl]	v.	总体的，全面的，综合的
overshoot	[ˌəuvəˈʃuːt]	v.&n.	超过；超调量
derivative	[diˈrivətiv]	n.	派生物，引出物，导数
differentiation	[ˌdifəˌrenʃiˈeiʃən]	n	区别，分化，微分
oscillation	[ˌɔsiˈleiʃən]	n.	摆动，振动
in contrast			相比之下
in the absence of			缺乏，不存在
trade-off			交换，协定，交易，权衡
transient response			瞬态响应，动态响应
steady state			稳定状态

NOTES

1. The PID control scheme is named after its three correcting terms, whose sum constitutes the manipulated variable (*MV*).

   译文：PID 控制器是根据其 3 个恰当的关系来命名的，其总和由操纵变量组成。"is named after" 意思是 "以……命名"。"whose" 是关系代词 who 的所有格，引导一个定语从句，在从句中做定语。

2. In the absence of disturbance, pure proportional control will not settle at its target value, but will retain a steady state error that is a function of the proportional gain and the process gain.

   译文：当不存在干扰时，纯比例控制不会获得其目标值，但将会保持一个稳态误差，其值取决于比例增益和过程增益。

3. However, since the integral term is responding to accumulated errors from the past, it can cause the present value to overshoot the setpoint value.

   译文：尽管如此，对信号进行微分放大了噪声，因而控制器中的此关系对噪声高度敏感。噪声和微分增益十分大，可能导致过程变得不稳定。

4. The trade-off is larger overshoot: Any negative error integrated during transient response must be integrated away by positive error before we reach a steady state.

   译文：其代价是超调量更大。在瞬态响应过程中，在达到稳态之前，积分产生的任何负误差都必须被整合成正误差。

EXERCISES

Ⅰ. **Translate the following words into Chinese.**

1. response   2. magnitude

3. duration
4. overshoot
5. derivative
6. differentiation
7. transient response
8. steady state

II. Complete the following sentences.

1. _____ makes a change to the output that is proportional to the current error value.
2. In contrast, a small gain results in a small output response to _____. If the proportional gain is too low, _____ may be too small when responding to the system disturbance.
3. The integral term accelerates the movement of the process towards _____ and eliminates _____ that occurs with a proportional only controller.
4. The outputs from the three terms, the _____, the _____ and the _____ terms are summed to calculate the output of the PID controller.

III. Translate the following text.

Control engineering is the engineering discipline that focuses on mathematical modeling of systems of a diverse nature, analyzing their dynamic behavior, and using control theory to create a controller that will cause the systems to behave in a desired manner.

Modern control engineering is closely related to electrical, electronic and computer engineering, as electronic circuits can often be easily described using control theory techniques. At many universities, control engineering courses are primarily taught by electrical or electronics faculty members; in others it is connected to computer science, as most control techniques today are implemented through computers, often as embedded systems (as in the automotive field). Previous to modern electronics, process control devices were devised by mechanical engineers using mechanical feedback along with pneumatic and hydraulic control devices, some of which are still in use today.

Supplementary Reading

Reading 21 Control Engineering

Control engineering is the engineering discipline that focuses on mathematical modeling of systems of a diverse nature, analyzing their dynamic behavior, and using control theory to create a controller that will cause the systems to behave in a desired manner.

Modern control engineering is closely related to electrical, electronic and computer engineering, as electronic circuits can often be easily described using control theory techniques. At many universities, control engineering courses are primarily taught by electrical or electronics faculty members; in others it is connected to computer science, as most control techniques today are implemented through computers, often as embedded systems (as in the automotive field). Previous to modern electronics, process control devices were devised by mechanical engineers using mechanical feedback along with pneumatic and hydraulic control devices, some of which are still in use today.

The field of control within chemical engineering is often known as process control. It deals primarily with the control of variables in a chemical process in a plant. It is taught as part of the undergraduate curriculum of any chemical engineering program, and employs many of the same principles in control engineering.

Other engineering disciplines also overlap with control engineering, as it can be applied to any system for which a suitable model can be derived.

Control engineering has diversified applications that include science, finance management, and even human behaviour. Students of control engineering may start with a linear control system course which requires elementary mathematics and Laplace Transforms (called classical control theory). In linear control, the student does frequency and time domain analysis. Digital control and nonlinear control courses require Z Transformations and algebra respectively, and could be said to complete a basic control education. From here onwards there are several sub branches.

Control engineering is the engineering discipline that focuses on the modelling of a diverse range of dynamic systems (e.g. mechanical systems) and the design of controllers that will cause these systems to behave in the desired manner. Although such controllers need not be electrical, many are and hence control engineering is often viewed as a subfield of electrical engineering. However, the falling price of microprocessors is making the actual implementation of a control system essentially trivial. As a result, focus is shifting back to the mechanical engineering discipline, as intimate knowledge of the physical system being controlled is often desired.

Electrical circuits, digital signal processors and microcontrollers can all be used to implement control systems. Control engineering has a wide range of applications from the flight and propulsion systems of commercial airliners to the cruise control present in many modern automobiles.

In most of the cases, control engineers utilize feedback when designing control systems. For example, in an automobile with cruise control the vehicle's speed is continuously monitored and fed back to the system which adjusts the motor's torque accordingly. Where there is regular feedback, control theory can be used to determine how the system responds to such feedback. In practically all such systems stability is important and control theory can help ensure stability is achieved.

Although feedback is an important aspect of control engineering, control engineers may also work on the control of systems without feedback. This is known as open loop control. A classic example of open loop control is a washing machine that runs through a pre-determined cycle without the use of sensors.

Chapter 5
Process Control Systems

Unit 22
Importance of Process Control

Importance of
Process Control
翻译

Control in process industries refers to the regulation of all aspects of the process. Precise control of level, temperature, pressure and flow is important in many process applications. Refining, combining, handling, and otherwise manipulating fluids to profitably produce end products can be a precise, demanding, and potentially hazardous process. Small changes in a process can have a large impact on the end result. Variations in proportions, temperature, flow, turbulence, and many other factors must be carefully and consistently controlled to produce the desired end product with a minimum of raw materials and energy. Process control technology is the tool that enables manufacturers to keep their operations running within specified limits and to set more precise limits to maximize profitability, ensure quality and safety.

Process

Process as used in the terms process control and process industry, refers to the methods of changing or refining raw materials to create end products. The raw materials, which either pass through or remain in a liquid, gaseous, or slurry (a mix of solids and liquids) state during the process, are transferred, measured, mixed, heated or cooled, filtered, stored, or handled in some other ways to produce the end product.

Process industries include the chemical industry, the oil and gas industry, the food and beverage industry, the pharmaceutical industry, the water treatment industry, and the power industry.

Process control

Process control refers to the methods that are used to control process variables when we manufacture a product. For example, factors such as the proportion of one ingredient to another, the temperature of the materials, how well the ingredients are mixed, and the pressure under which the materials are held can significantly impact the quality of an end product. Manufacturers control the production process for three reasons:

- Reduce variability;
- Increase efficiency;
- Ensure safety.

Reduce variability

Process control can reduce variability in the end product, which ensures a consistently high-quality product. Manufacturers can also save money by reducing variability. For example, in a gasoline blending process, as many as 12 or more different components may be blended to make a specific grade of gasoline. If the refinery does not have precise control over the flow of the separate components, the gasoline may get too many of the high-octane components. As a result, customers would receive a higher grade and more expensive gasoline than they paid for, and the refinery would lose money. The opposite situation would be customers receiving a lower grade at a higher price.

With accurate, dependable process control, the setpoint (desired or optimal point) can be moved closer to the actual product specification and thus save the manufacturer money.

Increase efficiency

Some processes need to be maintained at a specific point to maximize efficiency. For example, a control point might be the temperature at which a chemical reaction takes place. Accurate control of temperature ensures process efficiency. Manufacturers save money by minimizing the resources required to produce the end product.

Ensure safety

A run-away process, such as an out-of-control nuclear or chemical reaction, may result if manufacturers do not maintain precise control of all of the process variables. The consequences of a run-away process can be catastrophic. Precise process control may also be required to ensure safety. For example, maintaining proper boiler pressure by controlling the inflow of air used in combustion and the outflow of exhaust gases is crucial in preventing boiler implosions that can clearly threaten the safety of workers.

In process systems a commonly used control device called a programmable logic controller, or a PLC, is used to read a set of digital and analog inputs, apply a set of logic statements, and generate a set of analog and digital outputs. For example, the room temperature would be an input to the PLC. The logical statements would compare the setpoint with the input temperature and determine whether more or less heating was necessary to keep the temperature constant. A PLC output would then either open or close the hot water valve, an incremental amount, depending on whether more or less hot water was needed. Larger more complex systems can be controlled by a Distributed Control System (DCS) or SCADA system.

In practice, process control systems can be characterized as one or more of the following forms:

- Discrete—Found in many manufacturing, motion and packaging applications. Robotic assembly, such as that found in automotive production, can be characterized as discrete process control. Most discrete manufacturing involves the production of discrete pieces of product, such as metal stamping.
- Batch—Some applications require that specific quantities of raw materials be combined in specific ways for particular durations to produce an intermediate or end result. One example is the production of adhesives and glues, which normally require the mixing of raw materials in a heated vessel for a period of time to form a quantity of end products. Other important examples are the production of food, beverages and medicine. Batch processes are generally used to produce a relatively low to intermediate quantity of products per year (a few pounds to millions of pounds).
- Continuous—Often, a physical system is represented through variables that are smooth and uninterrupted in time. The control of the water temperature in a heating jacket, for example, is an example of continuous process control. Some important continuous processes are the production of fuels, chemicals and plastics. Continuous processes, in manufacturing, are used to produce very large quantities of products per year(millions to billions of pounds).

TECHNICAL WORDS AND PHRASES

refine	[ri'fain]	v.	精炼，精制，使纯净
profitable	['prɔfitəbl]	adj.	有利可图的，有益的
hazardous	['hæzədəs]	adj.	冒险的，有危险的，有害的
turbulence	['tə:bjuləns]	n.	扰动，湍流
manufacturer	[ˌmænju'fæktʃərə]	n.	制造商，制造厂
gaseous	['geisjəs]	adj.	气态的，似气体的

slurry	[ˈslə:ri]	n.	泥浆，浆
beverage	[ˈbevəridʒ]	n.	饮料
pharmaceutical	[ˌfɑ:məˈsju:tikəl]	adj.&n.	制药的；药品，制药学
ingredient	[inˈgri:djənt]	n.	成分，因素
consequence	[ˈkɔnsikwəns]	n.	结果，后果
catastrophic	[ˌkætəˈstrɔfik]	adj.	悲惨的，灾难的
combustion	[kəmˈbʌstʃən]	n.	燃烧，烧毁，氧化
exhaust	[igˈzɔ:st]	v.	弄空，取出，使非常疲倦
process control			过程控制
chemical industry			化学工业
run-away process			失稳过程
programmable logic controller			可编程逻辑控制器
distributed control system			集散控制系统
discrete process control			离散过程控制
continuous process control			连续过程控制

NOTES

1. Process control technology is the tool that enables manufacturers to keep their operations running within specified limits and to set more precise limits to maximize profitability, ensure quality and safety.

   译文：过程控制技术是一种工具，使制造商能够在规定的范围内保持运转，并设置更精确的限制，以最大限度地提高营利能力，确保质量和安全。

   句中"that"引导的是限制性定语从句，修饰"tool"。

2. Process as used in the terms process control and process industry, refers to the methods of changing or refining raw materials to create end products.

   译文：过程被用在术语（过程控制和过程工业）中，指的是对原材料进行改变和精炼，创造终端产品的方法。

3. The raw materials, which either pass through or remain in a liquid, gaseous, or slurry state during the process, are transferred, measured, mixed, heated or cooled, filtered, stored, or handled in some other ways to produce the end product.

   译文：在整个过程中，原材料或在液态、气态，或浆料状态之间变化，或就处于其中的某一状态，对它们进行传输、测量、混合、加热，或冷却、过滤、储存，或者经过某些其他方式处理生产出终端产品。

   句中"which"引导的是非限制性定语从句，"either…or…"指"两者之一"。

4. A run-away process, such as an out-of-control nuclear or chemical reaction, may

result if manufacturers do not maintain precise control of all of the process variables.

译文：如果制造商不能保持对所有过程变量的精确控制，那么就有可能导致过程失控，如失控的核或化学反应。

"run-away"的意思是"失去稳定的"，"out-of-control"的意思是"失去控制"。

EXERCISES

Ⅰ. **Translate the following words into English.**

1. 过程控制　　　　　　　　　2. 可编程逻辑控制器
3. 集散控制系统　　　　　　　4. 连续过程控制
5. 逻辑语句　　　　　　　　　6. 批处理
7. 过程变量　　　　　　　　　8. 失稳过程

Ⅱ. **Complete the following sentences.**

1. _____ in proportions, temperature, flow, turbulence, and many other factors must be carefully and consistently controlled to produce the _____ with a minimum of raw materials and energy.

2. Process control refers to the methods that are used to _____, when manufacturing a product.

3. In process systems a commonly used control device called a _____, is used to read a set of digital and analog inputs, apply _____, and generate a set of analog and digital outputs.

4. When there is _____ in the end product, manufacturers are forced to pad the product to ensure that _____ are met, which adds to the cost.

Supplementary Reading

Reading 22　What Is Industrial Automation?

Automation (ancient Greek: = self dictated), robotization or industrial automation or numerical control is the use of control systems such as computers to control industrial machinery and processes, replacing human operators. In the scope of industrialization, it is a step beyond mechanization. Whereas mechanization provided human operators with machinery to assist them with the physical requirements of work, automation greatly reduces the need for human sensory and mental requirements as well.

Currently, for manufacturing companies, the purpose of automation has shifted from increasing productivity and reducing costs, to broader issues, such as increasing quality and flexibility in the manufacturing process.

The old focus on using automation simply to increase productivity and reduce costs was seen to be short-sighted, because it is also necessary to provide a skilled workforce who can make repairs and manage the machinery.

Moreover, the initial costs of automation were high and often could not be recovered by the time entirely new manufacturing processes replacing the old. (Japan's "robot junkyards" were once world famous in the manufacturing industry.)

Automation is now often applied primarily to increase quality in the manufacturing process, where automation can increase quality substantially. For example, automobile and truck pistons used to be installed into engines manually. This is rapidly being transitioned to automated machine installation, because the error rate for manual installment was around 1%–1.5%, but has been reduced to 0.000,01% with automation. Hazardous operations, such as oil refining, the manufacturing of industrial chemicals, and all forms of metal working, were always early contenders for automation.

Another major shift in automation is the increased emphasis on flexibility and convertibility in the manufacturing process. Manufacturers are increasingly demanding the ability to easily switch from manufacturing Product A to manufacturing Product B without having to completely rebuild the production lines.

Unit 23
Process Control Loops

Process Control Loops 翻译

Control loops can be divided into two categories: Single variable loops and multi-variable loops.

Single variable loops

Feedback control loops

A feedback loop measures a process variable and sends the measurement to a controller for comparison with the setpoint. If the process variable is not at setpoint, control action is taken to return the process variable to the setpoint. Fig. 5.23.1 illustrates a feedback loop in which a transmitter measures the temperature of a fluid and, if necessary, opens or closes a hot steam valve to adjust the fluid's temperature.

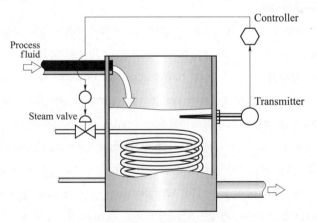

Fig. 5.23.1　A feedback loop

An everyday example of a feedback loop is the cruise control system in an automobile. A setpoint is established for speed. When the car begins to climb a hill, the speed drops below setpoint and the controller adjusts the throttle to return the car's speed to the setpoint. Feedback loops are commonly used in the process control industry. The advantage of a feedback loop is that it directly controls the desired process variable. The disadvantage to feedback loops is that the process variable must leave the setpoint for action to be taken.

Pressure control loops

Pressure control loops vary in speed—that is, they can respond to changes in load or to control action slowly or quickly. The speed required in a pressure control loop may be dictated by the volume of the process fluid. High-volume systems (e.g., large natural gas storage facilities) tend to change more slowly than low-volume systems (Fig. 5.23.2).

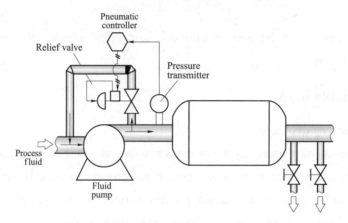

Fig. 5.23.2   Pressure control loops

Flow control loops

Generally, flow control loops are regarded as fast loops that respond to changes quickly. Therefore, flow control equipment must have fast sampling and response times. Because flow transmitters tend to be rather sensitive devices, they can produce rapid fluctuations or noise in the control signal. To compensate for noise, many flow transmitters have a damping function that filters out noise. Sometimes, filters are added between the transmitter and the control system. Because the temperature of the process fluid affects its density, temperature measurements are often taken with flow measurements and compensation for temperature is accounted for in the flow calculation. Typically, a flow sensor, a transmitter, a controller, and a valve or pump are used in flow control loops (Fig. 5.23.3).

Level control loops

The speed of changes in a level control loop largely depends on the size and shape of the process vessel (e.g., larger vessels take longer to fill than smaller ones) and the flow rate of the input and outflow pipes. Manufacturers may use one of many different measurement technologies to determine level, including radar, ultrasonic, float gauge, and pressure measurement. The final control element in a level control loop is usually a valve on the input and/or outflow connections to the tank (Fig. 5.23.4). Because it is often critical to avoid tank overflow, redundant level control systems are sometimes employed.

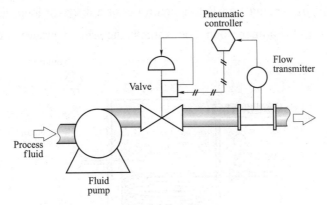

Fig. 5.23.3   Flow control loops

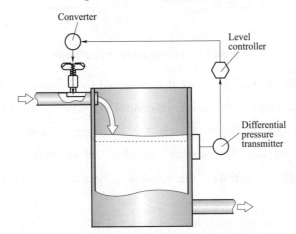

Fig. 5.23.4   Level control loops

Temperature control loops

Because of the time required to change the temperature of a process fluid, temperature loops tend to be relatively slow. Feedforward control strategies are often used to increase the speed of the temperature loop response. RTDs or thermocouples are typical temperature sensors. Temperature transmitters and controllers are used, although it is not uncommon to see temperature sensors wired directly to the input interface of a controller. The final control element for a temperature loop is usually the fuel valve to a burner or a valve to some kind of heat exchanger. Sometimes, cool process fluid is added to the mix to maintain temperature (Fig. 5.23.5).

Multi-variable loops

Multi-variable loops are control loops in which a primary controller controls one process variable by sending signals to a controller of a different loop that impacts the process variable of the primary loop. For example, the primary process variable may be

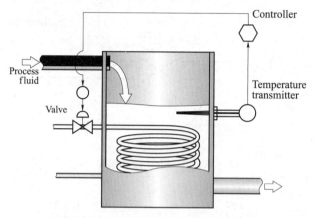

Fig. 5.23.5   **Temperature control loops**

the temperature of the fluid in a tank that is heated by a steam jacket (a pressurized steam chamber surrounding the tank). To control the primary variable (temperature), the primary (master) controller signals the secondary (slave) controller that is controlling steam pressure. The primary controller will manipulate the setpoint of the secondary controller to maintain the setpoint temperature of the primary process variable.

When tuning a control loop, it is important to take into account the presence of multi-variable loops. The standard procedure is to tune the secondary loop before tuning the primary loop because adjustments to the secondary loop impact the primary loop. Tuning the primary loop will not impact the secondary loop tuning.

TECHNICAL WORDS AND PHRASES

category	['kætigəri]	n.	种类，类别
illustrate	['iləstreit]	v.	说明，阐明，表明
transmitter	[trænz'mitə]	n.	变送器
establish	[is'tæbliʃ]	v.	建立，成立，确立，制定
throttle	['θrɔtl]	n.	（控制油、气流的）节流阀，油门
compensate	['kɔmpenseit]	v.	补偿，报酬
filter	['filtə]	n.	过滤，过滤器

Unit 23　Process Control Loops 253

vessel	['vesəl]	n.	容器，血管，脉管，导管
ultrasonic	[ˌʌltrə'sɔnik]	adj.&n.	超声的，超音波（的）；超声波
gauge	[geidʒ]	n.	厚度，直径，规格，尺度
redundant	[ri'dʌndənt]	adj.	多余的，不需要的
thermocouple	['θəːməuˌkʌpl]	n.	热电偶
secondary	['sekəndəri]	adj.	次要的，次等的
process control loop			过程控制回路
single variable loop			单变量回路
multi-variable loop			多变量回路
pressure control loop			压力控制回路
flow control loop			流量控制回路
damping function			阻尼函数
level control loop			物位控制回路
temperature control loop			温度控制回路
RTD			热电阻

NOTES

1. Fig. 5.23.1 illustrates a feedback loop in which a transmitter measures the temperature of a fluid and, if necessary, opens or closes a hot steam valve to adjust the fluid's temperature.

   译文：图 5.23.1 演示了一个反馈回路，其中变送器测量液体的温度，必要时，打开或关闭热汽阀调节液体的温度。

   "If" 引导的条件状语从句中省略了主语和 be 动词。通常当状语从句中的主语和主句的主语一致时，从句中的主语和 be 动词可以省略。

2. Because the temperature of the process fluid affects its density, temperature measurements are often taken with flow measurements and compensation for temperature is accounted for in the flow calculation.

   译文：由于过程流体温度影响其密度，所以温度测量通常测量流量，而对流量的计算需要进行温度补偿。

3. Multi-variable loops are control loops in which a primary controller controls one process variable by sending signals to a controller of a different loop that impacts the process variable of the primary loop.

   译文：多变量回路的控制回路中，主控制器控制着一个过程变量，该变量通过将信号传递给另一个不同回路中的控制器来影响主回路中的过程变量。

EXERCISES

Ⅰ. **Translate the following words into English.**

1. 主回路
2. 变送器
3. 过程变量
4. 超声波
5. 流量控制回路
6. 单变量回路
7. 热电阻
8. 过程控制回路

Ⅱ. **Complete the following sentences.**

1. An everyday example of a _____ is the cruise control system in an automobile. A setpoint is established for speed. When the car begins to climb a hill, the speed _____ and the controller adjusts the throttle to return the car's speed to the setpoint.
2. Pressure control loops vary in speed—that is, they can _____ changes in load or to control action _____.
3. Because the temperature of the process fluid affects its density, temperature measurements are often taken with _____ and _____ temperature is accounted for in the flow calculation.
4. The standard procedure is to tune _____ before tuning _____ because adjustments to the secondary loop impact the primary loop.

Ⅲ. **Translate the following text.**

The ability of digital computers to make precise calculations and decisions at high speeds has made it possible to use them as parts of control systems. The first example of the use of a computer in a large control system was the SAGE Air Defense System. In this system, data from a network of radar stations, which are used to detect the positions of all aircraft in the area, are fed via communication links into a high-speed computer. The computer stores all the incoming positional information from the radar stations and from this calculates the future positions of the aircraft, their speed and altitude, and all other pertinent information.

A number of other types of information are also relayed into the computer, including information from picket ships, AEW aircraft, Ground Observer Corps, aircraft spotters, flight plans for both military and civilian aircraft, and weather information.

A single computer receives all this information and from it calculates a composite picture of the complete air situation. The computer then generates displays on special oscilloscopes which are used by members of the military services to make tactical decisions. The computer further aids these operators by calculating the most effective use of the interceptor aircraft, antiaircraft guns, and also antiaircraft missiles. By means of radio links, the computer automatically guides both the interceptor aircraft and missiles to their targets.

Supplementary Reading

Reading 23   Distributed Control System (DCS)

The DCS is a control system which collects the data from the field and decides what to do with them. Data from the field can either be stored for future reference, used for simple process control, or be used in conjunction with data from another part of the plant for advanced control strategies.

What must be in the DCS for it to be able to do so much?

Operator console

These are like the monitors of our computers. They provide us with the feedback of what they are doing in the plant as well as the command we issue to the control system. These are also the places where operators issue commands to the field instruments.

Engineering stations

These are stations for engineers to configure the system and also to implement control algorithms.

History modules

This is like the harddisk of our PCs. They store the configurations of the DCS as well as the configurations of all the points in the plant. They also store the graphic files that are shown in the console and in most systems these days they are able to store some plant operating data.

Data historian

These are usually extra pieces of software that are dedicated to store process variables, set points and output values. They are usually of higher scanning rates than the available in the history module.

Control modules

These are like the brains of the DCS. Specially customized blocks are found here. These are customized to do control functions like PID control, ratio control, simple arithmetic and dynamic compensation. These days, advanced control features can also be found in them.

I/Os

These manage the input and output of the DCS. Input and output can be digital or analogue. Digital I/Os are those like on/off, start/stop signals. Most of the process measurements and controller outputs are considered analogue. These are the points where the field instruments are hard-wired to.

All above mentioned elements are connected by using a network. Nowadays very often used network is Ethernet.

The practical and technological boundaries between a Distributed Control System DCS, Programmable Logic Controller PLC and Personal Computer PC control are blurring. Systems traditionally associated with process control are being used in discrete applications. Likewise, traditionally discrete solutions are used increasingly in both batch and continuous process control.

Today's control hardware is constructed from many of the same standard industry components such as Intel processors. Therefore the only real difference between control systems is at the software level.

Unit 24
Advanced Control Loops

Advanced Control Loops 翻译

Feedforward control

Feedforward control is a control system that anticipates load disturbances and controls them before they can impact the process variable. For feedforward control to work, the user must have a mathematical understanding of how the manipulated variables will impact the process variable. Fig. 5.24.1 shows a feedforward loop in which a flow transmitter opens or closes a hot steam valve based on how much cold fluid passes through the flow sensor.

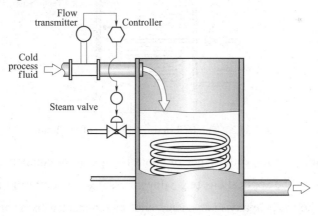

Fig. 5.24.1　The feedforward loop

An advantage of the feedforward control is that error is prevented, rather than corrected. However, it is difficult to account for all possible load disturbances in a system through feedforward control. Factors such as outside temperature, buildup in pipes, consistency of raw materials, humidity, and moisture content can all become load disturbances and cannot always be effectively accounted for in a feedforward system.

In general, feedforward systems should be used in cases where the controlled variable has the potential of being a major load disturbance on the process variable ultimately being controlled. The added complexity and expense of feedforward control may not be equal to the benefits of increased control in the case of a variable that causes only a small load disturbance.

Feedforward plus feedback control

Because of the difficulty of accounting for every possible load disturbance in a feedforward system, feedforward systems are often combined with feedback systems. Controllers with summing functions are used in these combined systems to total the input from both the feedforward loop and the feedback loop, and send a unified signal to the final control element. Fig. 5.24.2 shows a feedforward-plus-feedback loop in which both a flow transmitter and a temperature transmitter provide information for controlling a hot steam valve.

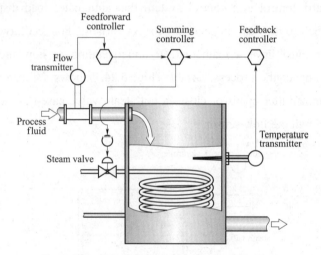

Fig. 5.24.2　The feedforward-plus-feedback loop

We have discussed specific types of control loops, what components are used in them, and some of the applications (e.g., flow, pressure, temperature) they are applied to. In practice, however, many independent and interconnected loops are combined to control the workings of a typical plant. Next we will acquaint you with some of the methods of control currently being used in process industries.

Cascade control

Cascade control is a control system in which a secondary (slave) control loop is set up to control a variable that is a major source of load disturbance for another primary (master) control loop. The controller of the primary loop determines the setpoint of the summing controller in the secondary loop (Fig. 5.24.3).

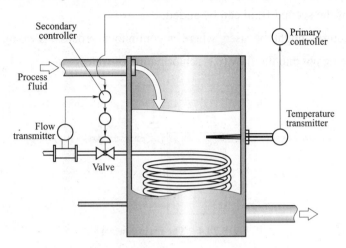

Fig. 5.24.3   The cascade control

Batch control

Batch processes are those processes that are taken from start to finish in batches. For example, mixing the ingredients for a juice drink is often a batch process. Typically, a limited amount of one flavor (e.g., orange drink or apple drink) is mixed at a time. For these reasons, it is not practical to have a continuous process running. Batch processes often involve getting the correct proportion of ingredients into the batch. Level, flow, pressure, temperature, and often mass measurements are used at various stages of batch processes. A disadvantage of batch control is that the process must be frequently restarted. Start-up presents control problems because, typically, all measurements in the system are below setpoint at start-up. Another disadvantage is that as recipes change, control instruments may need to be recalibrated.

Ratio control

Imagine a process in which an acid must be diluted with water in the proportion two parts water to one part acid. If a tank has an acid supply on one side of a mixing vessel and a water supply on the other, a control system could be developed to control the ratio of acid to water, even though the water supply itself may not be controlled. This type of control system is called ratio control (Fig. 5.24.4). Ratio control is used in many applications and involves a controller that receives input from a flow measurement device on the unregulated (wild) flow. The controller performs a ratio calculation and signals the appropriate setpoint to another controller that sets the flow of the second fluid so that the proper proportion of the second fluid can be added.

Ratio control might be used where a continuous process is going on and an additive is being put into the flow (e.g., chlorination of water).

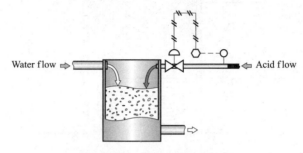

Fig. 5.24.4　The ratio control

Selective control

Selective control refers to a control system in which the more important of the two variables will be maintained. For example, in a boiler control system, if fuel flow outpaces air flow, then uncombined fuel can build up in the boiler and cause an explosion. Selective control is used to allow for an air-rich mixture, but never a fuel-rich mixture. Selective control is most often used when equipment must be protected or safety maintained, even at the cost of not maintaining an optimal process variable setpoint.

Fuzzy control

Fuzzy control is a form of adaptive control in which the controller uses fuzzy logic to make decisions about adjusting the process. Fuzzy logic is a form of computer logic where whether something is or is not included in a set is based on a grading scale in which multiple factors are accounted for and rated by the computer. The essential idea of fuzzy control is to create a kind of artificial intelligence that will account for numerous variables, formulate a theory of how to make improvements, adjust the process, and learn from the result.

Fuzzy control is a relatively new technology. Because a machine makes process control changes without consulting humans, fuzzy control removes from operators some of the ability, but none of the responsibility, to control a process.

TECHNICAL WORDS AND PHRASES

valve	[vælv]	n.	阀，真空管
intermediate	[ˌintəˈmiːdjət]	adj.	中间的，中级的
objective	[əbˈdʒektiv]	n.	目标，目的
thermostat	[ˈθəːməstæt]	n.	恒温（调节）器
dictate	[dikˈteit]	v.	指示，指定，指令
upper	[ˈʌpə]	adj.	上的，上面的，较高的
condense	[kənˈdens]	v.	缩合，凝聚，压缩
overshoot	[ˌəuvəˈʃuːt]	n.	超调量，超调
bandwidth	[ˈbændwidθ]	n.	带宽，频宽，误差
combination	[ˌkɔmbiˈneiʃən]	n.	合作，结合，组合
on/off control			开/关控制
continuous control			连续控制
in balance			平衡
control action			控制作用，控制动作
two step control			双级控制
two-position control			双位调节，双位控制
in-built			内置的，固定的，嵌入的
operating differential			运行误差
modulating control			调幅控制，调节控制

NOTES

1. For feedforward control to work, the user must have a mathematical understanding of how the manipulated variables will impact the process variable.

   译文：对于前馈控制的工作原理，用户必须从数学上理解操纵量会对过程变量产生怎样的影响。

   句中"of"引导了一个特殊疑问句来修饰"a mathematical understanding"。

2. An advantage of feedforward control is that error is prevented, rather than corrected. However, it is difficult to account for all possible load disturbances in a system through feedforward control.

   译文：前馈控制的优点是能够预防误差的发生，而并非对误差进行纠正。尽管如此，很难通过前馈控制来预测系统中所有可能出现的负载扰动。

   该句由两个分句组成，前一个分句中，"that"引导了一个表语从句，"rather than"意思是"并非，而不是"。

3. If a tank has an acid supply on one side of a mixing vessel and a water supply on the other, a control system could be developed to control the ratio of acid to water, even though the water supply itself may not be controlled.

译文：如果罐中容器的一边提供酸，一边提供水，就可以开发一个控制系统来控制酸和水的比例，但是水的供应不能控制。

句中，"if"引导的是一个条件状语从句。"even though"引导了一个让步状语从句。

4. Fuzzy logic is a form of computer logic where whether something is or is not included in a set is based on a grading scale in which multiple factors are accounted for and rated by the computer.

译文：模糊逻辑是计算机逻辑的一种形式，其中，某件事件是否包含在集合中取决于分级标准，在分级标准中须考虑多种因素，其由计算机分级。

句中，"where"引导的是一个定语从句，在该从句中，"whether"引导的是一个主语从句。

EXERCISES

Ⅰ. **Translate the following words into English.**

1. 恒温器
2. 双级控制
3. 带宽
4. 运行误差
5. 连续控制
6. 平衡
7. 调幅控制
8. 开/关控制

Ⅱ. **Complete the following sentences.**

1. In general, _____ should be used in cases where the controlled variable has the potential of being a major load disturbance on the process variable _____.

2. Because of the difficulty of accounting for _____ in a feedforward system, feedforward systems are often combined with _____.

3. The controller performs a _____ and signals the appropriate setpoint to another controller that sets the flow of the second fluid so that _____ of the second fluid can be added.

4. Because a machine makes process control changes without _____, fuzzy control removes from _____, but none of the responsibility, to control a process.

Ⅲ. **Translate the following sentences.**

1. The added complexity and expense of feedforward control may not be equal to the

benefits of increased control in the case of a variable that causes only a small load disturbance.
2. Controllers with summing functions are used in these combined systems to total the input from both the feedforward loop and the feedback loop, and send a unified signal to the final control element.
3. Cascade control is a control system in which a secondary (slave) control loop is set up to control a variable that is a major source of load disturbance for another primary (master) control loop.
4. The essential idea of fuzzy control is to create a kind of artificial intelligence that will account for numerous variables, formulate a theory of how to make improvements, adjust the process, and learn from the result.

Supplementary Reading

Reading 24   Tools for Advanced Process Control

For Advanced Process Control applications, you need powerful tools to do the job right. ExperTune's PID Loop Optimizer includes the following tools:
- Coordinated tuning of multiple loops;
- Model & tune feedforward controls;
- Develop MPC model vectors;
- Frequency domain models;
- Full integration with PlantTriage.

PID loop optimizer goes far beyond the basics of PID tuning. It helps you to address all aspects of PID loop performance. Make sure that you have the tools to do your job properly.

Coordinated tuning of multiple loops

Add as many extra variables as you want on the faceplate. Let you monitor other variables on the same faceplate trend to see how other process variables affect the loop. These can be configured for the modeling and the tuning of interactions or other loops. Defining extra loops helps you work with these systems:
- Monitor, tune and analyze multiple loops from one tag;
- Add as many extra trends as you want. Let you monitor other variables on the same faceplate to see how other process variables affect the loop;
- Create extra loops from the extra trends for extra modeling, analysis, simulation and tuning;

- Multi-variable: Model and decouple multi-variable systems 2×2, 3×3, 2×3, etc.;
- Feedforward: Model load processes for feedforward compensation;
- Cascade loops and RRT analysis;
- Interacting loops and RRT analysis.

Relative response time

Only in ExperTune, this is a new cutting edge tool for decoupling interacting loops. The relative response time (RRT) makes it easy to set interacting and cascade loops to work together. The RRT in each interacting or cascade should be a factor of 3 away from the others. Change RRT by adjusting the safety factor or lambda time. The relative response time is the period at the peak amplitude ratio in the closed loop frequency response (to load upsets).

Cascade: Use ExperTune PID Analyzer to model and tune cascade systems simultaneously with one test. The master (outer) loop should have a relative response time that is 3 times slower (larger) than the slave (inner) loop.

Interacting loops: Use cross-correlation to see how one loop affects another. To prevent interaction, adjust the safety factor or lambda value (set point speed) in the interacting loops so that the relative response time is different by a factor of 3.

Feedforward compensator design and modeling

ExperTune allows you to build a robust feedforward system. First use ExperTune's Advanced PID Loop Optimizer to model both the feedback and load or feedforward system. Then use Loop Simulator to design the compensator and simulate time responses with and without the compensator in place.

Development of MPC model vectors

You can use ExperTune to support the development of MPC models. Each loop's model exists as a Laplace, frequency domain, and MPC model vector. Model vectors can be exported in standard CSV format, and can be imported directly into your MPC controller.

Frequency domain models

Get more detailed analysis with frequency-domain models of the process. With a graphical frequency-domain model, you can determine the effect of load upsets, determine closed-loop natural frequency, and much more.

Full Integration with PlantTriage

ExperTune's PlantTriage provides 24×7 control loop monitoring, for every control loop in your plant. With PlantTriage, you can ensure that the benefits of your work are sustained. PlantTriage monitors:

- Controller performance;
- Instrument performance;
- Valve performance.

All PID Loop Optimizer features are included with PlantTriage, and they are tightly integrated within PlantTriage.

Use PlantTriage to monitor and diagnose issues, then resolve them directly using all the power of PID Loop Optimizer.

Unit 25
Computers in Control

Computers in Control 翻译

Single loop controllers date back to pneumatic controllers, which, through the ingenious use of flaps and nozzles, could approximate the basic PID functions. These complex and expensive controllers were often found in large petrochemical plants where accurate control of the process, as well as intrinsic safety (the absence of sparks which could initiate a fire) was essential.

Often, these processes were individually connected to local circular chart recorders (Fig. 5.25.1); alternatively, a number of processes were connected to multi-pen recorders in control rooms (Fig. 5.25.2). While the multi-pen recorders enabled a number of parameters to be reviewed together, the mechanisms in the instrument and the number of lines on one chart effectively limited their use to approximately twelve inputs.

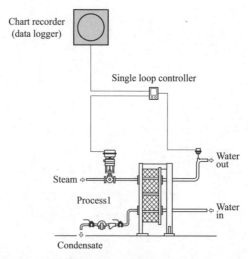

Fig. 5.25.1 The single loop controller with chart recorders

The first computers used in control systems replaced the main control room chart recorders. They gathered information (or data) from a much greater number of points around the plant. They were generally referred to as "data loggers" (Fig. 5.25.3), and had no input to the plant operation.

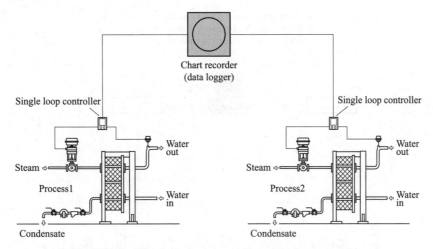

Fig. 5.25.2 The single loop controller with chart recorders

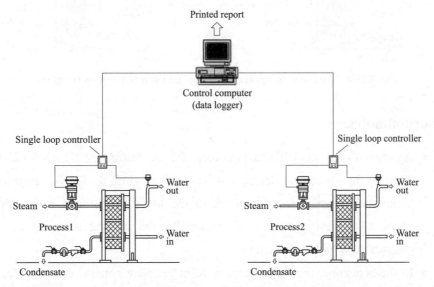

Fig. 5.25.3 A number of single loop controllers with a central data logging computer

These early computers were usually programmed to print out reports at specific time intervals on continuous computer listing paper. By manually extracting the data from the computer print-outs, the plant manager was able to review the operation of his plant as a whole, comparing the performance of different parts of the plant, looking for deterioration in performance, which would indicate the need for a shutdown, etc.

In the mid 1970's, a number of well-known instrument companies began marketing digital control systems. These systems utilized a central computer unit, which took inputs from sensors, performed mathematical routines, and provided an output to various relevant controlling devices. They also maintained a record of events for review (Fig. 5.25.4).

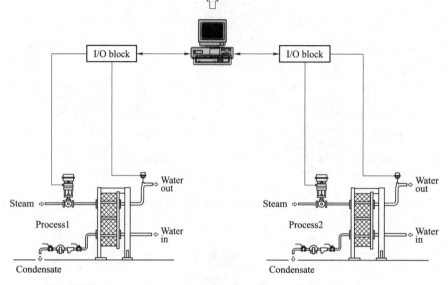

Fig. 5.25.4 A central computer gathering data and controlling the plant

Important notes:

- A personal computer (PC) cannot accept the raw instrument signals (4–20 mA, 0–10 V) from a control device. An Input/Output (I/O) device was required to "translate" between the two. Each of the I/O manufacturers had a unique means of achieving this, which meant that the systems were not quite as compatible as had been intended.
- In the beginning, the I/O devices were in the plant's main control room, and each individual piece of equipment was connected to the main control room by its own individual signal cable. This meant that in a large plant, the cable installation and management was an important issue, in terms of its physical volume and corresponding cost.
- As technology progressed, the I/O device moved out to the plant, and the amount of cabling to the control room was reduced, but was still significant.

These digital control systems led to the development of:

- Distributed control systems (DCS) (Fig. 5.25.5);
- Supervisory control and data acquisition (SCADA) systems;

- Building management systems (BMS).

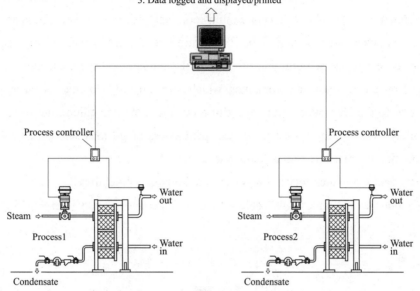

Fig. 5.25.5 A distributed control system

A giant leap forward occurred in the late 1980s with the introduction of the PC and the Windows screen environment and computer operating system. This provided a standard platform for the earlier digital control systems, as all the instrument companies needed to work in a common format. The advantage of the "Windows" based systems was that information was exchangeable in the same way that today's personal computer user can freely exchange data between Word, "Excel" and "PowerPoint." This data exchange "language" was termed Dynamic Data Exchange (DDE), and subsequently developed into Object Linking and Embedding (OLE). This was further modified for process control to become OLE for Process Control (OPC), which is still used at the time of writing.

The use of PCs also meant that the options for viewing history were considerably easier. Instead of being confined to print-outs and manual transfer data, the plant manager could use powerful graphing programs, analyze trends, add colors, adjust scales and use symbols.

Modern automation systems utilize the computer as a "Window" in the process. The operator uses the computer to monitor what is happening in the plant as a whole, and revise set-points and control parameters, such as PID, of individual plant based controllers, thus leaving the individual controllers to run the PID algorithms and control logic.

Consequently stand-alone controllers still have a place in modern automation systems as they are in final control, but the controller usually takes the form of a PLC (Programmable Logic Controller) or a multi-loop rack mounted device. These are quite different in appearance to single loop PID controllers. Rather than an operator using a keypad to change the setpoint and other control parameters at the controller, they are changed by an operator at a computer, which electronically downloads the required parameter to the controller. In the event of a central computer failure, the stand-alone controller would continue with its current parameters or go to a safe condition, thus ensuring that the plant continued to operate safely.

The next major step forward was a system known as "Fieldbus."

Fieldbus uses a single digital cable system, which connects every item (Fig. 5.25.6).

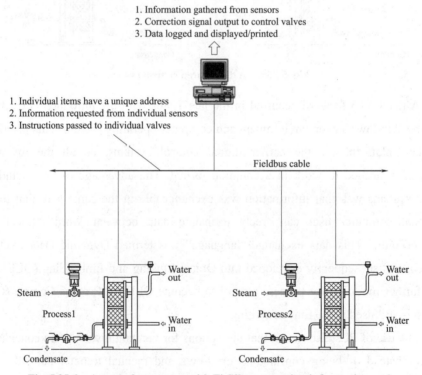

Fig. 5.25.6 A central computer with Fieldbus accepting information and transmitting correction signals via Fieldbus

Each item (sensor, controller and controlled device) is given a unique address, which is used to either request information (perhaps from a sensor) or to take some action (perhaps close a control valve).

However, these systems are complex and can be expensive. A Fieldbus network needs a master controller to organize the communications and control logic on the Fieldbus. It also needs a way of interfacing the Fieldbus to computer networks so information can be shared (Fig. 5.25.7). A device that combines the role of Fieldbus controller and provides the bridge to a PC network is called a "bridge" or "master controller" (Fig. 5.25.8).

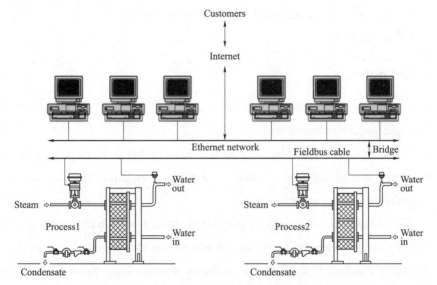

Fig. 5.25.7   The process control computer communicating with other computers over a network and the Internet

Fig. 5.25.8   A bridge

On the process side the bridge can:

- Request and receive data from a number of sensors.
- Use this information in complex mathematical routines to determine and transmit the required corrective action to control devices such as valves.
- Request the equipment to initiate a diagnostic routine, and report.

On the computer network side it can provide:

- Historical data of equipment, such as date and result of recent diagnostic routines.
- Alarms when the process or equipment exceeds set parameters.
- Detailed historical and current data on plant performance.
- Safety interlocks.

Important notes:

- Bridges vary in complexity but may control 50+ processes; the equivalent of 50 single loop PID controllers.
- If more processes are to be controlled, then more than one bridge may be used.
- Names commonly encountered in Fieldbus bridge(s) may be located at convenient points around a plant.
- The bridge does not usually display information, nor have any buttons to press. It is simply an electronic gateway; all interaction with it is made via the PC.

Although Fieldbus is theoretically a common technology, there are differences between the products and protocols used by different manufacturers.

Names commonly encountered in Fieldbus include:

- HART;
- CAN;
- PROFIBUS;
- Interbus.

TECHNICAL WORDS AND PHRASES

alternatively	[ɔːlˈtəːnətivli]	adv.	作为选择，二者择一地
mechanism	[ˈmekənizəm]	n.	机械装置，构造，机制
shutdown	[ˈʃʌtdaun]	n.	关闭，倒闭
routine	[ruːˈtiːn]	n.	例行公事，惯例，惯常程序
leap	[liːp]	n.	跳跃，剧增，急变
platform	[ˈplætfɔːm]	n.	平台，讲台，舞台，戏台
exchangeable	[iksˈtʃeindʒəbl]	adj.	可交换的，可转换的
considerably	[kənˈsidərəbəli]	adv.	相当地
consequently	[ˈkɔnsikwəntli]	adv.	所以，因此
keypad	[ˈkiːpæd]	n.	键盘，按键，键区

Unit 25　Computers in Control

fieldbus	[ˈfiːldbʌs]	n.	现场总线
gateway	[ˈgeitwei]	n.	方法，手段，途径，大门口
interaction	[ˌintərˈækʃən]	n.	合作，配合，相互作用
single loop controller			单回路控制器
date back to			追溯到……，从……开始
pneumatic controller			气动控制器
intrinsic safety			原有安全度，本质安全
circular chart			圆形图
time interval			时间间隔，时程，时节
digital control system			数字控制系统
supervisory control and data acquisition system			监控和数据采集系统
building management system			建造管理系统
dynamic data exchange			动态数据交换
object linking and embedding			对象链接与嵌入
OLE for process control			过程控制的对象链接和嵌入
rack mount			机架固定件
stand-alone			单机，卓越
diagnostic routine			诊断程序
safety interlock			安全联锁装置，保险联锁装置

NOTES

1. By manually extracting the data from the computer print-outs, the plant manager was able to review the operation of his plant as a whole, comparing the performance of different parts of the plant, looking for deterioration in performance, which would indicate the need for a shutdown, etc.

   译文：从计算机的打印输出中提炼出数据，工厂经理能够总体地检查工厂的运行情况，比较工厂不同部门的工作效能，发现效能恶化，其预示着有关闭的需要，等等。

   "By"引导的介词短语做方式状语，现在分词"comparing"和"looking"做状语，"which"引导的是非限制性定语从句。

2. As technology progressed, the I/O device moved out to the plant, and the amount of cabling to the control room was reduced, but was still significant.

   译文：随着技术的发展，输入/输出设备搬迁出工厂，连到控制室内的电缆数量有所减少，但仍然可观。

3. Instead of being confined to print-outs and manual transfer data, the plant manager

could use powerful graphing programs, analyze trends, add colors, adjust scales and use symbols.

译文：不再局限于打印图表和手动传输数据，工厂经理可以使用强大的绘图程序，分析趋势，增加颜色，调整比例并使用符号。

"be confined to" 的意思是 "局限于"、"受限于"。

4. Rather than an operator using a keypad to change the setpoint and other control parameters at the controller, they are changed by an operator at a computer, which electronically downloads the required parameter to the controller.

译文：操作员不再使用键盘控制器的设定点和控制参数，操作员通过一台计算机，用电子方式把所需的参数下载到控制器中。

EXERCISES

Ⅰ. **Translate the following words into English.**

1. 数字控制系统
2. 气动控制器
3. 二者择一地
4. 机架固定件
5. 诊断程序
6. 安全联锁装置
7. 动态数据交换
8. 对象链接与嵌入

Ⅱ. **Complete the following sentences.**

1. While _____ enabled a number of parameters to be reviewed together, the mechanisms in the instrument and the number of lines on one chart effectively _____ to approximately twelve inputs.

2. Early computers were usually _____ to print out reports at specific time intervals on continuous _____.

3. In the beginning, _____ were in the plant's main control room, and each individual piece of equipment was connected to _____ by its own individual signal cable.

4. Consequently _____ still have a place in modern automation systems as they are in final control, but the controller usually takes the form of a PLC or _____.

Ⅲ. **Translate the following text.**

Control engineering has diversified applications that include science, finance management, and even human behavior. Students of control engineering may start with a linear control system course which requires elementary mathematics and Laplace Transforms (called classical control theory). In linear control, the student does frequency and time domain analysis. Digital control and nonlinear control courses require Z Transformations and algebra respectively, and could be said to complete a basic control education. From here onwards there are several sub-branches.

Control engineering is the engineering discipline that focuses on the modelling of a diverse range of dynamic systems (e.g. mechanical systems) and the design of controllers that will cause these systems to behave in the desired manner. Although such controllers need not be electrical, many are and hence control engineering is often viewed as a subfield of electrical engineering. However, the falling price of microprocessors is making the actual implementation of a control system essentially trivial. As a result, focus is shifting back to the mechanical engineering discipline, as intimate knowledge of the physical system being controlled is often desired.

Supplementary Reading

Reading 25 Computer Control

Computer-control systems can be viewed as approximations of analog-control systems, but this is a poor approach because the full potential of computer control is not used. At best the results are only as good as those obtained with analog control. It is much better to master computer-control systems, so that the full potential of computer control can be used. These are also phenomena that occur in computer-control systems that have no correspondence in analog systems. It is important for an engineer to understand this.

The computer interprets the converted signals, as a sequence of numbers, processes the measurements using an algorithm, and gives a new sequence of numbers. The events are synchronized by the real-time clock in the computer. The digital computer operates sequentially in time and each operation takes some time. The D-A converter must, however, produce a continuous-time signal. This is normally done keeping the control signal constant between the conversions. In this case the system runs open loop in the time interval between the sampling instants because the control signals are constant irrespective of the value of the output.

The mixture different types of signals sometimes cause difficulties. In most cases it is, however, sufficient to describe the behavior of the system at the sampling instants. The signals are then of interest only at discrete times. Such systems will be called discrete-time systems. Discrete-time systems deal with sequences of numbers, so a natural way to represent these systems is to use difficult equations.

The idea of using digital computers for process control emerged in the mid-1950s. Serious work started in March 1956 when the aerospace company Thomson Ramo Woodridge (TRW) contacted Texaco to set up a feasibility study. After preliminary discussions it was decided to investigate a polymerization unit the Port Arthur, Texas, refinery. A group of engineers from TRW and Texaco made a thorough feasibility study, which required about 30 people-years. A computer-controlled system for the polymerization unit was designed based on the RW-300 computer. The control system went on-line on March 12, 1959. The system controlled 26 flows, 72 temperatures, 3 pressures, and 3 compositions. The essential functions were to minimize the reactor pressure, to determine an optimal distribution among the feeds of 5 reactors, to control the hot water inflow based on the measurement of the catalyst activity, and to determine the optimal recirculation.

The pioneering work done by TRW was noticed by many computer manufacturers, who saw a large potential market for their products. Many different feasibility studies were initiated and vigorous development was started. To discuss the dramatic development, it is useful to introduce six periods:

- Pioneering period—1955
- Direct-digital-control period—1962
- Minicomputer period—1967
- Microcomputer period—1972
- General use of digital control—1980
- Distributed control—1990

It is difficult to give precise dates, because the development was highly diversified. There was a wide difference between different application areas and different industries; there was also considerable overlap. The dates given refer to the emergence of new approaches. An overview of Direct-Digital-Control Period follows.

The early installation of control computers operated in a supervisory mode, either as an operator guide or as a set-point control. The ordinary analog-control equipment was needed in both cases. A drastic departure from this approach was made by Imperial Chemical Industries (ICI) in England in 1962. A complete analog instrumentation for process control was replaced by one computer, a Ferranti Argus. The computer measured 224 variables and controlled 129 valves directly. This was the beginning of a new era in process control: Analog technology was simply replaced by digital technology; the function of the system was the same. The name direct digital control (DDC) was coined to emphasize that the computer controlled the process directly.

Unit 26
Introduction to Sensors

Introduction to Sensors 翻译

Resistance

Electrical resistance is the easiest electrical property to measure precisely over a wide range at moderate cost. A simple digital multimeter costing a few tens of dollars can measure resistances in the range from 10 ohm to 10 megohm with a precision of about 1% using a two-wire technique (Fig. 5.26.1). The precision of the two-wire method is limited by uncertainties in the values of the lead resistances R_{L_1} and R_{L_2}.

Providing R_{L_1} and R_{L_2} are well-matched, the three-wire technique can be used. Fig. 5.26.2 employs two matched current sources, I_1 and I_2, to eliminate the effects of the lead resistance. Fig. 5.26.3 is an AC-bridge that is in-balance when $R_X=R_Y$. If a lock-in amplifier is used as a null-detector, determination of R_X with an extremely low excitation current is possible.

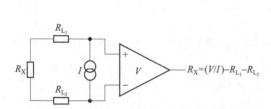

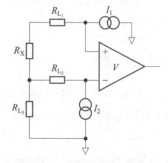

Fig. 5.26.1 The 2-wire resistance measurement technique

Fig. 5.26.2 The 3-wire resistance measurement technique

The 4-wire "Kelvin" method (Fig. 5.26.4) is used in difficult cases when lead resistances vary, R_X is very small, or when very high accuracy is required. The method is immune to the influence of lead resistance and is limited by the quality of the constant current source and voltage measurement. Thermo-electric voltages can be eliminated by averaging two measurements with the polarity of the excitation current reversed.

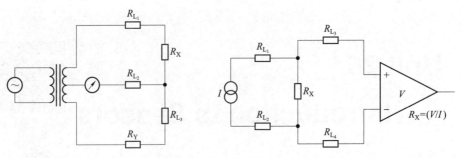

Fig. 5.26.3 The bridge method   Fig. 5.26.4 The 4-wire "Kelvin" resistance measurement technique

Resistive temperature detectors

Resistance temperature detectors (RTD) exploit the fact that the electrical resistivities of metals and alloys vary in a reproducible way with temperature. Platinum, with a temperature coefficient of about $0.003,9\ \text{K}^{-1}$, is the most popular material used in this application. An RTD consists of a coil of wire, or a thin-film, with four-wire electrical connections supported in a way that is a compromise between robustness and thermal time-constant. RTDs have excellent accuracy (e.g. $0.025\ \text{K}$ at room temperature) over a wide temperature range. At cryogenic temperatures the resistance of metals becomes constant, and it is usual to use a sample of doped-semiconductor as the sensing element. When we use RTDs, it is always important to check that the measured resistance is independent of excitation current in order to avoid errors caused by self-heating.

Strain gauges

At constant temperature, the resistance R of a metal or semiconductor element of area A, length l, resistivity ρ, is

$$R = l\rho / A$$

and when the element is strained this changes by an amount:

$$\Delta R = \left(\frac{dR}{dl}\right)\Delta l + \left(\frac{dR}{d\rho}\right)\Delta\rho + \left(\frac{dR}{dA}\right)\Delta A = \frac{\rho}{A}\Delta l + \frac{l}{A}\Delta\rho + \frac{\rho l}{A^2}\Delta A$$

$$\frac{\Delta R}{R} = \frac{\Delta l}{l} + \frac{\Delta \rho}{\rho} - \frac{\Delta A}{A}$$

A typical strain gauge consists of a metal foil, photo-etched to form a serpentine pattern, and mounted on a resin backing film. Metal sensor-elements are dominated by the geometric terms in the above equation and therefore they are relatively temperature independent and have a modest gauge factor (i.e. responsivity) of about 2.

Semiconductor elements can exploit a large piezo-resistive effect yielding gauge factors of about 150. However, this is at the expense of temperature stability and some sort of compensation scheme is usually required in practice.

Strain gauges are widely used in many applications; they are small, cheap and reliable, and many variables (e.g. pressure) can be used to cause strain.

Capacitance

Capacitance can also be measured over a wide range at moderate cost. A simple hand-held meter, and some digital multimeters use a two-wire technique to measure the capacitance in the range from 100 pF to 1 F with an accuracy of about 1%. Such meters often work by incorporating the unknown capacitor into a relaxation oscillator such as the ramp generator experiment in PHY2003. This charges the unknown capacitance with a known constant current, and the capacitance is calculated from the charging time required for it to reach the threshold voltage.

Stray capacitance, typically in the range from 10 pF to 10 nF, is the major source of error in capacitance measurement, and must be dealt with using "guarding" techniques. Fig. 5.26.5 shows how the influence of the stray capacitance to ground associated with a piece of coaxial cable can be eliminated by reconnecting its shield to a low impedance node.

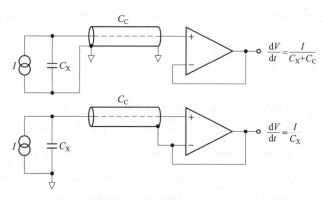

Fig. 5.26.5 Unguarded (top) and guarded (bottom) configurations

Capacitive sensors are the most precise of all electrical sensors. A capacitive sensor can be designed to be:
- Non-dissipative and therefore free of thermal noise;
- Free from self-heating;
- Linear with applied voltage;
- Temperature independent.

Simple but very precise sensors can be based on the change in geometry of a pair of capacitor plates, or on the effects of introducing conducting material into the capacitor gap.

Capacitive pressure sensors

Capacitive pressure sensors use a thin diaphragm, usually metal or metal-coated quartz, as one plate of a capacitor. The diaphragm is exposed to the process pressure on one side and to a reference pressure on the other. Changes in pressure cause it to deflect and change the capacitance. The change may or may not be linear with pressure and is typically a few percent of the total capacitance. The capacitance can be monitored by using it to control the frequency of an oscillator or to vary the coupling of an AC signal. It is good practice to keep the signal-conditioning electronics close to the sensor in order to mitigate the adverse effects of stray capacitance. Fig. 5.26.6 is a schematic example.

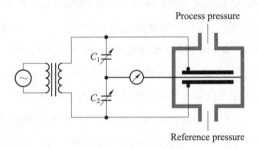

Fig. 5.26.6 A schematic capacitive pressure sensor

Development in silicon-based micro- machine technology has lead to several significant improvements in the performance and usability of capacitive pressure sensors.

Inductance

Inductors are probably the least-ideal of discrete components and circuit designers try to avoid using them. As a result, inexpensive handheld inductance meters are available, but not are particularly common (or useful). Their resolution is a few microhenries, limited by the connection leads. Only rather sophisticated impedance analyzers can be expected to characterize inductors automatically.

Inductive displacement sensors

The voltage at the output of Fig. 5.26.7 depends on the position of the high-permeability core which is changed with a mechanical linkage. The output signal must be monitored with a phase-sensitive detector. There is a null position at the midway point between the two detection coils, which are connected in series-opposition. Inductive displacement transducers can be purchased with integral electronics that internally generates the alternating current and converts the measured signal into a calibrated DC output.

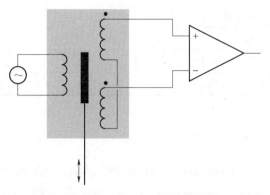

Fig. 5.26.7 A schematic inductive position sensor

Thermoelectric effects

Thermoelectric voltages are the most common source of error in low-level voltage measurement. They arise when circuit connections are made using dissimilar metals at different temperatures. In this context, two thermoelectric effects are important. Firstly, the Seebeck effect is the flow of current which arises when the junctions of a circuit made of two different metals are at different temperatures. Secondly, the Thomson effect describes the production of an electromotive force between two points at different temperatures in the same material.

Each metal-to-metal junction generates an EMF proportional to its temperature and precautions must be taken to minimize thermocouple voltages and temperature variations in low-level voltage measurement. The best connections are formed using copper-to-copper crimped connections. Tab. 5.26.1 lists thermoelectric voltages for junctions between copper and other metals commonly found in electronics.

Tab. 5.26.1 Thermoelectric voltages for junctions between copper and other metals commonly found in electronics

Copper-to-	EMF /(μV K^{-1}) (approx)
Aluminum	5
Beryllium Copper	5
Brass	3
Copper	< 0.3
Copper-Oxide	1,000

Copper-to-	EMF /(μV K^{-1}) (approx)
Gold	0.5
Silicon	500
Silver	0.5
Solder (Cadmium-Tin)	0.2
Solder (Tin-Lead)	5

Temperature measurement

Thermocouples are reproducible, small and cheap. It is not surprising therefore that they are commonly used to measure temperatures (Fig. 5.26.8).

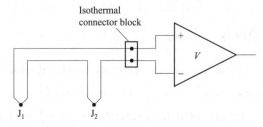

Fig. 5.26.8 Thermocouples

If the reference junction J_2 is held at a known temperature, the temperature of J_1 can be deduced from the measured voltage difference by using standard tables. Maintaining a constant reference temperature is often inconvenient but specialized integrated circuits (e.g. the AD594/5) known as "electronic cold-junctions" are available. They create and monitor the reference junction within their own packaging, including a precision DC amplifier and linearization circuitry.

Hall effects

The phenomenon known as the Hall Effect occurs when a current-carrying conductor is placed in a magnetic field and an EMF (the "Hall voltage") is generated in the direction mutually perpendicular to both the field and the current flow. Depending on the application, the Hall voltage can be detected with an instrumentation amplifer (DC excitation current) or a lock-in amplifier (AC excitation current). A large range of Hall Effect sensors is available commercially, and facilitates the measurement of magnetic fields at frequencies from DC to about 100 kHz, and resolutions of about 10 μT.

The high bandwidth and sensitivity of Hall Effect sensors can be exploited in many applications.

Electric power meter

The Hall voltage is proportional to the product of the excitation current and magnetic field. Fig. 5.26.9 exploits this property to monitor the power delivered to a load. A coil generates a magnetic field that is proportional to the load current; the sensor excitation current passes through R_1 and is proportional to the load voltage. The output voltage is therefore proportional to the instaneous power dissipated by the load.

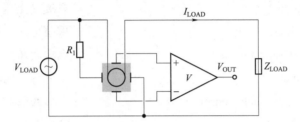

Fig. 5.26.9 The schematic wattmeter based on Hall Effect sensors

TECHNICAL WORDS AND PHRASES

sensor	['sensə]	n.	传感器，灵敏元件
multimeter	['mʌlti,mi:tə]	n.	万用表
megohm	['megəum]	n.	兆欧
excitation	[eksi'teiʃən]	n.	激发，激动，励磁
immune	[i'mju:n]	adj.	有免疫力的，不受影响的
coefficient	[,kəui'fiʃənt]	n.	系数
cryogenic	[,kraiəu'dʒenik]	adj.	低温学的
geometric	[dʒiə'metrik]	adj.	几何的，几何学的
capacitance	[kə'pæsitəns]	n.	电容，电容量
capacitive	[kə'pæsitiv]	adj.	电容的，电容性的
oscillator	['ɔsileitə]	n.	振荡器
inductance	[in'dʌktəns]	n.	电感，感应系数，感抗
microhenry	['maikrə,henri]	n.	微亨
permeability	[,pə:miə'biliti]	n.	磁导率，导磁系数
electromotive	[ilektrəu'məutiv]	adj.	电动的，电测的
thermocouple	['θə:məu,kʌpl]	n.	热电偶
thermoelectric	[,θə:məui'lektrik]	adj.	热电的

perpendicular	[ˌpə:pən'dikjulə]	adj.	垂直的，成直角的
resolution	[ˌrezə'lu:ʃən]	n.	分辨率
null-detector			零值检测器，零位探测器
thermo-electric			热电的
resistance temperature detector			电阻式温度检测器
time constant			时间常数
strain gauge			应变仪，变形测量器
gauge factor			仪器常数，仪表灵敏度
relaxation oscillator			弛张振荡器
ramp generator			斜坡发生器
threshold voltage			阈值电压，临限电压
capacitive pressure sensor			电容式压力传感器
inductance meter			亨利计，电感表
inductive displacement sensor			电感式位移传感器
thermoelectric effect			热电效应
electromotive force			电动势
Hall Effect			霍尔效应
magnetic field			磁场
electric power meter			电功率表，电表

NOTES

1. Resistance temperature detectors (RTD) exploit the fact that the electrical resistivities of metals and alloys vary in a reproducible way with temperature.

   译文：电阻温度探测器利用了一个事实：金属和合金的电阻率随温度的变化以可重复的方式变化。

   句中"that"引导了一个同位语从句，修饰"the fact"。

2. Inductive displacement transducers can be purchased with integral electronics that internally generates the alternating current and converts the measured signal into a calibrated DC output.

   译文：电感式位移传感器可以与整体电子设备一同购买，在其内部产生交流电，将被测量信号转换成标准的直流输出。

3. The Hall device is shown in light blue; a coil (in red) generates a magnetic field that is proportional to the load current; the sensor excitation current passes through R_1 and is proportional to the load voltage. The output voltage is therefore proportional to the instaneous power dissipated by the load.

译文：霍尔装置如亮蓝色部分所示，线圈（红色）产生磁场，其与负载电流成比例，传感器激励电流流过 R_1，并与负载电压成比例，因此输出电压与加在负载上的瞬间功率成比例。

EXERCISES

Ⅰ. **Translate the following words into English.**

1. 万用表
2. 零位探测器
3. 霍尔效应
4. 变形测量器
5. 电功率表
6. 电感式位移传感器
7. 电感表
8. 弛张振荡器

Ⅱ. **Complete the following sentences.**

1. A simple digital multimeter costing a few tens of dollars can measure resistances in the range from 10 ohm to 10 megohm with a _____ of about 1% using a _____.

2. The method is immune to the influence of _____ and is limited by the quality of the constant current source and _____.

3. An RTD consists of _____, or _____, with four-wire electrical connections supported in a way that is a compromise between robustness and thermal time-constant.

4. Each metal-to-metal junction generates an EMF _____ its temperature and precautions must be taken to _____ thermocouple voltages and temperature variations in low-level voltage measurement.

Ⅲ. **Translate the following sentences.**

1. At cryogenic temperatures the resistance of metals becomes constant, and it is usual to use a sample of doped-semiconductor as the sensing element.

2. Simple but very precise sensors can be based on the change in geometry of a pair of capacitor plates, or on the effects of introducing conducting material into the capacitor gap.

3. Inductors are probably the least-ideal of discrete components and circuit designers try to avoid using them.

4. The phenomenon known as the Hall Effect occurs when a current-carrying conductor is placed in a magnetic field and an EMF (the "Hall voltage") is generated in the direction mutually perpendicular to both the field and the current flow.

Supplementary Reading

Reading 26　Sensors

A sensor is a device that measures a physical quantity and converts it into a signal which can be read by an observer or by an instrument. For example, a mercury-in-glass thermometer converts the measured temperature into expansion and contraction of a liquid which can be read on a calibrated glass tube. A thermocouple converts temperature to an output voltage which can be read by a voltmeter. For accuracy, all sensors need to be calibrated against known standards.

Use

Sensors are used in everyday objects such as touch-sensitive elevator buttons and lamps which dim or brighten by touching the base. There are also innumerable applications for sensors of which most people are never aware. Applications include cars, machines, aerospace, medicine, manufacturing and robotics.

A sensor's sensitivity indicates how much the sensor's output changes when the measured quantity changes. For instance, if the mercury in a thermometer moves 1 cm when the temperature changes by 1 ℃, the sensitivity is 1 cm/℃. Sensors that measure very small changes must have very high sensitivities. Sensors also have an impact on what they measure; for instance, a room temperature thermometer inserted into a hot cup of liquid cools the liquid while the liquid heats the thermometer. Sensors need to be designed to have a small effect on what is measured, making the sensor smaller often improves this and may introduce other advantages. Technological progress allows more and more sensors to be manufactured on a microscopic scale as microsensors using MEMS technology. In most cases, a microsensor reaches a significantly higher speed and sensitivity compared with macroscopic approaches.

Classification of measurement errors

A good sensor obeys the following rules:
- Is sensitive to the measured property.
- Is insensitive to any other property.
- Does not influence the measured property.

Ideal sensors are designed to be linear. The output signal of such a sensor is linearly proportional to the value of the measured property. The sensitivity is then defined as the ratio between the output signal and the measured property. For example, if a sensor measures temperature and has a voltage output, the sensitivity is a constant with the unit [V/K]; this sensor is linear because the ratio is constant at all points of measurement.

Sensor deviations

If the sensor is not ideal, several types of deviations can be observed:
- The sensitivity may in practice differ from the value specified. This is called a sensitivity error, but the sensor is still linear.
- Since the range of the output signal is always limited, the output signal will eventually reach a minimum or maximum when the measured property exceeds the limits. The full scale range defines the maximum and minimum values of the measured property.
- If the output signal is not zero when the measured property is zero, the sensor has an offset or a bias. This is defined as the output of the sensor at zero input.
- If the sensitivity is not constant over the range of the sensor, this is called nonlinearity. Usually this is defined by the amount the output differs from ideal behavior over the full range of the sensor, often noted as a percentage of the full range.
- If the deviation is caused by a rapid change of the measured property over time, there is a dynamic error. Often, this behavior is described with a bode plot showing sensitivity error and phase shift as function of the frequency of a periodic input signal.
- If the output signal slowly changes independent of the measured property, this is defined as drift (telecommunication).
- Long term drift usually indicates a slow degradation of sensor properties over a long period of time.
- Noise is a random deviation of the signal that varies in time.
- Hysteresis is an error caused when the measured property reverses direction, but there is some finite lag in time for the sensor to respond, creating a different offset error in one direction in comparison with that in the other.
- If the sensor has a digital output, the output is essentially an approximation of the measured property. The approximation error is also called digitization error.
- If the signal is monitored digitally, limitation of the sampling frequency also can cause a dynamic error.

- The sensor may to some extent be sensitive to properties other than the property being measured. For example, most sensors are influenced by the temperature of their environment.

All these deviations can be classified as systematic errors or random errors. Systematic errors can sometimes be compensated for by means of some kind of calibration strategy. Noise is a random error that can be reduced by signal processing, such as filtering, usually at the expense of the dynamic behavior of the sensor.

Resolution

The resolution of a sensor is the smallest change it can detect in the quantity that it is measuring. Often in a digital display, the least significant digit will fluctuate, indicating that changes of that magnitude are only just resolved. The resolution is related to the precision with which the measurement is made. For example, a scanning tunneling probe (a fine tip near a surface collects an electron tunneling current) can resolve atoms and molecules.